CUTTING
EDGE

THIRD EDITION

INTERMEDIATE

STUDENTS' BOOK

WITH DVD-ROM

CONTENTS

Pronunciation	Task	Language live/ World culture	Study, Practice & Remember
Sentence stress in questions Using intonation to show interest	Discuss the way you spend your time **Preparation:** Listening and reading **Task:** Speaking	**Language live** **Speaking:** Keeping a conversation going **Writing:** An informal email	Study & Practice 1, page 132 Study & Practice 2, page 132 Remember these words, page 134 Study tips, page 134
Past simple -*ed* endings	Describe a personal memory **Preparation:** Listening and vocabulary **Task:** Speaking **Follow up:** Writing	**World culture** **Video and research:** Flashbulb memories	Study & Practice 1, page 135 Study & Practice 2, page 136 Remember these words, page 137 Study tips, page 137
Stress and /ə/ sounds in comparative phrases Sentence stress in polite questions	Provide an insider's guide **Preparation:** Listening **Task:** Speaking	**Language live** **Speaking:** Travel problems **Writing:** A travel blog	Study & Practice 1, page 138 Study & Practice 2, page 139 Remember these words, page 140 Study tips, page 140
Strong and weak forms of *have* Linking in time phrases	Nominate someone for an award **Preparation:** Listening **Task:** Speaking **Follow up:** Writing	**World culture** **Video and research:** Charles Dickens: Writer and campaigner	Study & Practice 1, page 141 Study & Practice 2, page 142 Remember these words, page 143 Study tips, page 143
Word stress in word families Polite intonation in questions	Choose who to hire or fire! **Preparation:** Reading and listening **Task:** Speaking and listening	**Language live** **Speaking:** Making a formal telephone call **Writing:** A CV	Study & Practice 1, page 144 Study & Practice 2, page 145 Remember these words, page 146 Study tips, page 146
Hearing the difference between Past simple and Past perfect in connected speech	Retell a story **Preparation:** Listening and vocabulary **Task:** Speaking and listening **Follow up:** Writing	**World culture** **Video and research:** A story that rocked the world	Study & Practice 1, page 147 Study & Practice 2, page 148 Remember these words, page 149 Study tips, page 149

CONTENTS

Pronunciation	Task	Language live/ World culture	Study, Practice & Remember
Word stress Sentence stress	Talk about a show you love or hate **Preparation:** Vocabulary and listening **Task:** Speaking	**Language live** **Speaking:** Making a social arrangement **Writing:** A review	Study & Practice 1, page 150 Study & Practice 2, page 150 Remember these words, page 152 Study tips, page 152
Polite intonation in requests	Give tips on how to behave **Preparation:** Listening **Task:** Speaking **Follow up:** Writing	**World culture** **Video and research:** Addicted to games	Study & Practice 1, page 153 Study & Practice 2, page 154 Remember these words, page 155 Study tips, page 155
Stress in compound nouns	Talk about things you couldn't live without **Preparation:** Reading **Task:** Speaking	**Language live** **Speaking:** Buying things **Writing:** A short thank-you message	Study & Practice 1, page 156 Study & Practice 2, page 157 Remember these words, page 158 Study tips, page 158
Shifting stress in word families *'ll* or *'d* in connected speech	Balance the budget **Preparation:** Listening **Task:** Speaking	**World culture** **Video and research:** In orbit	Study & Practice 1, page 159 Study & Practice 2, page 160 Remember these words, page 161 Study tips, page 161
Modal verbs in connected speech	Discuss new laws **Preparation:** Reading and listening **Task:** Speaking	**Language live** **Speaking:** Expressing and responding to opinions **Writing:** An opinion essay	Study & Practice 1, page 162 Study & Practice 2, page 163 Study & Practice 3, page 163 Remember these words, page 164 Study tips, page 164
Past modal forms in connected speech	Discuss dilemmas **Preparation:** Reading **Task:** Speaking **Follow up:** Writing	**World culture** **Video and research:** Life in a new country	Study & Practice 1, page 165 Study & Practice 2, page 166 Remember these words, page 167 Study tips, page 167

01

YOUR WORLD

Language focus 1
Questions and short answers

1a Match situations 1–3 with photos A–C.

   1 someone answering questions to complete a form
   2 someone who has just arrived in a foreign country and is greeting an old friend she hasn't seen for a long time
   3 someone getting to know a classmate on a new course

b Work in pairs. Think of two questions that the people in each situation might ask.

2a 🎧 1.1 Listen to nine short conversations. Match them with situations 1–3 in exercise 1a.

   1 _1_ 2 __ 3 __ 4 __ 5 __ 6 __ 7 __ 8 __ 9 __

b Work in pairs. How many questions from the conversations can you remember? Make a list. Then listen again and check.

GRAMMAR

Forming questions

Many questions begin with *wh-* words and phrases:
What? Where? Which part? (also *How?*)

1 Think of four more *wh-* question words/phrases.

2 Cross out the question with incorrect word order.
   1 Where do live your parents?
   2 Where do your parents live?

Short answers

3 Rewrite the answers to these questions using *did*, *do* and *doesn't*.
   A: Did you have a good journey?
   B: ~~Yes, I had a good journey.~~ Yes, I did.

   1 A: Do all your family live near here?
     B: My parents live near here, but my sister doesn't live near here.
   2 A: Does your father work in London?
     B: No, he works from home.

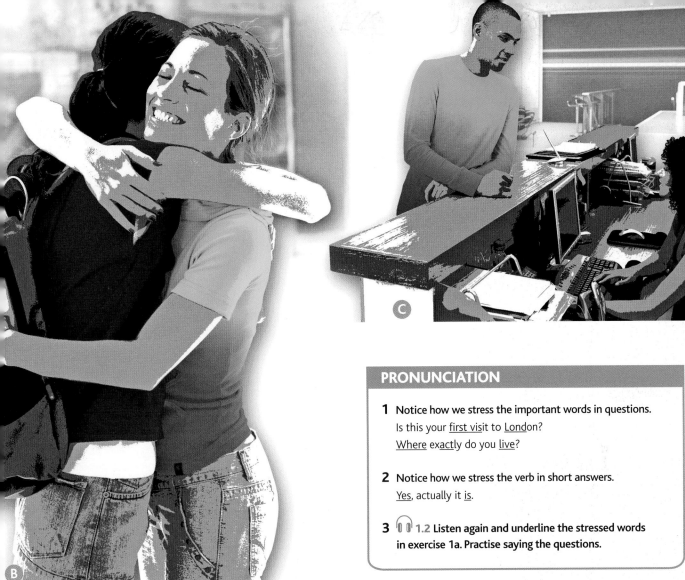

PRACTICE

1a Complete the questions and answers with the verbs in the box. You may need to use some verbs more than once. One verb isn't used.

are   could   do   don't   did   have   haven't   is ('s)

A: Is this your first visit to London?
B: Yes, actually it is.

1 What your postcode, please?
2 Where exactly you live?
3 How your job going?
4 A: You speak any other languages apart from English?
   B: No, I.
5 All your family speak English?
6 You tell me your date of birth?
7 A: You have a nice holiday?
   B: Yes thanks, I.
8 A: You got any brothers and sisters?
   B: No, I.

b Look back at the situations in exercise 1a on page 6. Match the questions and answers with the photos.

c 🎧 1.2 Listen and check.

PRONUNCIATION

1 Notice how we stress the important words in questions.
Is this your <u>first</u> <u>visi</u>t to <u>Lond</u>on?
<u>Where</u> ex<u>act</u>ly do you <u>live</u>?

2 Notice how we stress the verb in short answers.
<u>Yes</u>, actually it <u>is</u>.

3 🎧 1.2 Listen again and underline the stressed words in exercise 1a. Practise saying the questions.

2 Work in pairs. Act out two conversations from the photos using questions from exercise 1a and your own ideas.

3a Discuss what questions to ask your teacher in the situations below.

You don't know what 'colleague' means.
What does 'colleague' mean?

1 You don't know the English word for ⬭.
2 You don't know how to pronounce a word.
3 You don't know how to spell your teacher's name.
4 You don't know which page to look at.
5 You didn't understand an explanation.
6 You didn't hear what your teacher said.
7 You want to know what today's homework is.
8 You want your teacher to write a word on the board.

b 🎧 1.3 Listen and check.

4 Work in pairs. Choose four questions from exercise 1a. Then think of two more questions of your own. Take turns to ask and answer the questions.

Unit 1, Study & Practice 1, page 132

Vocabulary
People around you

1a Which word doesn't belong in each group? Cross it out and write it in the correct group.

Family	older sister	stepmother
	relative	stranger
	grandchild	half-brother
	grandparents	
Work/school	classmate	boss
	colleague	employee
	niece	
Friends	best friend	old school friend
	acquaintance	mother-in-law
Other	neighbour	flatmate
	cousin	ex-girlfriend

b Add more words to the table.

2a 🎧 1.4 Listen to eight instructions. Write your answers in any of the spaces below.

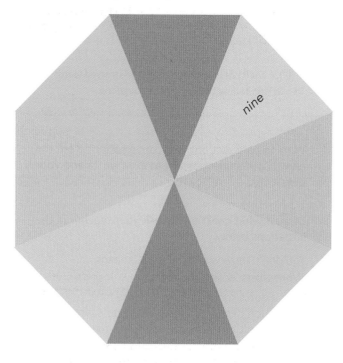

nine

b Work in pairs and swap books. Ask questions to find the meaning of the names/numbers that your partner has written.

Why did you write 'nine'?

Because I've got nine cousins.

Who's Roberta?

She's my colleague.

🛜 WIFI

Lydia, Jess, Tom, Saliba

Isabel, John

Language focus 2
Present simple and Present continuous

1a Look at the photos from Jess's birthday party last weekend. What do you think her relationship is to each person in the photos?

b 🎧 1.5 Jess is showing the photos to a colleague. Listen and check your answers to exercise 1a.

Lydia – best friend

2 Listen again and find five mistakes in the sentences below.

Jess is showing her photos to L~~ydia~~. *Ann*

1 Lydia is working in a restaurant at the moment.
2 She wants to become a social worker.
3 She's applying for lots of jobs.
4 Isabel is getting old.
5 She always pulls faces in photos.
6 Jess's grandparents go out a lot.
7 Luxmmi is training to be a dentist.
8 Joe is wearing sunglasses.
9 Joe's living in a student house at the moment.
10 He doesn't like the city very much.

Jess, Luxmmi

Joe, Jess, Pete, Harriet, Andy

3a Underline the Present simple verbs and circle the Present continuous verbs in exercise 2. How do we form the Present continuous?

b Find another example in exercise 2 for each use below.

GRAMMAR

Present simple

1 habits, repeated actions and permanent situations
Isabel always pulls faces in photos.
Saliba lives near Jess.

2 'states'
He doesn't like the city.
(other state verbs: *be*, *have* (*got*), *want*, *think*, *love*, etc.)

Present continuous

1 actions happening at this moment
Jess is showing her photos to Ann.

2 actions happening in the present period (but not at this moment)
She's applying for lots of jobs.

3 situations we see as temporary
Joe's living in a student house.

4 situations that are gradually changing
Grandpa's getting old.

PRACTICE

1 Choose the correct answers.

  1 Raoul *wears* / *is wearing* a suit today – it*'s* / *is being* really smart.
  2 Eva is a fantastic musician – she *plays* / *is playing* the piano, the guitar and the violin.
  3 Ben *doesn't smoke* / *isn't smoking* – he *hates* / *is hating* cigarettes.
  4 I *don't like* / *am not liking* this coffee very much – what *do you think* / *are you thinking* of it?
  5 Amy *works* / *is working* in a hotel this summer.

2a Complete the questions with *you* and either the Present simple or the Present continuous.

  1 _____ (like) meeting new people?
  2 _____ (read) a good book at the moment?
  3 _____ (read) a daily newspaper?
  4 _____ (study) for any exams at the moment?
  5 _____ (prefer) smart or casual clothes?
  6 _____ (usually get up) late at the weekend?
  7 _____ (plan) anything special at the moment?

b Ask other students the questions. Find someone who answers *yes* to each question. Report back to the class.

Yasuko is reading a good book. It's called …

3 Rewrite the sentences where necessary to make them true for you. Compare your answers in pairs.

I'm losing weight.
I'm gaining weight.

  1 The weather's getting colder.
  2 I'm getting taller.
  3 My hair's going grey.
  4 My English is getting better.
  5 I'm getting hungry.

4a Find photos on your mobile phone of people you know <u>or</u> write the names of six important people in your life on a piece of paper.

b Make notes about your relationship with the people, what they do and their lives at the moment.

Tomas   – best friend
*   – not working and really fed up*

c Work in groups. Tell other students about the people in your photos or on your list. They can ask questions.

> This is Tomas – he's my best friend. He's not working at the moment.

Unit 1, Study & Practice 2, page 132

Reading and speaking

1a **Look at the photos and discuss the questions.**

- Is there a lot of advice about lifestyle in newspapers and magazines in your country?
- Which photos remind you of yourself?

> The photo of the woman exercising reminds me of myself. I hate exercising.

b **Which opinions (a–d) do you think are true?**

- **a** young people spend too much time on the internet
- **b** people who get up early are more productive
- **c** multitasking is an essential modern skill
- **d** there's no such thing as too much exercise

2a **Read the article. Choose a phrase from exercise 1b to complete the gaps.**

b **According to the article, is each phase a fact or a myth?**

3a **Read the article again and answer the questions.**

1. How does the writer feel about his own lifestyle?
2. When are night owls more productive?
3. What kind of people had damage to their heart muscles?
4. Which group spends the most time online in the USA?
5. What are older people better at doing online than younger people?
6. Is it impossible to multitask well? Why / Why not?

b **Work in pairs. Tell your partner which paragraph you think is the most surprising and interesting. Give reasons for your answer.**

4a **What common beliefs do people have about lifestyle in your country? Make a list.**

People often say that you should sleep at least eight hours a day.

You often hear that eating late at night makes you fat.

b **Work in pairs and compare your lists. Do you think each belief is a fact or a myth? Why?**

The myths that make you feel guilty

by Lester Johnson

Every time I open a newspaper, I read a new piece of advice about what I'm doing wrong. I don't drink enough water, I sleep too much, I don't sleep enough … it can get depressing. So I decided to do some research myself to find out if I should really feel so guilty.

I've always felt bad because I find it difficult to get up in the morning – mainly because I can never sleep before 2 a.m. So while my colleagues arrive for work looking bright and fresh at 8 o'clock, I arrive at ten, feeling grumpy. And everyone knows that ¹_____ , right? Wrong actually, according to a report from the University of Liege. Two hours after waking, researchers found that early birds and night owls are equally productive. But ten hours after waking, night owls like me are less tired and better able to concentrate! So next time I'm late for work, I won't apologise; I'll just tell my boss that I'm a night owl – and that's good!

Like many people, I constantly worry about the amount of exercise I take … or rather don't take. I know I should spend hours in the gym every day and run marathons just for fun. After all, ²_____ , is there? Actually, according to a recent study, there is. Researchers studied top athletes who are now in their fifties and found that some of them had damage to their heart muscles. Men of the same age who didn't exercise so intensively had no damage. So perhaps I'm doing the best thing by sitting at home on the sofa? Unfortunately not. It seems the best advice is still the old saying: moderation in all things.

Everyone says that ³_____ , and as someone who grew up with technology – a 'digital native' – I often worry that I might be an internet addict. But apparently, a recent study of Americans shows that it's not young people who go online the most, it's the middle-aged. The study found that 18- to 24-year-olds spend around 32 hours a week online, but for 45- to 54-year-olds it's 40 hours! However, it's not all good news for digital natives. According to research, we are not as good as older people at actually using the internet. It seems we are too impatient and believe what we read too easily!

I'm not the kind of person who can talk on the phone, shop online and cook dinner all at the same time, but I keep reading that ⁴_____ . Does this mean there is something wrong with me? I googled the subject and felt a little better. It seems, after all, that the human brain can't do several things at the same time: it can only switch quickly from one task to another. If you try to do several things at once, experts say that you simply do each thing less well. According to workplace psychologist Steven Nguyen, we should stop worrying about multitasking. 'Concentrate on what you are doing and do fewer things better,' he says. Now that's advice that I'm happy to follow!

"Concentrate on what you are doing and do fewer things better

Vocabulary
Everyday activities

1a Underline the activities in the box that you never do or hardly ever do.

going to the gym	hanging out with friends
doing your hair	going on social networking sites
looking after children	commuting
chatting to friends	going shopping
doing paperwork	relaxing
tidying up	doing the ironing
playing video games	texting
putting on make-up	doing nothing

b Work in pairs and compare your answers.

I never (go to the gym).
I hardly ever (iron).

2 Write the activities from exercise 1a in the correct category below. Some activities can go in more than one category. Then think of more activities to add to each category.

Sport/fitness:
Social:
Domestic:
Personal care:
Other:

3 Match the phrases in A with their opposites in B. Which verb form is used in all of these phrases?

A
1 I really love …
2 … is very important to me
3 I spend a lot of time …
4 I'm quite good at …
5 I'm really into …

B
a I don't spend much time …
b I'm not very good at …
c I'm not very interested in …
d I can't stand …
e … isn't very important to me

4 Use the phrases in exercise 3 to write eight true sentences for you about the activities in exercise 1a.

Shopping isn't very important to me.
I can't stand doing paperwork in the morning.

5 Work in pairs. Choose five activities from exercise 1a and ask your partner about them.

> Do you ever play video games?

> Not very often. I find them a bit boring.

FIND OUT MORE Go online to find out more about early birds and night owls or Steven Nguyen and multitasking.

11

Task

Discuss the way you spend your time

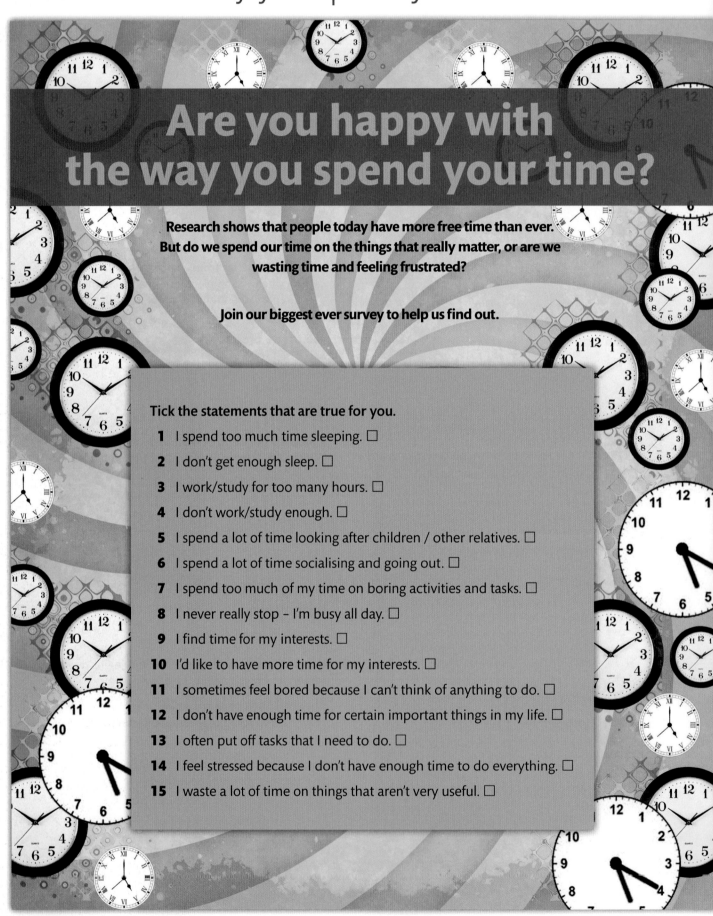

Are you happy with the way you spend your time?

Research shows that people today have more free time than ever. But do we spend our time on the things that really matter, or are we wasting time and feeling frustrated?

Join our biggest ever survey to help us find out.

Tick the statements that are true for you.

1 I spend too much time sleeping. ☐

2 I don't get enough sleep. ☐

3 I work/study for too many hours. ☐

4 I don't work/study enough. ☐

5 I spend a lot of time looking after children / other relatives. ☐

6 I spend a lot of time socialising and going out. ☐

7 I spend too much of my time on boring activities and tasks. ☐

8 I never really stop – I'm busy all day. ☐

9 I find time for my interests. ☐

10 I'd like to have more time for my interests. ☐

11 I sometimes feel bored because I can't think of anything to do. ☐

12 I don't have enough time for certain important things in my life. ☐

13 I often put off tasks that I need to do. ☐

14 I feel stressed because I don't have enough time to do everything. ☐

15 I waste a lot of time on things that aren't very useful. ☐

Preparation Listening and reading

1a Read the introduction to the questionnaire. What is the questionnaire trying to find out?

b Read the statements and complete the questionnaire. How many statements are true for you?

2a  1.6 Listen to five respondents talking about their answers. Which statements are they discussing? Make notes about what they say.

> Speaker 1   – spends too much time commuting
>   – journey takes one and a half hours, or three hours on a bad day
>   – really boring

b Listen again and tick the phrases you hear in the first part (a) of the Useful language box.

Task Speaking

1 You are going to talk about your answers to the questionnaire. Think about how to explain them. Ask your teacher for any words/phrases you need.

> Useful language a

2a Work in pairs and swap questionnaires. Look at the statements your partner has ticked and think of five questions to find out more information.

> Useful language b

b Take turns to tell your partner about your answers to the questionnaire. Answer his/her questions. Make brief notes about your partner.

> Useful language a and b

3 Tell the class about your partner. Think about:

- which activities are most important in his/her life and why.
- the things he/she is happy about.
- the changes he/she would like to make.

> Useful language c

Writing
An informal email

1 Work in groups and discuss.

- Do you use online social networks a lot? Why / Why not?
- Have people from your past got in touch with you through the internet?
- If so, did you meet up with them? What happened?

2 Read the online message that Katarina sent to her old friend Grace. How do they know each other? What does Katarina want to do?

MESSAGE from Katarina

Hi Grace,

Long time no see! It's been a few years but I hope you remember me! After we left university I lost your details, so I was really happy to find you again on this website. You look great in your photo. ¹_____ .

²_____ ? What are you doing now? Are you still living in Manchester? Sorry for all the questions but ³_____ ! And how is your family? Is your brother still training to be a lawyer? And what are your parents doing? ⁴_____ that holiday I spent at your house with your family. Happy days!

⁵_____ , after university I moved back to Slovakia. I'm still there now. I live in Bratislava with my husband, Hendrik. He's a TV producer. I work for a media company now. Life changes so quickly! I really love my life here but I still miss our time together at university. It was so much fun!

⁶_____ . My company is sending me to Manchester for three days next week. Hendrik is coming with me. While we're there we would really love to meet up with you. Is that possible? ⁷_____ .
Take care. ⁸_____ ,
Katarina
⁹_____ .

REPLY

---

3 Read Katarina's message again and complete it with the phrases below.

- **a** As you know,
- **b** Lots of love,
- **c** I want to hear all your news!
- **d** I really hope you're well.
- **e** PS You can see some photos of me now on my profile page.
- **f** So how are things with you?
- **g** There's another reason I wanted to get in touch.
- **h** Please let me know.
- **i** I still remember

4 Match topics a–d with the paragraphs in Katarina's message.

- **a** Questions for her old friend   *para. 2*
- **b** Reasons for getting in touch now
- **c** Why she hasn't been in touch before
- **d** News about her own life

5a You are going to write a similar message. Think of an old friend you haven't seen for a long time and invent a reason to contact him/her.

b Use the topics in exercise 4 to make notes for your message. Add any other information that you want to include.

6 Write a first draft of your message. Follow the same structure as Katarina's message and use the checklist below to help you.

- Are there clear paragraphs? (e.g. the topics in exercise 4)
- Are you using appropriate phrases? (see exercise 3)
- Are you using present tenses and questions correctly?
- Have you checked spelling and punctuation?

7a Work in pairs. Read each other's messages and suggest improvements. Use the checklist above to help you.

b Read your partner's comments and ask him/her for more information if necessary. Then write the final draft of your message.

Speaking
Keeping a conversation going

1 Look at the picture and answer the questions.

- Do you enjoy meeting new people?
- Do you find it easy to talk to people you don't know?
- What questions can you ask someone when you have just met him/her?

2 ⊙ Grace is meeting Katarina and Hendrik in a café. Watch the video and tick the topics that Grace and Hendrik talk about.

- where they are from
- how they met Katarina
- university
- their home towns
- a holiday in the past
- the weather

3 Watch again and match the auxiliary questions in A with the phrases in B.

A	B
1 Were you?	a Did you meet at university?
2 Did you?	b That sounds fun.
3 Haven't you?	c That's amazing!
4 Was it?	d I see!
5 Do you?	e When was that?
6 Don't you?	f Why's that?
7 Was he?	g Wow!
8 Did he?	h Really?

PRONUNCIATION

1 ⊙ Watch and listen to the key phrases. Repeat the auxiliary questions and phrases. Notice how the speakers use intonation to show interest.

We were working for the same company.

Were you? When was that?

4 Work in pairs. Take turns to read out the statements below and show interest. Use the auxiliary questions and phrases in exercise 3 to help you.

1 I'm reading a really good book about love.
2 My brother has just bought a big house.
3 We're moving to a little village.
4 My grandparents go on holiday five times a year!
5 An old friend of mine was on TV this week.
6 I've got some important news for you.

> We're going to New York on holiday next week.
>
> Are you? Wow!

5a Work in pairs. Act out the situations below. How long can you keep each conversation going? Which do you think is the most difficult situation?

- You have joined a photography class and when you arrive there is only one other student. You try to keep a conversation going until the teacher arrives.
- A school friend who you haven't seen for five years sits opposite you on the train. You have to keep the conversation going until you reach your stop.
- You have just been introduced to a friend of your mother's and have to keep a conversation going with her while your mother is making coffee.

b Work in groups and take turns. Pair A: Act out a conversation from exercise 5a. Pair B: Listen and note things they did well and ways they could improve.

AFTER UNIT 1 YOU CAN ...

Provide detailed personal information.

Describe in detail people you know.

Describe how you spend your time.

Write a message to an old friend.

Keep a conversation going.

02
MEMORY

IN THIS UNIT

- **Grammar:** Past simple and Past continuous; *used to* and *would*
- **Vocabulary:** Childhood and upbringing; Remembering and forgetting
- **Task:** Describe a personal memory
- **World culture:** Flashbulb memories

The secrets of your memory

Memory expert Professor Jemima Gryaznov answers your most common questions about memory.

1 Why can I remember events in my childhood but not what happened last week?
We remember the things that have strong connections in our mind, especially emotional connections. Childhood memories are often very emotional: we experience things for the first time so we have strong feelings of fear or excitement. Retelling events also helps to fix them in our memories and interesting or funny stories from our childhood are often told again and again!

2 Do some people really have a photographic memory?
It is well known that some people have an extraordinary memory. Daniel Tammet, for example, can remember the first 22,500 digits of pi and Stephen Wiltshire can draw a detailed picture of a city from memory after flying over it in a helicopter. However, neither Daniel nor Stephen have a photographic memory. They are good at remembering particular things for a limited time. A person with a photographic memory could remember every detail of a picture, a book or an event many years later. No one has yet proved that they have a photographic memory in a scientific test.

3 Is computer memory better than human memory?
That depends what you mean by 'better'! Information in a computer is stored in separate pieces. Human memory is stored in a different way. Each piece of information is connected to many other pieces. That's why a particular smell can bring back memories of a holiday or a person. The problem with human memory is that it is messy and not very accurate. The problem with computer memory is that it can't make connections between pieces of information – it isn't creative.

4 I'm 24. Is my memory getting worse?
Not yet, but it will do soon. Our memory reaches its full power at the age of 25. At that point we can remember up to 200 pieces of information a second. After this age, however, the brain starts to get smaller. By the age of 40 we are losing 10,000 brain cells every day. By middle age our memory is significantly worse than when we were young.

5 Is it possible to remember early childhood?
Scientists used to believe that it was impossible to remember very early childhood, but recent research shows that babies are much cleverer than we previously thought. Some people really can remember being a baby. Others, however, remember nothing before the age of five or even ten!

> **FIND OUT MORE** Go online to find out more about Daniel Tammet and Stephen Wiltshire.

Reading and speaking

1a Work in pairs and discuss. Which of these things are you good/bad at remembering?

- names and faces
- pin numbers, passwords, etc.
- facts and information
- messages and arrangements
- things that happened long ago
- things that happened recently

b Do you think you have a good memory?

2 Read the comments below. Do you have the same or similar experiences to any of the speakers?

a I can't remember anything before I started school when I was six.   **Emilia, 19**

b I'm not as young as I used to be and I definitely think my memory is getting worse. I sometimes go into a room to look for something, but then I can't remember what I'm looking for.   **Alex, 41**

c I can remember the holiday we had when I was ten really clearly; it was the first time I went abroad, and it was really exciting. But I can't remember what I did last summer very well at all.   **Jasmine, 34**

d My grandma's dead now, but I have this really strange association with her. Whenever I smell ironing, I remember her. I think it's because she used to tell us stories while she was ironing.   **Rosina, 23**

3 Read the text on page 16 quickly. Then match paragraphs 1–5 with comments a–d. There is one extra paragraph.

4 Read the text again and decide if the statements are true (T) or false (F). Correct the false statements.

1 We remember certain events in our childhood because we felt strongly about them at the time.
2 When we tell a story many times, we forget important details.
3 Stephen Wiltshire never forgets anything.
4 Scientists have proved that some people have a photographic memory.
5 Our brain stores each piece of information separately.
6 Our memory starts to get worse in middle age.
7 It is impossible to remember anything accurately before the age of five.

5 Work in pairs and discuss. Is there any information in the text that you find surprising? Why?

6 Read the tips for improving your memory. Are the ideas in the box associated with remembering or forgetting? Write R or F next to each idea.

doing crossword puzzles   lack of sleep   doing new things
imagining strange pictures   short, regular revision
oxygen going to your brain   asking yourself questions

Seven tips for improving your memory

1 **Sleep well:** If we don't sleep properly, we 'lose' many of our memories.
2 **Do physical exercise:** When you exercise, more oxygen goes to your brain and that makes your memory work better.
3 **Do mental exercise:** It is important to exercise your brain just like your body. New activities are more challenging than familiar ones.
4 **Be interested:** Ask yourself questions about what you are learning. We learn better if we are interested.
5 **Keep reviewing:** Review information regularly rather than trying to remember it all at once.
6 **Have a cup of coffee:** Caffeine, like exercise, sends oxygen to your brain and helps you concentrate.
7 **Form a mental picture:** For example, if you want to remember the name 'John Keys', imagine his face with a big key on it. The stranger the picture the better!

7 Work in pairs and discuss.

- Which tips seem the most/least useful?
- Which, if any, would be useful in learning English?
- Do you have any other ways of remembering new words in English?

Language focus 1
Past simple and Past continuous

1 Work in pairs. Test your memory by answering the quiz questions as quickly as you can. Give brief details for each answer.

> I remember my grandfather, and he died when I was two and a half.

> I was working in a shop when I met my partner.

How well do you **remember** the **past?**

① Can you remember anything that happened to you before you were three?

② What were you doing at 3 o'clock last Saturday afternoon?

③ How did you meet your oldest friend, or your partner?

④ What was the name of your first teacher and what did he/she look like?

⑤ What was the first word you learnt in English?

⑥ What were you wearing in your last English lesson?

⑦ What did you have for breakfast the day before yesterday?

⑧ What were you doing when you heard about an important piece of world news? (e.g. the death of a very famous person)

2 🎧 2.1 Listen to five people discussing the quiz. Which question is each speaker discussing?

3a Can you remember what the speakers said? Complete the listening extracts below.

   1 Last English lesson I was wearing jeans and a _____ shirt.

   2 I was about _____ months old and I was walking with my parents – they were holding my hands. Suddenly, my favourite _____ appeared at the door and I walked towards her.

   3 At that time I was watching _____ on TV.

   4 She had very dark _____ and dark _____ , and she always wore a lot of make-up on her _____ .

   5 While I was shopping in town, I saw the news on the TVs in a _____ _____ . I went into the shop and asked the _____ what was happening. Everyone in the shop was talking about it.

b Listen again and check.

4a Underline eight Past simple verbs in the sentences in exercise 3a. Which verbs are regular and which are irregular?

b Circle seven examples of the Past continuous in exercise 3a. How do we form the Past continuous?

GRAMMAR

1 Look at the timeline and examples. Then choose the correct answers to complete the rules.

I saw the news on TV while I was shopping.

At 3 o'clock last Saturday I was watching football.
I was walking with my parents when my favourite aunt appeared.

   1 The **Past simple** / **Past continuous** shows complete actions, usually the main events in a story.

   2 The **Past simple** / **Past continuous** shows actions in progress at a point in the past. They start before and often continue after the main events.

   3 We can link Past simple and Past continuous actions with the words 'when' and _____ .

2 Notice that we do not usually use the Past continuous to describe states or repeated actions.

She had dark hair and always wore a lot of make-up.

PRACTICE

1a Here are some more answers to the quiz questions. Which question is each person answering?

1 At exactly that time I *sat / was sitting* in a traffic jam! I *drove / was driving* to a big football match with my mate, but the traffic was really terrible and tragically we *missed / were missing* the first half of the match!

2 When I was a young child, my sister and I *always watched / were always watching* TV together on a Sunday morning. One Sunday we *came / were coming* downstairs and *switched on / were switching on* the TV, but they *didn't show / weren't showing* all our usual favourite programmes. Instead every channel *showed / was showing* pictures of ... and all the presenters were very serious. We *didn't understand / weren't understanding* why.

3 I can remember when I was about two and a half, I *sat / was sitting* at the kitchen table while my mum *cooked / was cooking* dinner. I *cut out / was cutting out* pictures from a magazine, then suddenly, for no reason, I *fell / was falling* off my chair and *banged / was banging* my head quite badly. My mum *took / was taking* me to hospital!

b Read the answers in exercise 1a again. Choose the correct verb forms to complete each answer.

2 🎧 2.2 Read the story of how Vicki's grandparents met. Complete the text with the correct form of the verb in brackets. Then listen and check.

A true story!

The most romantic story I know is the way my grandparents ¹_____ (meet). They ²_____ (travel) from London to Newcastle by train, and in those days it ³_____ (be) a long journey, so after a while they ⁴_____ (start) talking. They soon ⁵_____ (discover) that they ⁶_____ (have) a lot in common. Both of them ⁷_____ (be) from Newcastle, but both of them ⁸_____ (train) to be journalists in London, and both of them ⁹_____ (go) home to see their families for Christmas.

The weather was terrible; apparently it ¹⁰_____ (snow) really badly all the way to Newcastle. At one point, the train ¹¹_____ (stop) for quite a long time, but it obviously ¹²_____ (not be) a problem, because somehow during the journey, they ¹³_____ (fall) in love and ¹⁴_____ (decide) to get married. By the time they ¹⁵_____ (reach) Newcastle, they were engaged! The wedding ¹⁶_____ (take) place a few weeks later, and amazingly they are still happily married 50 years later!

PRONUNCIATION

1a 🎧 2.3 Listen and count the number of syllables in the past forms below.

start-ed 2   discovered   stopped   decided   reached

b In which words is *-ed* pronounced as a separate syllable? Why?

2 🎧 2.4 Here are some more *-ed* past forms. How are they pronounced? Listen and check. Write the words with the same pronunciation in groups.

arrived   asked   invited   remembered   expected
studied   visited   offered   hoped   watched
worked   noticed   travelled

3a You are going to test your partner's memory further by asking him/her about a time when he/she met someone important in his/her life (a good friend, a partner, etc.). Use the prompts to form questions.

1 Where / you meet?   *Where did you meet?*
2 What / happen in your life at that time?
3 What / happen in your friend's/partner's life at that time?
4 What / be the first thing you noticed about him/her?
5 What / you talk about?
6 What / your friend/partner look like then?
7 What / he/she / wear?
8 Be / anyone else there?
9 How / you feel after you first met?
10 How / you meet again?

b Choose an important person in your life and work in pairs. Take turns to ask and answer the questions.

> Where did you meet?
>
> I think we met at a football match, but I can't really remember. It seems like a long time ago!

Unit 2, Study & Practice 1, page 135

Listening and vocabulary
Childhood and upbringing

1 Read about Mi-Sun/Emily and Rafael. You will hear them describe their upbringing. What topics do you think they will mention?

Rafael Martin (27), who is half Spanish and half British, grew up and went to school in the same part of London as Mi-Sun (Emily) Kim (28), whose family is Korean. However, their upbringings were very different.

2 🎧 2.5 Listen to Mi-Sun/Emily and Rafael. Which things below were:

a things their parents permitted?
b things they didn't permit?
c things they insisted on?

Rafael
1 going to bed on time
2 being mean to his sister
3 playing in the street with his friends
4 hanging out in town with his friends
5 staying out late at the weekend

Mi-Sun/Emily
1 playing at friends' houses
2 going for sleepovers
3 going out in the evenings
4 playing the piano
5 getting A's in schoolwork

3 Can you remember anything Rafael and Mi-Sun/Emily said about the topics in exercise 2?

4 Check the meaning of the words in bold in a dictionary. Who said these things? Write R (Rafael) or M (Mi-Sun/Emily) next to the ideas below.

My parents were very **strict.** M
1 My parents **punished** us sometimes – we **got into trouble** if we were rude.
2 If we **behaved badly**, our parents stopped our **pocket money**.
3 If I **argued with** my mum, my dad **told** me **off** and I felt really **ashamed**.
4 My parents **got angry** if we got into trouble at school.
5 In our culture, you should always **respect** your parents.
6 Our parents only **praised** us if we did something really excellent.
7 Our parents **encouraged** us a lot.
8 They didn't often **criticise** us.
9 They **gave** me a lot of **confidence**.

5 Work in pairs and discuss. Use the words in exercise 4 to explain your answers.

• Was your upbringing more similar to Mi-Sun/Emily's or Rafael's? In what ways?
• How will/do you bring up your children? Is this different from your upbringing?

> My parents were strict – they punished us a lot.

> I'll praise and encourage my children a lot, but they'll get into trouble if they're rude.

Language focus 2
used to and *would*

1 Read the extracts about Mi-Sun/Emily and Rafael's after-school activities. Underline four verbs with *used to* and two with *would* ('*d*).

My mum decided that my brother and I should both learn the piano, so that's what we did. We used to practise for two hours every day after school and more at the weekend. Occasionally, I argued with my mum about piano practice and then my dad would tell me off, and I used to feel very ashamed.

After school we used to play in the street with our friends – football or skateboarding – or we'd go inside and play games on the computer. When I was about 11, I used to love hanging out in town with my friends. I thought I was really cool!

GRAMMAR

1 Complete the rules below with examples from exercise 1.

1 *Used to* and *would* describe habits in the past:

_____

_____

2 *Used to* describes states in the past:

_____

3 The Past simple (but not the Past continuous) also describes habits and states in the past:

_____

2 Notice how to compare the past to the present.

*I **still** feel ashamed if I argue with my parents.*

*I don't practise the piano **anymore**.*

PRACTICE

1 Complete the sentences with *used to* or *didn't use to* to make them true for you.

When I was 11 or 12 ...
1 I _____ play the piano.
2 my parents _____ give me pocket money.
3 I _____ have a regular bedtime.
4 I _____ play football with my friends.
5 I _____ go skateboarding.
6 my parents _____ get angry with me.

At secondary school ...
1 I _____ wear uniform.
2 I _____ get into trouble.
3 I _____ work hard.
4 I _____ get A's in all my exams.

2 Work in pairs and discuss.

- Which things in exercise 1 do you still do?
- Which things don't you do anymore?
- Think of five more things you used to do when you were a child / at secondary school.

3 Write a short description of your upbringing/ schooldays using *used to* and *would*.

Unit 2, Study & Practice 2, page 136

Vocabulary
Remembering and forgetting

1 The verbs below relate to memory. Cross out the phrases which cannot follow each verb. Use a dictionary to help you.

a Remember
- meeting someone for the first time
- when something happened
- a person, a word, an appointment, etc.
- to phone someone
- ~~someone to phone you~~

b Remind
- someone to phone you
- to do something
- someone about a message
- someone of another person

c Forget
- that you did something
- to do something
- a birthday, a message, an appointment, etc.
- of something
- about something

d Recognise
- someone / someone's face
- to do something
- a piece of music, a painting, etc.

2 Complete the questions below with one word where necessary.

1 Did anyone important forget _____ your birthday this year?
2 Who usually reminds you _____ do things?
3 Can you remember anything about _____ you were at nursery school? What can you remember?
4 Have you forgotten _____ do anything important this week?
5 Does anyone in your class remind you _____ of someone famous?
6 Do you usually recognise _____ pop songs quickly?
7 Is there anyone you must remember _____ phone today?
8 Have you ever seen anyone famous in the street? How did you recognise _____ him/her?

3 Work in pairs. Choose four of the questions above to ask your partner.

Task

Describe a personal memory

Preparation Listening and vocabulary

1a You are going to hear three people describe a personal memory related to the pictures below. Find these things in the pictures.

an anchor	a branch	a budgie
a cherry tree	a sailing boat	a swing

b Check the meaning of the verbs and phases in the box. Which things in exercise 1a do you think they relate to?

to be tame	to fall off	to fly off	to float
to get tangled	to perch	to black out	to get choppy
to rescue			

2 🎧 2.6 Listen to the three stories and match them with the pictures. Choose the best title for each story.

- A memorable celebration
- A story about a childhood pet
- Meeting someone important in my life
- Meeting a famous person
- A time I got into trouble
- A time I was really frightened
- A childhood accident
- A trip I'll never forget
- A day when everything went wrong

3 Listen again and answer as many of these questions as you can for each story.

1 When/Where did the story happen?
2 What other background information do you learn?
3 What happened?
4 How did the speaker feel?

4 Listen again and tick the phrases you hear in the Useful language box.

Task Speaking

1a Think of an important memory of your own. Use the titles in exercise 2 on page 22 to help you.

b Think about how to tell your story. Use the questions below and make notes. Ask your teacher for any words/phases you need.

  1 What kind of event was it and why do you still remember it?
  2 What was the background to the event?
  3 What were the main things that happened?
  4 How did it end?

> Useful language a–d

2a Work in pairs or groups. Take turns to tell your stories. Use your notes to help you.

b Listen to each other's stories. Show interest and ask questions.

> Useful language e

Follow up Writing

1 Write a paragraph about your important memory. Include the information in exercise 1b above.

USEFUL LANGUAGE

a Introducing the story
I remember when …
This is the story of something that happened to me when (I was about 11).
It was about (two) years ago.
At that time I was living/working/studying in …
I was with (my sister).
I used to (come home from school) …
The sun was shining.

b Describing the events
One day …
Suddenly …
Then …
After a while …
At the same time …

c Describing how you felt
It was so (embarrassing).
It was a bit (sad).
At the time we were very (worried).

d Ending the story
Eventually …
In the end …

e Listening with interest
How funny/amazing/sad!
Really?
So what happened?

SHARE YOUR TASK

Practise telling your story until you feel confident.

Film/Record yourself telling your story.

Share your film/recording with other students.

FLASHBULB MEMORIES

Find out first

1a Match the photos with the events below.

- the Beijing Olympic Games
- the Berlin Wall coming down
- the death of Diana, Princess of Wales
- the assassination of John F. Kennedy
- the first person on the moon

b Can you put the events in the order in which they happened?

c Go online to check your answers or ask your teacher. Which events do you think people remember the most?

View

2a You are going to watch a video about memories of important events. Before you watch, match the words and phrases in A with their meanings in B.

A
1 psychologist
2 striking
3 vivid
4 amygdala
5 lay down a memory
6 idiosyncratic
7 recall

B
a remember
b a part of the brain
c unique to one person and not true of everyone
d someone who studies the human mind
e very attractive or memorable
f makes strong, clear images in the mind
g make a new memory

b ▶ Watch the video. Which events from exercise 1 are mentioned? Are any other events mentioned?

3a Watch the video again and answer the questions.

1 What are the characteristics of a flashbulb memory?
2 How long do flashbulb memories last?
3 What is the purpose of the amygdala?
4 How many flashbulb memories do most people have?
5 What sort of news or event is associated with a flashbulb memory?
6 Why are deaths often the subject of flashbulb memories?

b Work in pairs and compare your answers.

World view

4a ▶ Watch three people talking about a flashbulb memory. Write notes in the table for each speaker.

	The public event	The personal associations
Sion		
Anna		
Martin		

b What did each person say? Work in pairs and compare your answers.

5a Work in small groups and discuss.

- What events in your country's recent history are likely to cause flashbulb memories?
- What global events from the 21st century are likely to cause them?
- Do you have any flashbulb memories? If so, what are they? Try to remember all the details of when you heard the news.

b Do any people in your class share flashbulb memories of the same event or piece of news? Are there any similarities in their memories?

🔊 FIND OUT MORE

6a Work in pairs. How much do you know about memory? Try to answer the questions below.

1 How can we improve our memory?
2 How does sleep affect your memory?
3 What is amnesia and what causes it?

b Go online to find out more information about one of the questions above.

Search: how to improve memory / effect of sleep on memory / causes of amnesia

▶ Write up your research

7 Write a paragraph about the question you researched in exercise 6. Use the prompts below to help you.

- One of the best ways to ... is to ...
- Another useful tip is to ...
- (Sleep) causes us to ...
- (Amnesia) happens when ...

03

ACROSS THE GLOBE

The big wide world quiz

Language focus 1
Comparatives and superlatives

1a Work in groups. Do the quiz above to test your world knowledge.

b  3.1 Listen and check your answers. Remember one more piece of information about each question.

2 Underline all the comparatives and superlatives in the quiz.

GRAMMAR

Revision of basic forms

1 What are the comparative and superlative forms of these adjectives?

long   tall   happy   popular   far   hard-working

2 Write the rules for one-, two- and three-syllable adjectives.

3 Think of two more irregular adjectives like *far*.

Big and small differences

4 Match the sentences with the correct picture.

1 *X* is much higher than *Y*.
2 *X* is a (little) bit higher than *Y*.
3 *X* is a lot higher than *Y*.
4 *X* is slightly higher than *Y*.

Superlative phrases

5 Complete the missing words in the superlative phrases.
1 It's the tallest city _____ the world.
2 It's the second/third biggest city _____ the USA.
3 It's one _____ the biggest countries in South America.
4 It's got _____ far the longest coastline in the world.
5 The _____ happy people in the world are the citizens of Togo.

Part 1: People

There are over six billion people in the world.
Find out more about them. Look at the nationalities in the box.

> Americans   Danes   Germans   Indians   Mexicans

1 Who are happier and more satisfied than any other nationality in the world?

2 Who work harder than any other people in the world?

3 Who are more likely to go to the cinema than any other nationality in the world?

4 Who discuss politics more often than any other nationality in the world?

5 Who are the funniest people in the world, according to a survey of 30,000 people of different nationalities?

Part 2: Countries and cities

It's a big wide world. What do you know about it?
Choose the correct country or city (a–d).

6 Which city is more popular with tourists than London, New York or Rome?
 a Rio de Janeiro   b Paris   c Shanghai   d Moscow

7 Which is the third largest country in South America after Brazil and Argentina?
 a Colombia   b Peru   c Ecuador   d Chile

8 Which US city is the furthest north?
 a Chicago   b San Francisco   c Dallas   d New York

9 Which country has the longest coastline?
 a Indonesia   b India   c Japan   d Canada

10 Which is the tallest city in the world (the city with the most skyscrapers)?
 a Tokyo   b London   c Hong Kong   d New York

 FIND OUT MORE Go online to find out more about how hard each nationality works. Search for the OECD report into working hours and household chores.

PRACTICE

1 Add two words to each sentence to complete the information from the quiz. Use the correct form of the adjective in brackets.

Canada's coastline is _much longer_ (long) than the coastline of Indonesia or Russia.

1 Paris, with 15 million tourists, is a lot _____ _____ (popular) than New York, which has 10 million.

2 Argentina is the _____ _____ (large) country in South America.

3 Chicago is _____ _____ (far) north than New York.

4 Mexicans are the _____ _____ (hard-working) people in the world.

5 The Danes are a _____ _____ (happy) than the people of Togo.

6 The people of India are a lot _____ _____ (likely) to go to the cinema than the people of Malaysia.

7 Americans are considered _____ _____ (funny) other nationalities.

8 The Germans discuss politics much _____ _____ (often) than the British.

2a 🎧 3.2 Listen to eight instructions and write your answers in random order on a piece of paper.

b Work in pairs and swap answers. Take turns to ask and answer questions about the places you wrote about. Were any of your answers the same?

> Why did you write … ?
>
> Because I think it's one of the ugliest buildings in this town.

3a 🎧 3.3 Look at the information about France, Ireland and the UK on page 128. Then listen to six statements and decide if they are true (T) or false (F). Correct the false statements.

b Work in pairs. Use the information on page 128 to write six more true or false statements about the three countries. Read your sentences to another pair. Can they say which are true?

4a Write six sentences comparing your country to a nearby country or an English-speaking country you know. Use the prompts in the box.

> cities   climate   cost of living   population   scenery   size

b Compare your ideas in groups.

> … is a lot more expensive than …
>
> … is a bit bigger than …

France is a lot more expensive than Poland.
Spain is a bit bigger than Germany.

> Unit 3, Study & Practice 1, page 138

Vocabulary

Features and sights

1a Look at the words in the box. Where do you <u>usually</u> find these features and sights? Put them in the correct place in the diagram below.

> ancient ruins   a bay   a beach   a bridge   a canal
> a cathedral   a cliff   docks   a factory   farmland
> a festival   a (rain)forest   a harbour   a hill   an island
> a lake   a market   a monument   a mosque   a museum
> a palace   a shopping mall   a skyscraper   a temple
> a view   a village   a waterfall (falls)

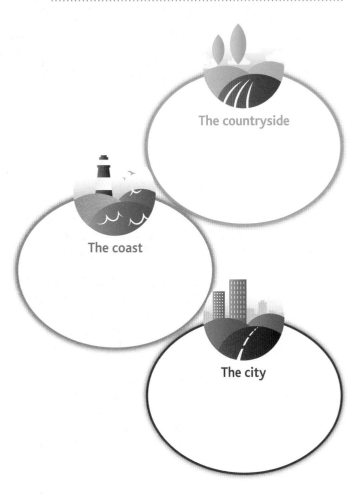

The countryside

The coast

The city

b Add two more features and sights to each group.

2a Work in groups. How many of these world-famous places can you match with words from exercise 1a?

the Amazon *rainforest*

1 the Cannes Film _____
2 Buckingham _____
3 Sydney _____
4 _____ Ontario
5 the Hermitage _____
6 the Canary _____
7 the Blue _____
8 Iguazu _____
9 the Suez _____

b 🎧 3.4 Listen and check.

Reading

1 Work in pairs and discuss. Which of these things do you look for in a holiday destination? What else do you look for?

- sunshine and beautiful beaches
- nature (mountains, forests, waterfalls, etc.)
- ancient ruins and historical sights
- nightlife and shopping
- art and culture (festivals, palaces, etc.)

2 Read the website quickly. Would you prefer Landon's holiday or Valentina's holiday? Why?

3 Work in pairs. Which pair can find the following information in the text first?

1 Landon's university course: _____
2 Where in Thailand the Grand Palace is located: _____
3 When Angkor Wat was rediscovered: _____
4 Where Halong Bay is in Vietnam: _____
5 The place where 'full moon' parties happen: _____
6 Valentina's favourite activity: _____
7 The name of a festival in Dubai: _____
8 How long it takes to fly from Santiago to Dubai: _____
9 The number of shops in Dubai Mall: _____
10 The name for a traditional market in Dubai: _____

4a Look at the readers' comments. Are the comments for Landon or Valentina? Is each comment suggesting *visit* or *avoid*?

b What places would you recommend or not recommend? Write your own comment for Landon or Valentina to add to the website.

5 Underline these phrases in the text. Then choose the correct meaning, a or b.

1 ... it's **a must-see**!
   a You should definitely go and see it.
   b It's necessary to go and see it.
2 There's ... **nowhere quite like it**.
   a It's similar to other places.
   b It's different from other places.
3 Dubai is **right up her street**.
   a It's very close to her.
   b It's the kind of place she'll like a lot.
4 ... they're **worth visiting** ...
   a It's a good idea to visit them.
   b They can be very expensive.
5 ... **you can't beat** these two cities.
   a You won't like these two cities.
   b They're the best.

6 Work in groups. Take turns to talk about your ideal holiday. Other members of the group listen and recommend places to visit/avoid. Try to use the phrases from exercise 5.

VISIT OR AVOID?

What's the right type of holiday for you?
Get the advice of our travel experts and readers.

Landon is from Australia. He's 24 and he's studying archaeology at university. Landon wants a holiday with lots of local history and culture ... and a few sandy beaches to relax. He hates crowds and noise.

VISIT *Thailand, Cambodia and Vietnam*

It sounds like a lot of travelling, but there's so much to see! Fly into Bangkok and spend a few days visiting the beautiful floating markets, the Old City and, of course, the Grand Palace – the historic heart of Thailand. With its temples, halls and extraordinary architecture, it's a must-see!

Then travel overland to Angkor Wat in Cambodia. Angkor Wat is a huge temple complex which contains the largest religious building in the world. About 500 years ago, Angkor Wat was mysteriously abandoned and only rediscovered 150 years ago.

After that, fly to Halong Bay in the north of Vietnam. Thousands of tiny islands seem to float in the blue waters of the bay. Some people call it the Eighth Wonder of the World. There's certainly nowhere quite like it.

AVOID the 'party islands' like Koh Samui. With their 'full moon' parties these are great for some people, but not for people like you who hate noise!

Valentina is from Chile. She's 27 years old and she loves shopping and sun. She wants to go somewhere special in January or February.

VISIT *Dubai*

It's one of the fastest-growing cities in the world, and it's also one of the best for shopping. What other city has an annual shopping festival? It's a long flight for Valentina, over 17 hours from Santiago, but if she has a couple of weeks to spare, she'll find that cosmopolitan Dubai is right up her street.

The weather makes it too hot to walk outside for much of the year (though it should be fine in January) so shopping malls are one way to escape the heat. Dubai Mall, for example, has over 1,200 shops – more than some small cities. And just like small cities, some of its malls have theatres, art galleries and even indoor ski slopes.

If all this seems a bit too artificial, Valentina could try the Dubai 'souks', which are a kind of traditional market. They aren't quite as beautiful as the bazaars in Turkey and Morocco, but they're worth visiting anyway. It's where the locals go and it's a good place to learn to haggle and pick up some bargains!

AVOID most of Europe. Cities like Edinburgh, London, Paris and Berlin are great for shopping, but there's not much chance of seeing the sun in January or February!

COMMENTS

I've just come back from two weeks in Turkey. The ancient ruins at Ephesus are amazing. I think it's exactly what you're looking for.
Lulu_RT, Germany, 6.10 p.m.

Try Los Angeles. You'll find plenty of places to shop till you drop!
LucyLane, USA, 4.09 p.m.

You should spend a couple of weeks in St Petersburg and Moscow. I've been around the world and to my mind you can't beat these two cities. There are hundreds of malls so you won't be disappointed.
Yuri55, Russia, 3.35 p.m.

If you're looking for a quiet time, you should come to Luton. It's just won an award (for Britain's most boring city!).
Cal_M, UK, 2.23 p.m.

"I think I'm very lucky compared to my mum's generation."

3a 🎧 3.5 Listen to Pan (49) and her daughter Jasmine (24) as they talk about how Shanghai has changed. Check your answers to exercise 1. Did they say the same things as you?

b Listen again. Overall, are Pan and Jasmine positive about the changes or negative? Give reasons for your answer.

Language focus 2
Different ways of comparing

1 Look at the two photos showing the same part of Shanghai 20 years ago and now, then read 'It's a fact!' Work in pairs and answer the questions.

- Where is Shanghai and what do you know about it?
- Why do you think the population of the city has changed so much in 20 years?
- What are the main differences between how the city looked then and now?

2 Try to guess the correct answers.

In Shanghai 25 years ago:

1 the streets were *very similar to / completely different from* the streets now.
2 the historic buildings are *the same as / different from* how they were.
3 older people play *exactly the same / completely different* games on the street.
4 younger people were *not as busy as / the same as* they are now.
5 clothes were *more / less* colourful than they are now.
6 shops were *better / worse* than they are now.
7 there were *fewer / more* cars than there are now.

GRAMMAR

1 Read the sentences in exercise 2 again. Complete the phases for comparing in box A with the prepositions in box B.

A different   similar   the same   worse   not as busy
fewer   less

B than (x3)   as (x2)   from   to

2 Choose the correct answers and give reasons.
1 There were *fewer / less* cars then.
2 There was *fewer / less* traffic then.

3 Put the phrases in the best place on the line.

completely different from   about the same as
exactly the same as   a bit different from   very similar to

the same
1 _____
2 the same as
3 _____
4 _____
5 similar to
6 _____
7 different from
different
8 _____

PRACTICE

1a 🎧 **3.6** Look at the photos of Times Square in New York, USA. Listen and decide if the statements you hear are true (T) or false (F). Correct the false statements.

b Work in pairs. Can you think of any other differences?

2a Think about your town now and at some point in the past. Write six sentences comparing the things in the box then and now.

clothes	the cost of living	historic buildings	people
pollution	public transport	restaurants	shops
the streets	traffic		

b Work in pairs and compare your answers.

> I guess pollution wasn't as bad as it is now.

> The historic buildings are exactly the same as before.

PRONUNCIATION

1 🎧 **3.7** Listen and write down the six sentences you hear.

2 🎧 **3.8** Notice the stress and /ə/ sounds in the comparative phrases. Practise saying the phrases.

1 /ə/ /ə/		4 /ə/ /ə/	
better than ...		not as **good** as ...	
2 /ə/ /ə/ /ə/		5 /ə/ /ə/	
a **lot bus**ier than ...		the **same** as ...	
3 /ə/ /ə/		6 /ə/	
different from ...		**sim**ilar to ...	

3 Practise the sentences you wrote down, paying attention to the /ə/ sounds.

Unit 3, Study & Practice 2, page 139

Vocabulary
Adjectives for describing places

1 Look at the words in box A. Which words, if any, do you associate with the cities in box B? Compare your answers in pairs.

A arty colourful cosmopolitan crowded dangerous dirty expensive friendly historic industrial lively modern old-fashioned peaceful polluted poor romantic smart spectacular touristy

B Bangkok Cairo Hong Kong Moscow New York Paris Rio de Janeiro Venice

2 🎧 **3.9** Listen to three descriptions and match them with photos A–C on page 126. Which cities do you think are being described? Check your answers on page 129.

3 Listen again and tick the words that you hear from exercise 1.

4a Write a short description of a town or city you know, or know about, but don't name it. Include at least three adjectives, and include a clue at the end!

It's a lively, arty city on the west coast of the USA. It's quite spectacular with steep hills and it's where the Golden Gate Bridge is.

b Work in groups. Take turns to read your descriptions and guess the places which are being described.

Task

Provide an insider's guide

Preparation Listening

1 Name three famous tourist attractions in London. Have you ever visited London? If so, which places did you see?

2 🎧 3.10 Carla is visiting London for the first time and asks her friend Tom for advice. Listen to the first part of the conversation and choose the best summary.

Carla is asking advice because she wants to know:
a the most popular tourist attractions.
b the places that locals go to.
c the cheapest places to eat out and shop.

3 🎧 3.11 Listen to the second part of the conversation. Match the places Tom recommends with the ideas in the box.

1 the South Bank
2 Brick Lane market
3 Richmond Park
4 the Sherlock Holmes Museum

theatres and concert halls *1*	ethnic food
free exhibitions	the 19th century
street entertainers	picnics
deer	views of famous buildings
vintage stuff	individually designed clothes
clubs and nightlife	a lively atmosphere

4 Listen again and tick the phrases you hear in the Useful language box.

5 Which of the places that Tom mentions would/ wouldn't you like to visit? If you could visit only one, which would you choose? Why?

Task Speaking

1a You are going to recommend places to go to in your city, region or country (or another place you know well). Decide which place you are going to talk about.

b Make a list of five places to recommend in your city/ country. The places should be popular with locals.

2a Make notes about why you recommend these places. Ask your teacher for any words/phrases you need.

> *the Old Town – beautiful square; interesting old buildings; great atmosphere*

b Spend a few minutes planning what you will say about each place.

> Useful language a and b

3 Work in pairs. Act out conversations similar to Tom and Carla's. Take turns to ask for and give advice.

> Useful language c

LANGUAGE LIVE

10:15 | TRAIN 501 | DUE 10:48
10:25 | TRAIN 010 | DELAYED
10:25 | TRAIN 554 | CANCELLED
10:41 | TRAIN 214 | DELAYED

Speaking
Travel problems

1a Work in small groups and look at the picture. Which travel problems does it show? What travel problems have you experienced? What happened?

b ▶ Watch the video of three conversations. What problem is each passenger having? How does he/she resolve the problem?

2a Which conversation are these phrases from? Write T (taxi), B (bus) or Tr (train). Then watch again and check your answers.

1 Excuse me ... what was that announcement? *Tr*
2 One more question: is this ticket still valid?
3 Can I ask you a question? ... How do I get to the Manhattan shopping centre?
4 Do you know where I get off?
5 Could you tell me how much it will cost?
6 Do you know which platform the 4:38 goes from?
7 Do you know how long it will take?
8 Could you tell me where I have to change?
9 Do you know when the next one is?

b Which questions are useful on more than one form of transport?

Question 2 is useful on a bus or a train.

3 Look at the questions in exercise 2a again.

1 What phrases make questions 1–3 polite?
2 What phrases make questions 4–9 polite? What is different about the word order?

4 Rewrite the questions in a more polite form using the prompts in brackets.

Is this seat free? (a question)
Could I ask you a question? Is this seat free?

1 Where do I get on the bus? (know)
2 Which platform is the 6:30 to Paris? (tell me)
3 Can I use this ticket on the train? (excuse)
4 What time will the train arrive? (know)
5 How do I get to the airport? (last question)
6 Where do I have to change? (tell me)
7 Does this bus go to High Park? (a question)

5a Work in pairs. Choose a new travel problem and write a short dialogue. Try to use polite questions.

b Act out your conversation to the rest of class. Which conversation was the most entertaining?

Writing
A travel blog

1 Read the two travel blogs below. Which one do you think is better? Why?

2 Which of these things do Hannah and Florence do? Write H (Hannah), F (Florence) or HF (both).

1 Give first impressions
2 Mention some history
3 Talk about feelings
4 Describe the hotel
5 Mention places visited
6 Describe sights and sounds

Venice
Hannah Gormley, September 2nd

We arrived in Venice about midday on Friday. It's a nice old city. The only way to get around Venice is to walk. It's the best city in the world for couples. The first place we went to was Piazza San Marco. It was pretty. We ate an ice cream. Then we walked along the Grand Canal and saw the Bridge of Sighs. It's nice but busy. In the evening we had a meal in a restaurant and then we went to bed.

Escape from Alcatraz!
Florence Wall, September 3rd

We arrived in San Francisco on Tuesday afternoon. The first thing I noticed was how beautiful and cosmopolitan it is here. In the 1960s it was home to the hippy movement, but nowadays it's home to a lot of internet companies like Twitter. Because of this, some parts of San Francisco are very smart and expensive while other parts are a bit more old-fashioned and arty. Landmarks like the Golden Gate Bridge are world-famous, but seeing them for real is quite special. However, our hotel isn't special at all. We've got a tiny, dirty room and the beds are awful. I had a very restless night.

On Wednesday morning we took a boat to Alcatraz, the famous prison on an island in San Francisco Bay. It closed in 1963 and these days it's a popular tourist attraction. Jennifer was feeling a bit seasick by the time we arrived, but it was worth the trip. The island is small and rocky. You can hear the seagulls and smell the sea air even in the prison. The prison itself is like a huge factory. I would hate to be in prison there, but Jennifer thought that it was nicer than our hotel!

3a Read the tips for writing a good blog. Find examples of each tip in Florence's blog.

1 Be honest. Talk about the good and the bad times.
2 Use all your senses: write about what you saw, heard, smelt, felt and tasted.
3 Give some basic facts about the place you visited.
4 Use interesting adjectives to describe the place (e.g. old-fashioned, huge).

b Which tips did/didn't Hannah follow? Make six ordinary adjectives in her blog more interesting.

c Add the following facts to Hannah's blog in the correct place.

1 ... which was designed by Antonio Contino.
2 ... that was founded around 1,500 years ago.
3 Venetians call it 'the Piazza'.
4 ... because no cars, buses or trains are allowed in.

4a You are going to write a travel blog.
EITHER write a blog for a journey you made in the past (imagine you are there now).
OR write the blog of someone visiting your area for the first time.
Make notes under the headings in exercise 2.

b Write the first draft of your blog. Use the checklist below to help you.

- Have you followed all the tips for writing a good travel blog?
- Have you used past tenses and comparatives correctly?
- Have you used capital letters for place names?
- Have you checked your spelling?

5a When you have finished, swap with a partner and comment on his/her blog. Use the checklist above to help you. Would you like to read more of your partner's blog?

b Read your partner's comments and ask him/her for more information if necessary. Then write the final draft of your blog.

AFTER UNIT 3 YOU CAN ...

Describe and compare different places.

Make recommendations about places to visit and why.

Ask for information when travelling.

Give a written description of a place you have visited.

04

REAL LIVES

IN THIS UNIT

- **Grammar:** Present perfect and Past simple; Present perfect simple and Present perfect continuous

- **Vocabulary:** Life events; Personal qualities

- **Task:** Nominate someone for an award

- **World culture:** Charles Dickens: Writer and campaigner

Language focus 1
Present perfect and Past simple

1 Work in groups and discuss. Have you achieved anything the other students don't know about? For example, have you ever won an award, been in a newspaper or played in a band? What happened?

2a How many of the famous people in the photos do you recognise? Check your answers on page 131.

b Work in pairs. Can you match the people with the surprising achievements in the text?

The surprising achievements of famous people
1 _____ has published a best-selling book for children.
2 _____ wrote over 70 books and won the Nobel Prize for Literature.
3 _____ has learnt to speak six languages and has founded many schools for poor children.
4 _____ has studied architecture and has designed several buildings.
5 _____ has rowed from England to France.

c 4.1 Listen and check. One of the achievements was planned but didn't happen. Which one was it and why?

3 Choose the correct verb form. Listen again and check.

1 Barack Obama **published** / **has published** several books. In 2008, he **wrote** / **has written** a book for his two daughters.
2 Over the course of his life, Winston Churchill **painted** / **has painted** more than 500 pictures and **wrote** / **has written** over 70 books. In 1953, he **won** / **has won** the Nobel Prize for Literature.
3 Since 1995, Shakira **founded** / **has founded** schools for poor children all over Columbia. She **also raised** / **has also raised** many millions of dollars for charity.
4 Brad Pitt **was** / **has been** interested in architecture since he was young, and he **designed** / **has designed** a restaurant and an apartment building.
5 Before she **was** / **has been** engaged to Prince William, Kate Middleton **trained** / **has trained** to row across the English Channel in an all-woman team.

2a **4.2 Listen to five everyday conversations and match them with the descriptions below.**

a a teacher talking to some students
b a woman meeting her friend in the street
c two flatmates at home
d some business people meeting at a party
e some colleagues in an office

b **Complete these extracts from the conversations with the Present perfect form of a verb in the box.**

change   finish   not finish   go (x2)   lock   lose (x2)
meet   see

1 I _____ my mobile. _____ you _____ it anywhere?
2 You _____ your hair – it's really nice.
3 You _____ weight, haven't you?
4 She was here – perhaps she _____ just _____ out for a minute.
5 She _____ home. She left about ten minutes ago.
6 _____ she _____ her office?
7 We _____ the test. Can we go now?
8 Sorry, I _____ yet. Can I have another five minutes?
9 Pierre, _____ you _____ Karimah?

c **Listen again and check your answers.**

PRONUNCIATION

1 **4.3 Listen to the first conversation from exercise 2a. Find an example where:**
1 *have* is pronounced /hæv/ (= the strong form)
2 *have* is pronounced /həv/ (= the weak form)
3 *have* is pronounced /v/ (= the contracted form)

2 **Practise the following phrases, starting with the strong words. Use the recording to help you.**
1 lost → I've lost → I've lost my mobile.
2 seen → Have you seen → Have you seen it?
3 have → I have → Yes, I have.

3 **Look at audio script 4.3 on page 170. Practise reading it with a partner. Pay attention to the stress and to weak forms.**

GRAMMAR

1 **How do we form the Present perfect simple? Which verbs in exercise 3 are regular/irregular?**

2 **We use the Present perfect when a past action is connected to the present in some way. Choose the correct verb form in the rules below and find an example of each rule in exercise 3.**
1 If an action started in the past but continues into the present, we use the *Past simple / Present perfect*.
2 If we want to show that an action in the past is still relevant now, we use the *Past simple / Present perfect*.
3 If an action happened in a finished time period, or if we say when it happened, we use the *Past simple / Present perfect*.

3 **Which time phrases only go with the Past simple? Which go with the Present perfect?**

in 2010   ten minutes ago   since 2005   when?   so far
yesterday   when I was young   in the last ten years

PRACTICE

1 **Read about the surprising achievement of an ordinary person, Toby Ord. Complete the story with the correct form of the verb in brackets.**

The surprising achievements of an ordinary person

Toby Ord is an ordinary person, but he ¹_____ (decide) to do something extraordinary. He ²_____ (promise) to give away £1 million to charity over the course of his life. Toby isn't rich. He's a university researcher in the UK and he earns an average salary. But in the past year alone he ³_____ (give) away more than one-third of his earnings and last year he ⁴_____ (give) away his savings of £15,000, too.

So why does he do it? 'When I was a poor student I ⁵_____ (find) I was in the richest four percent of the world. When I ⁶_____ (realise) that, I ⁷_____ (decide) to change how I look at the world. I don't want more stuff. The money that I ⁸_____ (give) away this year ⁹_____ (buy) 4,000 extra years of life for people in developing countries.'

3 **Work in pairs. Find six things that you have done that your partner hasn't. Use the ideas on page 126 or your own ideas. Ask and answer questions like this:**

> Have you ever written a blog?
>
> Yes, I have. I wrote one when I was at college.

Unit 4, Study & Practice 1, page 141

37

Reading and speaking

1 Work in groups and discuss.

- Did your parents have any ambitions or plans for you when you were growing up?
- What did they do to help you achieve them?

2 Look at the photos of Andre Agassi and read the text below. What do you learn about:

- the reasons for his fame?
- his parents and childhood?
- his career?
- his personal problems?
- his marriage and children?

ANDRE AGASSI

Andre Agassi is generally considered one of the greatest tennis players of all time and the greatest returner of the ball in the history of tennis.

Agassi was introduced to tennis by his father, Mike, who had been a tennis groundsman during his youth. Mike Agassi trained all four of his children intensively to become tennis professionals, but only Andre, the youngest, showed great talent.

Andre went on to win numerous championships and became one of the biggest stars in the history of the game. However, he also suffered from drug and other personal problems.

Andre Agassi is now married to one of the greatest women players ever, Steffi Graf, whose father also trained her hard as a child. Since he retired from tennis, Agassi has dedicated himself to helping poor and abused young people, giving them the chance to have a good education. Agassi and Graf have not taught their children how to play tennis.

 FIND OUT MORE Go online to find out more about Andre Agassi and pushy parents.

3 Work in pairs and discuss.

- How old do you think Agassi was when he started playing tennis?
- What kind of childhood and upbringing do you think he had?

4 Read the extract from Agassi's autobiography and answer the questions.

1 What is Andre doing in this extract?
2 How does the young Andre feel about tennis?
3 How does he feel about his father?
4 What is 'the dragon'?

Pushed too far?

5 Read the text again and mark the statements below true (T), false (F) or not sure (NS). Underline the part of the text that gives you the answer.

1 Andre feels that no one cares about his opinion.
2 He hates his father.
3 His father wants him to be frightened of the dragon.
4 He feels worried because he can't do what his father wants.
5 He is more frightened of the dragon than of his father.

I'm seven years old. I'm talking to myself, because I'm scared and because I'm the only person who listens to me. Under my breath I whisper: just quit, Andre, just give up. Put down your racket and walk off this court right now. Go into the house and get something good to eat. … Wouldn't that feel like heaven, Andre? To just quit? To never play tennis again?

But I can't. Not only would my father chase me round the house with my racket, but something deep inside me won't let me. I hate tennis, hate it with all my heart, but still I keep playing, keep hitting all morning and all afternoon because I have no choice.

…

At the moment my hatred for tennis is focused on the dragon, a ball machine modified by my father. … The dragon looks, at first glance, like the ball machine in every tennis club in America, but to me it's actually a living, breathing creature straight out of my comic books. The dragon has a brain, a will, a black heart and a horrifying voice. … As the ball rises slowly to its mouth, … the dragon gives a terrifying roar then fires a ball at me at 170 km an hour. … I flinch every time.

My father has deliberately made the dragon fearsome. … At seven years old, I'm small for my age. … My father wants the balls that shoot from the dragon's mouth to land at my feet as if dropped from an aeroplane. The way the balls bounce makes them impossible to return in the normal way. …

> Hit earlier, my father yells. Damn it Andre, hit earlier. …

But even that's not enough for my father. Hit earlier, he yells, hit earlier. My father yells everything twice, sometimes three times, sometimes ten. Harder, he shouts, harder. But what's the use? No matter how hard I hit a ball, no matter how early, the ball comes back. Every ball I send across the net joins the thousands that already cover the court.

…

My father says if I hit 2,500 balls each day, I'll hit 17,500 each week and at the end of one year I'll hit nearly one million balls. He believes in math. Numbers, he says, don't lie. A child who hits one million balls each year will be unbeatable.

He's yelling directly in my ear. It's not enough to hit everything the dragon fires at me, my father wants me to hit it harder and faster than the dragon. He wants me to beat the dragon. The thought makes me panicky. I tell myself: you can't beat the dragon. How can you beat something that never stops? … The dragon is a lot like my father. Except my father is worse. At least the dragon stands in front of me, where I can see it. My father stays behind me. I rarely see him, only hear him day and night, yelling in my ear.

From Andre Agassi's autobiography *Open*, HarperCollins 2009

6 Find the words in the box in the text. Circle them in blue if they relate to tennis and in red if they relate to Andre's feelings of fear. Use the context to help you.

a racket   a court   to chase   horrifying
a terrifying roar   to flinch   fearsome   to bounce
to hit   to yell   unbeatable   to beat   panicky

7 Work in pairs and discuss.

- Do you think Andre's father was right to push his children in the way he did? Why do you think he did it?
- How are Andre Agassi and Steffi Graf's lives similar?
- How are they bringing up their own children? Why?

8a Work in groups. Read the statements below and decide whether you agree, disagree or partly agree. Think of examples (of famous people or people you know) to support your opinions.

- It's unhealthy for parents to push their children – it can really damage them.
- It's natural for parents to be closely involved in their children's activities and to do everything possible to help them to succeed.
- A lot of successful people have had pushy parents – that's often why people become successful.
- Parents shouldn't try to achieve their own dreams through their children. Everyone has the right to lead their own life.

b Compare your ideas with other students.

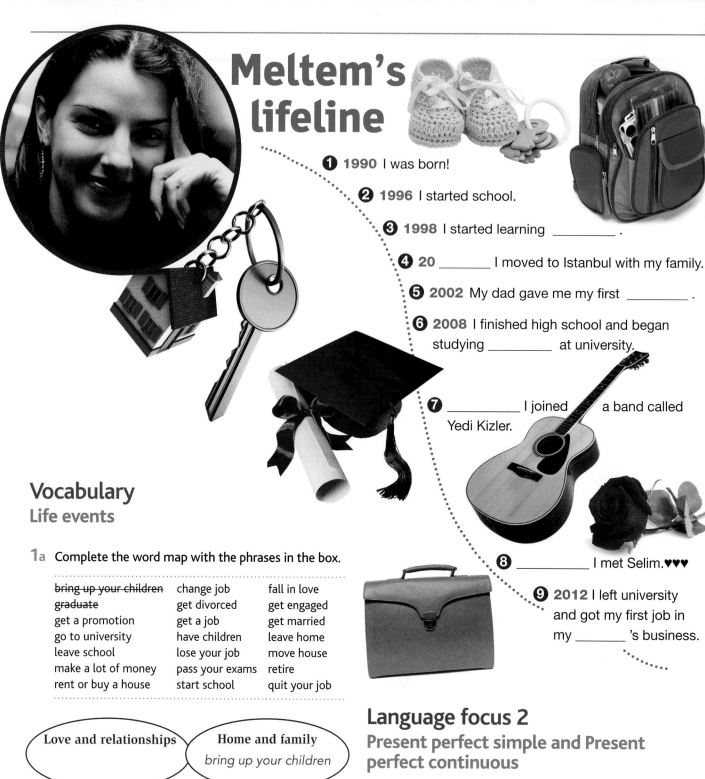

Meltem's lifeline

1 1990 I was born!

2 1996 I started school.

3 1998 I started learning _____ .

4 20_____ I moved to Istanbul with my family.

5 2002 My dad gave me my first _____ .

6 2008 I finished high school and began studying _____ at university.

7 _____ I joined a band called Yedi Kizler.

8 _____ I met Selim.♥♥♥

9 2012 I left university and got my first job in my _____ 's business.

Vocabulary
Life events

1a Complete the word map with the phrases in the box.

bring up your children	change job	fall in love
graduate	get divorced	get engaged
get a promotion	get a job	get married
go to university	have children	leave home
leave school	lose your job	move house
make a lot of money	pass your exams	retire
rent or buy a house	start school	quit your job

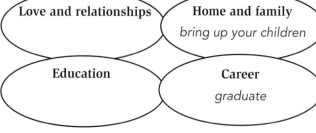

Love and relationships

Home and family
bring up your children

Education

Career
graduate

b Work in pairs and discuss.
- In what order do the things in each category usually happen? (There are different possibilities.)
- Which of these things have you done?
- Which haven't you done yet?
- Which of these things are you going/hoping to do in the future?

2 Look at the words/phrases in exercise 1a again. Then do the quiz on page 126 to check what you remember.

Language focus 2
Present perfect simple and Present perfect continuous

1 🎧 4.4 Read Meltem's lifeline above. Then listen and complete the gaps.

2 Use Meltem's lifeline and audio script 4.4 on page 170 to complete the sentences.

1 She lived in Ankara for _____ years.
2 She's been studying English since she was _____ .
3 She's been living in Istanbul for _____ years.
4 She studied business for _____ years at university.
5 She's been going out with Selim since 20_____ .
6 She's been working for her uncle for about _____ years.
7 She's been in the band for about _____ years.
8 They've played about _____ gigs.
9 She's been looking for a _____ recently and she thinks that she has finally found one.

GRAMMAR

1 Which sentences in exercise 2 are in the Present perfect simple? Which are in the Present perfect continuous? Read the rules.

1 We use the Present perfect continuous form in a similar way to the Present perfect simple: to talk about past actions that are connected to the present.
*Meltem's **been looking** for a flat.*
(= relevant now / continuing into the present)

2 However, the Present perfect continuous emphasises:
- that the action has duration or is repeated (it is often used with *for* and *since*).
*She's **been living** in Istanbul since she was 12.*
*She's **been playing** the guitar for a long time.*
- that we are interested in the activity itself rather than the result of the action.
*She's **been looking** for a flat. (activity)*
*She's **found** a flat. (result)*

3 We cannot use the Present perfect continuous if:
- we are describing a state.
*She's **been** in the band for three years.*
- we say how many times something has happened.
*They've played **20** gigs.*

2 *For* or *since*? Choose the correct answers to complete the rules and give an example from the sentences in exercise 2.

1 We use *for* / *since* with periods of time. _____
2 We use *for* / *since* with a point in time. _____

PRACTICE

1 Read more about Meltem and her family below. Complete the gaps with the correct form of the verb in brackets, using the Past simple, Present perfect simple or Present perfect continuous, and choose the correct answers.

1 Meltem _____ (learn) to drive *for* / *since* quite a long time. She _____ (take) a test in October last year, but unfortunately she failed, so recently her father _____ (give) her lessons.

2 Meltem's brother, Murat, _____ (study) medicine *for* / *since* four years. He wants to be a doctor. He _____ (pass) all his exams so far.

3 Meltem's mother _____ (be) an English teacher *for* / *since* over 20 years. Last year she _____ (get) a promotion to deputy head and *for* / *since* then she _____ (work) very long hours.

4 Meltem's father _____ (work) for a bank *for* / *since* over 30 years, but two years ago he retired. However, he's been very busy *for* / *since* he retired. Last year he _____ (buy) an old boat and for the last few months he _____ (try) to repair it.

PRONUNCIATION

In normal speech, if a word ends with a consonant sound and the next word begins with a vowel sound, the two sounds 'link'.
for about a month

1 🎧 4.5 Listen and mark the sounds that link.
1 a couple of minutes ago   2 since April
3 for a while   4 a long time ago
5 since eight o'clock

2 Practise saying the phrases, paying attention to the words that link together.

3 🎧 4.6 Listen and write down the six sentences you hear. Then practise saying them.

2a 🎧 4.7 Listen and answer the six questions. Write notes, not full sentences.
1 *3 months*

b How many of the questions can you remember? Listen again and check. Choose three of the questions to ask a partner.

3a Draw your own lifeline. Mark important dates and events in your life.

b You are going to explain your lifeline to other students. Spend a few minutes planning which verb forms to use.

c Work in small groups. Take turns to explain your lifelines and answer any questions.

I started skiing when I was four.

How long have you been working as a vet?

d Find a student from another group. Tell him/her about the people in your group.

Unit 4, Study & Practice 2, page 142

Vocabulary
Personal qualities

1 Read the descriptions below. Mark each one to show if it is a positive quality (+), a negative quality (–) or if you are not sure (NS).

- He/She's (extremely):
  - charming.
  - courageous.
  - creative.
  - dedicated.
  - determined.
  - egotistical.
  - inspiring.
  - obsessive.
  - original.
  - ruthless.
  - self-confident.
  - talented.
- He/She's got strong principles.
- He/She's a strong leader.
- He/She cares a lot about other people.
- He/She doesn't care about other people.
- He/She likes publicity.
- He/She inspires respect.

2a Add names to three of the categories.

1 A famous world leader: _____
2 A well-known business leader: _____
3 A writer, artist or musician who is famous at the moment: _____
4 A successful sports personality from your country: _____
5 A successful person you know personally: _____

b Choose at least three words or phrases to describe each person you have written down. Compare and explain your answers in groups.

3 Complete the sentences to make them true for you.

1 I really admire people who ... *are courageous and have strong principles.*
2 I never trust people who ...
3 I don't like people who ...
4 I wish I was (more) ...

Task

Nominate someone for an award

Each year the Inspiration Award is given to an individual who has done one or more of the following things:

- inspired others to follow their example
- done something remarkable to help others
- provided an outstanding role model for others
- achieved something remarkable against the odds.

Nominations can include artists, actors, musicians, leaders, sports personalities and TV personalities, as well as members of your local community.

Lionel Messi 4.9

Mark Zuckerberg 4.10

Preparation Listening

1 Read about the 'Inspiration Award'. What kind of person is it awarded to?

2 Look at the photos. Which people have you heard of? Why do you think they might be nominated for the Inspiration Award?

3a 🎧 4.8–4.12 Work as a class. Choose three people from the photos and listen to their nominations. What reasons do the speakers give for each nomination?

b Listen to the same three nominations again. Tick the phrases you hear in the Useful language box.

Emma Watson 4.8
Jamie Foxx 4.12
Aung San Suu Kyi 4.11

Task Speaking

1 Choose a person to nominate for the Inspiration Award. You can choose someone in the photos if you can't think of anyone else.

2 Make notes under these headings about why he/she deserves to win. Ask your teacher for any words/phrases you need.

Brief career details: Personal qualities:
Achievements: Influence on other people:

3 Plan a short nomination speech like the ones in the recording.

> Useful language a–d

4a Work as a class. Take turns to give your speeches. Listen and make notes about each person's achievements and qualities.

b Have a class vote to find:

1 the winner of the Inspiration Award.
2 the runner-up.
3 third place.

Follow up Writing

1 Write a paragraph about the person you nominated. Explain why you nominated him/her and include the details in exercise 2.

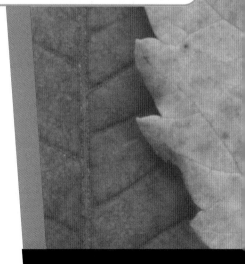

SHARE YOUR TASK

Practise giving your nomination speech until you feel confident.

Film/Record yourself giving the speech.

Share your film/recording with other students.

WORLD CULTURE

CHARLES DICKENS: Writer and campaigner

Find out first

1 Have you heard of Charles Dickens? Have you read any of his books or seen film adaptations of them? If so, what were they about?

2a Work in pairs. Try to answer the questions below.

    1 When did Dickens live?
    2 Which of these famous novels did he write?
      • *Anna Karenina*
      • *Oliver Twist*
      • *Huckleberry Finn*
      • *Emma*
      • *David Copperfield*
    3 What other novels is he famous for?
    4 Apart from his novels, what is Dickens known for?

b Go online to check your answers or ask your teacher.

Search: Charles Dickens + biography/facts

View

3a You are going to watch a video about Charles Dickens and how his childhood influenced his work. Before you watch, check you understand the meaning of the words and phrases in the glossary.

Glossary

the disadvantaged	poor people who have few opportunities
the oppressed	people who are treated unfairly and have few rights
a blacking factory	a factory in the past that made boot polish
compassion	caring about other people and their problems
to be in debt	to owe money that you cannot pay back

b ▶ Watch the video and read the statements below. Who do they describe: Dickens the child (C), Dickens the writer/man (W) or Dickens's father (F)?

    1 His work has always been popular. *W*
    2 He had a very successful career.
    3 He grew up in a comfortable home.
    4 He got into debt.
    5 He was sent to prison.
    6 He had to work long hours in a factory.
    7 He spent a lot of time walking the streets of London.
    8 He cared passionately about the poor.

4 Simon Callow is a famous British actor and a biographer of Dickens. Watch the video again and tick four reasons that he gives for admiring Dickens.

    • He seems very human and real.
    • He really wanted to make the world a better place.
    • He was an extremely popular and successful writer.
    • He was very passionate about what he believed in.
    • He was funny, clever and knowledgeable.
    • What he wrote about is still relevant today.

World view

5 ▶ Watch four people talking about a great writer, artist or leader that they would like to meet. Number the people 1–4 in the order they are mentioned. There are two extra names.

- Tom Hanks
- Florence Nightingale
- George Orwell
- Mother Teresa
- Frederico Garcia Lorca
- Desmond Tutu

6a Watch again. Why would each speaker like to meet this person and what do they admire about them?

b Work in groups and compare your answers.

7 Which writers, artists or leaders would you like to meet and why?

❝ There is no one in human history that I would rather meet than Charles Dickens.

Simon Callow

8a Work in pairs. What do you know about these famous campaigners? Complete the table.

	Mother Teresa	Florence Nightingale	Desmond Tutu
Where/when born			
Family background, etc.			
Job/role			
What they campaigned for / achieved			

b Go online to find out more about famous campaigners in history or a campaigner from your country.

Search: Mother Teresa / Florence Nightingale / Desmond Tutu + biography/facts

▶ Write up your research

9 Choose one of the people you have researched and write a short paragraph about his/her life and work. Use the prompts below to help you.

- He/She came from a ... background
- From an early age he/she ...
- He/She cared passionately about ...
- He/She (has) campaigned for ...
- He/She (has) managed to ...

AFTER UNIT 4 YOU CAN ...

Talk about achievements and experiences.

Explain important events in your life.

Talk about someone who inspires you.

Research simple biographical information online.

Getting ahead
in the
21ST CENTURY

Have you ever wondered whether you have the skill that you need to succeed in the 21st century? We have the answers.

1 Keep learning

Ten years ago, nobody was designing apps for mobile phones or using social media to reach new customers. Now these are popular jobs for graduates. As the world of work changes, we need to change, too. In the past, you just had to ask your uncle to get you a job in his company. These days we need to identify our strengths and constantly improve our skills. Business guru Heinz Landau suggests spending ten percent of your time on personal improvement; for example, learning a language or a new computer programme. As somebody once said, 'If you work hard on your job, you can make a living. But if you work hard on yourself, you can make a fortune.'

$e = mc^2$

2 Don't be afraid of failure

If you don't believe me, look at Thomas Edison, the inventor of the first light bulb, or Jimmy Wales, founder of Wikipedia. Edison tried at least 6,000 different materials for his light bulb before finding one that worked. That's 6,000 failures to find just one success. And before Wikipedia, Jimmy Wales had tried and failed to start several internet businesses, but none of them was profitable. Failure, however, didn't upset Wales. It gave him useful experience and knowledge. When you work for a company, though, it's worth remembering the words of famous British businessman, Alan Sugar: 'I don't mind mistakes. I just don't like people making them twice.'

 FIND OUT MORE Go online to find out more about Jimmy Wales and Nupedia or any of the other people in this article.

Reading

1 Work in groups. Think of three important ways to 'get ahead' in your career.

> I think the most important way to get ahead at work is to be nice to your boss!

> You should keep improving your skills.

2 Read the article. Did you come up with any of the same ideas as the author?

3 Learn how to manage your time

Whatever you do these days, you probably have more work and less time than you want. To meet these demands, everyone needs strategies to be effective and productive. That means, for example, avoiding distractions. Julie Morgenstern, author of *Never Check E-mail in the Morning*, recommends using the first hours of the working day to tackle your most important projects. Too often, she says, we start the day with our emails and before we realise, it's time for lunch. Other tips include shutting the door to your office (if you have one) and only going to meetings if they are essential.

4 Be discreet!

A woman known only as 'Lindsay' became internationally famous recently when she updated her online profile with the words 'I hate my job!' She then made some very personal and unkind remarks about her boss. But Lindsay had forgotten that she had recently added her boss as an online friend. He responded a few hours later: 'Don't bother coming in tomorrow … and yes, I'm serious.' A recent survey of 450 employers found that over half of them check Facebook before offering someone a job. The moral of the story is clear: even if your boss isn't on your friends list, be careful what you say online.

5 Build up a social network

Don't forget: it's not what you know, it's who you know. This saying is still as true today as it was in the past. Talent, imagination and hard work are important, but your contacts are also important. So keep in touch with as many people as possible, help them when you can and maybe one day they will be able to help you, too. And if that doesn't work, you can always ask your uncle for a job!

---

3 Read the article again and decide if the statements are true (T) or false (F). Correct the false statements.

1 The world of work is not the same as it was ten years ago.
2 Heinz Landau suggests spending ten percent of your time learning a language.
3 Edison didn't find the right material to make light bulbs.
4 Jimmy Wales started various internet businesses before Wikipedia.
5 Julie Morgenstern believes that we should deal with our emails before starting work.
6 Lindsay used her online profile to tell her boss that she wanted to quit.
7 Who you know is less important than what you know.
8 You should have more than your friends and family in your network.

4 Work in pairs and compare your ideas. Which advice in the article do you find most/least useful?

Vocabulary
Word families

1 Complete the table with nouns or adjectives from the article.

Verb	Noun	Adjective
experience	1 _____ (para. 2)	experienced
fail	2 _____ (para. 2)	
imagine	3 _____ (para. 5)	imaginative
improve	4 _____ (para. 1)	
know	5 _____ (para. 2)	knowledgeable
produce	production	6 _____ (para. 3)
succeed	7 _____ (para. 2)	successful

PRONUNCIATION

1 🎧 5.1 Mark the stressed syllable on each verb in the table in exercise 1. Listen and check.

im•agine

2 🎧 5.2 Now listen to the pronunciation of the verbs, nouns and adjectives. Is the same syllable stressed in all three words in each group?

im•agine   imagi•nation   ima•ginative

3 Practise saying the words, paying attention to the stressed syllable.

2a Work in pairs. Can you guess which nouns from exercise 1 complete the famous quotes below? Check your answers on page 126.

1 _____ is more important than knowledge. *Albert Einstein*
2 I don't know the key to _____ , but the key to _____ is trying to please everybody. *Bill Cosby*
3 _____ is power. *Sir Francis Bacon*
4 People are born with a liking for _____ . *Xunzi*

b Which quotes do you think are true? Which don't you agree with? Why?

Language focus 1
Future forms

1a Are you ambitious or not? Do the quiz to find out.

b Turn to page 127 and add up your score. Look at the quiz results to find out what it means.

2 Work in pairs and compare your results. Do you think this is an accurate description of your partner?

3a Read the quiz again and underline three future forms with *going to* + verb, three future forms with *will* + verb and two with the Present continuous.

b Can you find any other verbs or phrases in the quiz that express the future?

How ambitious are you?

Whether you're already in a career or you're just about to enter the world of work, find out if you're ambitious enough to succeed.

1 You find out that your local college is running a course next term that will be useful for your career. How do you react?

a You enrol immediately and pay for it yourself.
b You decide that you're going to do it and ask your company to pay.
c You're doing a lot in the next few months so you decide to wait until next year.

2 One of your colleagues gets a promotion. How do you feel?

a You're upset! You intend to find out why you didn't get the job.
b You feel a bit jealous, but you're not going to show it.
c You're really pleased for your colleague – you think he'll do a great job.

3 You are about to leave work and go away for the weekend with your family. At the last minute, something important comes up that needs dealing with over the weekend. What do you do?

a You call your family and say that you're not going.
b You call your colleagues and try to find someone else to deal with the problem.
c You leave a message for your boss and explain that your family will be upset if you don't spend the weekend with them.

4 One of your colleagues is due to go on maternity leave and you've always wanted her job. What happens?

a You ask your boss if you can do your colleague's job while she's away. Secretly, you hope to keep the job permanently.
b You're planning to speak to your boss about it soon, but you haven't found the right moment.
c You're thinking of asking your boss about it, but you don't want to upset your colleague.

5 What's your attitude towards hard work?

a It's the only way I'll achieve what I want.
b I'm only going to work hard if I'm paid well.
c Hard work interferes with my social life.

6 Which statement best summarises your attitude towards your future career?

a I intend to be successful whatever it takes.
b I'm going to do my best and see what happens.
c One day I hope I'll find a job that really suits me.

GRAMMAR

1 Choose the best verb form for each explanation. Find examples in the quiz.

1 We use *will* / *going to* / *the Present continuous* to describe actions in the future that are already arranged:

2 We use *will* / *going to* / *the Present continuous* to describe intentions for the future:

3 We use *will* / *going to* / *the Present continuous* to describe something you predict or see as a future fact. It is often used after verbs like *hope, think, know*:

2 Find examples in the quiz of these phrases for expressing the future.

to intend to	to be planning to	to hope to
to be thinking of	to be about to	to be due to

PRACTICE

1 Use the prompts to form sentences.

My brother / think / change / his job
My brother is thinking of changing his job.

1 My best friend / due / join the army / next month
2 My boss / about / go on maternity leave
3 I / hope / get a pay rise / soon
4 My dad / go / retire next month
5 Ally / not intend / work here for long
6 I / think / apply for a master's degree / next year

2 Write five sentences about yourself (or someone you know) using future forms and the prompts below.

1 (apply for) a job as a … / course in …
2 (take) … exams / driving test …
3 (get) married …
4 (train) to be a …
5 (go into) the army …
6 (travel) abroad …
7 (change) job/school …
8 (start/leave) university/school …

My brother's due to go into the army soon.
My cousin's going to start school next month.
I'm not planning to take my driving test until I'm 21.

3a Work in pairs. Student A: Choose three numbers from 1–12. Student B: Turn to page 127 and read out the corresponding instructions. Both students: Write answers to the instructions using appropriate future forms.

b Compare your answers.

Unit 5, Study & Practice 1, page 144

Vocabulary
Work

1 Write down three jobs you'd love to do, three jobs you wouldn't mind doing and three jobs you'd hate to do. Don't show anyone your list yet.

2a Use a dictionary to check the meaning of the words and phrases in bold in sentences 1–15. Write them in the groups below according to your preferences.

I would like a job like that.	*You have to be physically fit.*
I wouldn't mind doing a job like that.	
I wouldn't want a job like that.	

1 You have to be **physically fit**.
2 You have to be **good with money/numbers**.
3 You need good **communication skills**.
4 You have to be very **well organised**.
5 You have to be very **creative**.
6 You need **special training** and **qualifications**.
7 You have to **work long hours**.
8 It's very **secure**.
9 It's **well paid**.
10 It's **badly paid**.
11 It's **stressful**.
12 It's very **competitive**.
13 It's **challenging**.
14 There's a lot of **responsibility**.
15 There are lots of **opportunities to travel**.

b Work in pairs and compare your answers.

I'd like a job where you have to be physically fit.

3 Suggest some 'ideal jobs' to your partner based on what he/she has told you. Compare your suggestions with the list your partner made in exercise 1.

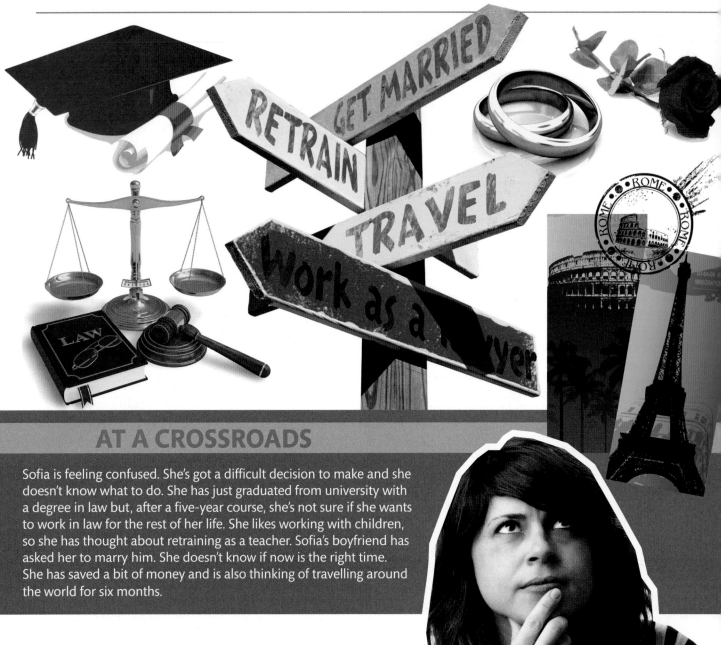

AT A CROSSROADS

Sofia is feeling confused. She's got a difficult decision to make and she doesn't know what to do. She has just graduated from university with a degree in law but, after a five-year course, she's not sure if she wants to work in law for the rest of her life. She likes working with children, so she has thought about retraining as a teacher. Sofia's boyfriend has asked her to marry him. She doesn't know if now is the right time. She has saved a bit of money and is also thinking of travelling around the world for six months.

Language focus 2

Future clauses with *if, when, unless, etc.*

1 Read about Sofia and the life choices she faces. Work in pairs and discuss what you think she should/shouldn't do and why.

2 Look at the picture. Which choice is Sofia talking about in each sentence? Some sentences may refer to more than one choice.

1 I'm going to see a bit of the world **before** I settle down and start a family.
2 I'll be qualified next year, **unless** I fail my exams of course.
3 **If** I still feel confused in a month's time, I'll just pack my bags and go.
4 I probably won't see David **until** I get back from travelling next year.
5 **As soon as** I make up my mind, he'll be the first person to know.
6 **When** we have children and they go to school, I'll have the same holidays as them.

GRAMMAR

These conjunctions join two clauses (parts) of a sentence.

as soon as   before   if   unless   until   when

1 Look at the conjunctions in bold in exercise 2. Underline the verb that follows the conjunction.

2 The sentences in exercise 2 are about the future, but what tense is used after the conjunctions? What verb forms are used in the other clause?

3 Is there a big difference in meaning between the pairs of sentences? If so, what is it?
   1 If I leave my job, my father will be angry.
      When I leave my job, my father will be angry.
   2 If he doesn't come with me, I won't go.
      Unless he comes with me, I won't go.

PRACTICE

1 Read what Sofia's friends say about her. Choose the best conjunction and complete the gaps with the correct form of the verb in brackets.

1 *If / When* she _____ (go) travelling, she _____ (still need) to get a job when she gets back.

2 She _____ (not be) happy *unless / before* she _____ (listen) to her heart.

3 She should become a teacher. I'm sure the children _____ (love) her *as soon as / until* she _____ (walk) in the classroom.

4 She should become a lawyer. *If / As soon as* she _____ (become) a teacher, she _____ (not earn) as much.

5 These decisions _____ (not get) easier for her *unless / until* she _____ (get) a bit older and knows what she wants.

6 *When / Before* she _____ (make) a decision, she _____ (feel) happier.

7 I don't think David _____ (be) happy *unless / if* Sofia _____ (go) travelling. He'll miss her.

8 Sofia _____ (need) to decide what she really wants *unless / before* she _____ (make) any big decisions.

2a Complete the sentences to make them true for you.

1 I'm going to buy a ... as soon as ...
2 I'll continue learning English until ...
3 I'll be able to relax when ...
4 I'll be at home by ... o'clock tonight if/unless ...
5 I'm (not) going to go out tonight if/unless ...
6 I'm going to ... next weekend if/unless ...
7 My English will/won't improve if/unless ...

b Work in pairs and compare your answers.

3 Work in small groups. Take turns to talk about the plans and ambitions of someone you know. The other students listen and think of possible consequences.

> My friend John wants to be a writer.

> If he wants to be a writer, he'll have to think of a good idea for a book.

> It won't be easy unless he's really good.

> He'll have to find an editor before he sends the book to publishers.

Unit 5, Study & Practice 2, page 145

Listening and speaking
Career crossroads

1 Work as a class and discuss.

- Is it easy to get a job in your country at the moment?
- How do people find jobs?

1 Gavin: advertising; Molly: graphic design; Delmar: he doesn't know yet
2 Gavin: no; Molly: yes; Delmar: no

2 🎧 5.3 Listen to a radio programme about people at a 'career crossroads'. Answer the questions.

1 What is each person's chosen career?
2 Are they working in it at the moment?

3a Listen again and decide if the questions describe Gavin (G), Molly (M) or Delmar (D). Who:

1 has already had a career for several years? D
2 checks job adverts regularly?
3 has found that lack of experience is a problem?
4 is currently working without pay?
5 had a nasty shock a few months ago?
6 is optimistic that he/she will get a permanent job offer soon?
7 is advertising his/her skills online?
8 is working for a charity?
9 is using social networking sites to help him/her find work?
10 is fulfilling one of his/her dreams?

b What details do they give about these things?

4 Work in groups and discuss.

- Do you think Gavin, Molly and Delmar have made good choices or not?
- Have you or any of your friends done the things that they mentioned? If so, what happened?

The Executive

In this popular reality TV show, 12 contestants compete to win the $75,000-a-year position as an executive in one of Sir Darren Sweet's highly successful companies. Each week the contestants work on business-related tasks in teams. These are designed to find out their strengths and weaknesses in the workplace. At the end of each programme, Sir Darren discusses the contestants with his board, then fires the least successful candidate.

TONIGHT

In tonight's semi-final only four contestants remain. They have completed their tasks and the board are reviewing their progress. Tonight, Sir Darren will decide which three will go through to the final next week.

SIR DARREN SWEET is the multi-millionaire owner of several international companies. However, he left school when he was 15 and has no qualifications. He started work on his uncle's market stall and from there he built up his first company.

PROFILE ⇒ Nikita Samra

Age: 28 Career: trained as dentist but works for charity

What she says about herself:

❝ I'm ambitious and extremely focused, but I care about other people.

Background:
- She was highly successful at school and gained A grades in all her exams.
- She studied dentistry for seven years at university, but then went to work for a children's charity.
- She has won a 'Woman of the Future' award after raising over half a million dollars for the charity.

PROFILE ⇒ Freddie Osborne-Davis

Age: 24 Career: investment banker

What he says about himself:

❝ I think of myself as charming but ruthless. I am absolutely determined to succeed. If Sir Darren doesn't give me a top job, someone else will.

Background:
- He comes from a wealthy background and attended a private school.
- He has a master's degree in business studies and works for a large international bank.
- He is single and has no children.

PROFILE ⇒ Mark Eastman

Age: 41 Career: unemployed supermarket executive

What he says about himself:

❝ I'm disciplined and extremely hard-working. I've got more experience than the other contestants, and I'm going to make a success of this.

Background:
- He was an officer in the army for ten years and still regularly runs marathons.
- He worked as a senior manager in a supermarket chain for 12 years until he lost his job.
- He is married with four children aged six to 16.

PROFILE ⇒ Melody Pelosi

Age: 27 Career: runs her own sandwich company

What she says about herself:

❝ I'm tough but honest and I've made my own way in life. If he gives me this opportunity, Sir Darren won't regret it.

Background:
- She comes from a very poor background and left school without any qualifications.
- She is the divorced mother of two young children.
- She started work on a supermarket checkout but now runs a successful small company.

Preparation Reading and listening

1 Read about the reality TV show *The Executive* and answer the questions.

  1 What are the contestants hoping to win?
  2 What do they have to do each week?
  3 Who judges the contestants?
  4 What kind of person is Sir Darren?
  5 How many contestants will be in the final?

2a 🎧 5.4 Listen to Sir Darren talking about the qualities he is looking for in the finalists. Which things does he mention?

  • business experience
  • potential
  • business sense
  • qualifications
  • clear-thinking
  • can take responsibility
  • achieves things
  • communication skills
  • assertive
  • works well in a team

  b Listen again. Which two qualities are most important to Sir Darren?

Task Speaking and listening

1a Read the profiles of the four semi-finalists. Memorise as much information as you can.

  b Work in groups. Close your books and see how much you can remember about the four candidates.

2 🎧 5.5 Listen to the board discussing the candidates' qualities and make notes. Compare your answers with other students.

3 Work in groups of four. Choose one candidate each. Go through your notes and underline the strengths and circle the weaknesses. Summarise your candidate's strengths and weaknesses for the group.

4 On your own, decide which three candidates should go through to the final and who should be fired. Discuss your ideas in your groups and make a final decision.

> Useful language a, b and c

5a Tell the class what you decided and why. Who do you think will be the eventual winner and the runner-up?

> Useful language d

  b 🎧 5.6 Listen to Sir Darren explaining who he has chosen and why. What order did he put the four candidates in? Was it the same as your group's order?

Writing
A CV

1 Work in pairs and read the job adverts. Which jobs would/wouldn't you like to do? Why?

JOB VACANCIES

TRAINEE MARKETING ASSISTANT:
Botswana Adventures

Wild African Adventures is a travel company that specialises in once-in-a-lifetime holidays to Botswana in Africa. We are looking for a trainee marketing assistant to join our team and help find new customers. Some travel to Africa may be required. A love of foreign adventure, an enthusiastic attitude and an ability to work in a team are essential.
Send your CV to Karen Bexley
karenb@wildafricanadventures.net

TRAINEE FITNESS INSTRUCTOR

Silver Fit Gym is a friendly, modern gym. We have a team of fitness instructors who help our customers to achieve their goals. We are currently looking for new trainee fitness instructors to join our team. No previous experience is required but a love of sport and fitness, a positive attitude and an ability to inspire people are essential.
Send your CV to Jim Price **enquiries@silverfitgym.com**

COMPUTER TRAINER

New Skills Training is a charity that helps the elderly and disadvantaged to get online. We are looking for an enthusiastic and outgoing person with excellent computer and interpersonal skills to join our team and help get people online. Previous experience not essential.
Send your CV to Marion Nelson **marion@newskillstraining.co.net**

SECRETARY

Gold Star Appliances sells top-quality domestic appliances. We are looking for a friendly, professional secretary with an excellent telephone manner. Must be able to type. No previous experience required, but enthusiasm is essential.
Send your CV to **info@goldstarappliances.net** or call **Wendy Yang on 0283 383 128**

CV
SEAN RICHARDSON

Flat 23, Portman House
Belfast Road
Manchester
M36 9EZ
T: 0161 599 376 **M:** 0788 548 3829
seanrichardson@totalmail.net

PROFILE
Final-year student in Information Technology at Leeds Metropolitan University.
Excellent computer skills **combined with** experience of one-to-one training.
Strong interpersonal skills and **the ability to work in a team**.

EXPERIENCE
Two-month **work placement** with an IT training company:
– learning how good IT trainers work; helping to train people in basic computer skills.
Volunteer for a local charity:
– working with disadvantaged teenagers and helping them to learn new computer skills.

EDUCATION AND QUALIFICATIONS
BA degree in Information Technology, Leeds Metropolitan University (due to graduate in July)
High school **graduate**, Thomas Manly Secondary School, Leeds

PERSONAL DETAILS
Full clean driving licence. **Non-smoker**. Languages: English and Hindi (**mother tongue**), Urdu (fluent), Spanish (conversational). Interests include sport, reading and photography.

REFERENCES
References available on request.

2a Read Sean's CV. How is it similar or different to CVs that people usually write in your country?

b Look at the words and phrases in bold in Sean's CV. Match them with the definitions below.

1 can get on well with people
2 working without being paid in order to get experience
3 someone who has completed their course at school or university
4 first language
5 can work with other people
6 someone who doesn't smoke
7 and

3a Sean adapts his CV for each job he applies for. Which of the four jobs in exercise 1 do you think he is applying for?

b Underline the phrases in his CV which show he is right for the job. Which phrases come directly from the advert?

4 Read the note below and find more examples in Sean's CV.

Note: In a CV we often miss out words which are unnecessary or obvious.
~~I am a~~ *final-year student in Information Technology* ~~at the~~ *Leeds Metropolitan University.*

I'd like to enquire about the... JOB

Speaking

Making a formal telephone call

1a ▶ Watch the video of two telephone conversations. Why is Sean Richardson calling? Which receptionist is more polite?

b Complete the phrases from the conversations with one word. Then watch again and check.

Conversation 1

1 Could I _____ to Marion Nelson, please?
2 I'll just see if she's _____ .
3 Can I ask who's _____ ?
4 Could I ask what the call is _____ ?
5 Can I take a _____ ?
6 Could you ask her to call me _____ ?
7 Could I _____ your number?
8 Could you tell her it's _____ ?
9 I'll _____ her know.

Conversation 2

10 I'd like to _____ to Wendy Yang, please.
11 I'm calling _____ the job advert in the newspaper.
12 Hello. Wendy Yang _____ .

PRONUNCIATION

1 ▶ Watch and listen to the key phrases. Notice how the speakers in the first conversation use intonation to make the questions polite. Repeat the questions and try to copy the intonation.

Could I speak to Marion Nelson, please?

---

2 Work in pairs. Watch and listen to conversation 2 again. Rewrite the secretary's part to make his conversation more polite.

Good morning. Gold Star Appliances. How can I help you?

3 Work in pairs. Student A: Turn to page 128. Student B: Turn to page 130. Read your instructions then act out the conversation.

5a Choose one of the job adverts on page 54 and plan your own CV for that job. Use the headings in Sean's CV to make notes. (You can invent experience and qualifications if you prefer.)

b Write the first draft of your CV. Use the checklist below to help you.

- Does your CV include your contact details?
- Does it fit onto one page?
- Have you sold yourself effectively in the 'Profile' section?
- Does it address all the requirements in the job advert?
- Have you used useful phrases from Sean's CV?
- Have you checked your punctuation and spelling?

6 Work in groups and swap CVs. Which CVs do you think would get an interview?

AFTER UNIT 5 YOU CAN ...

Talk about your plans, intentions and ambitions.

Talk about the consequences of future events.

Discuss your preferred choice of people for a job.

Write a CV.

Make a formal telephone call.

REAL LIVES
A twist of fate

When Tamara Rabi met Adriana Scott at a local McDonald's ® restaurant, their lives changed forever. 'I didn't know what to say except "hi". I was just so shocked – it was like seeing myself,' says Adriana. They were both students at neighbouring universities in Long Island, New York, and ¹_____ . They shared a birthday, they were exactly the same height and both loved hip hop. But the most important thing they shared was the same Mexican mother. Both girls grew up knowing that ²_____ , but they had no idea that they had an identical twin. Then, Justin Lattore, a friend of Adriana's, went to Tamara's twentieth birthday party. When he walked in and saw Tamara, he couldn't believe his eyes. 'I was just shocked – she looked so much like Adriana,' says Justin. Then it got clearer – they had to be sisters. In fact, ³_____ , clearly mistaking her for someone else.

Following the birthday, Justin put the two girls in touch and they arranged the McDonald's meeting by email. 'As she came towards me, she was walking like me, talking like me,' says Tamara. 'We have the same mannerisms, the same interests and got the same grades at school,' adds Adriana. The girls even discovered that as children ⁴_____ : of a really loud noise followed by a very quiet one. They had another sad factor in common. ⁵_____ a few years before they met.

Now the twins are finishing their studies, and they meet often. 'I feel she's my sister, but our relationship right now is more like friends,' says Tamara. She's optimistic and excited that their futures will be together: 'We will always have each other. We don't have any other brothers and sisters – we'll grow old together!'

Language focus 1
Past perfect

1a Work in groups. Think of examples of the types of story below from books, films or real life.

crime stories / mysteries	romantic stories	anecdotes
science fiction / fantasy	ghost stories	adventure stories
'human interest' stories	biographies	

b Which types of story are usually fictional? Write F if they are usually fictional, T if they are true and B if they can be both. Compare your answers with other students.

c Which types of story in exercise 1a do/don't you usually like? Give examples.
   I don't usually like fantasy stories like Alice in Wonderland.

2a Look at the article above. What kind of story is it?

b Read the article and answer the questions.

   1 Where did Tamara and Adriana first meet?
   2 Why was their first meeting shocking?
   3 Who first realised that they were sisters and when?
   4 Say three things that the girls had in common when they met.
   5 What kind of relationship do they have now?

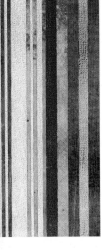

3 🎧 6.1 **Complete the story with the information below. Then listen and check.**

a Tamara had already noticed that strangers on her university campus often smiled and said hello
b Both of their adoptive fathers had died
c they had grown up only 30 kilometres apart
d their mother had given them up for adoption when they were born
e they had often had the same nightmare

4 **Work in pairs and discuss.**

- Why do you think the article is called 'A twist of fate'?
- Do you think their story is a sad or a happy one? In what ways?

5 **The story starts with the moment that the twins met. Did the actions in exercise 3 happen before or after they met?**

GRAMMAR

1 Which verb below is in the Past simple and which is in the Past perfect? How do we form the Past perfect? Which action happened first?

Both of their adoptive fathers had died a few years before they met.

2 Cross out the incorrect explanation below.

1 The Past perfect describes actions that happened a long time ago.
2 We use the Past perfect when we are describing past events and want to explain something that happened before that.

PRACTICE

1a **Read more about twins who were separated at birth. Complete the gaps below with the Past simple or Past perfect form of the verb in brackets.**

The 'Minnesota twins'

For over 30 years the Twin Family Study at the University of Minnesota has reunited twins separated at birth. Time and time again, they have discovered surprising similarities in their personalities, interests and lives.

Tom Patterson first ¹_____ (meet) his identical twin Steve Tazumi four years ago, but they ²_____ (soon find) that they ³_____ (have) a lot in common. They ⁴_____ (both / choose) the same career: at the time they met, both men ⁵_____ (own) a body-building gym, and before that, both ⁶_____ (compete) seriously as weightlifters, Steve ⁷_____ (even try) for the Olympics in his youth.

And when Daphne Goodship ⁸_____ (meet) her twin Barbara Herbert, they ⁹_____ (discover) that they ¹⁰_____ (have) the same number of children – three – and that their children ¹¹_____ (be born) in the same years.

But the very first pair of 'Minnesota twins' were the most amazing. Jim Springer ¹²_____ (meet) his identical twin Jim Lewis when they were 39 years old. It was a coincidence that their adoptive parents ¹³_____ (give) them both the same first name, but they ¹⁴_____ (soon / discover) a lot more amazing similarities in their pasts. Both men ¹⁵_____ (divorce) a woman named Linda and ¹⁶_____ (remarried) a woman named Betty. Both men ¹⁷_____ (have) a son called James Alan and a dog named Toy. And most strangely of all, in 2002, both men ¹⁸_____ (died) on the same day, of the same illness!

b **Work in groups and discuss. Do you think the similarities between the pairs of twins are really surprising or not?**

PRONUNCIATION

1 🎧 6.2 **Listen to eight sentences and write the form you hear: Past simple (PS) or Past perfect (PP).**

2 **Look at audio script 6.2 on page 171. Practise saying the sentences, paying attention to the tense.**

2a **Choose a story type from exercise 1a on page 56 and invent the introduction to a story. Include at least one Past simple and one Past perfect verb.**

Clara looked up and saw a tall dark stranger. She had never seen him before in her life.

b **Work in pairs. Take turns to read your introductions to each other and guess what types of story they are.**

Unit 6, Study & Practice 1, page 147

True coincidences

Do you have a favourite coincidence story?
Have any amazing coincidences happened to you?
Share your story below.

A few years ago I had an argument with my girlfriend. She said that I was obsessed by work. As I was driving home, I turned on the radio and the first thing I heard were the lyrics 'She said it wasn't working. She told me she was leaving.' …
Josh Lewis, Vancouver, Canada

My favourite coincidence story is about Mark Twain, the American author. He was born in 1835, two weeks after Halley's Comet appeared. In his autobiography, Twain said that he had come in with the comet and he expected to go out with it (Halley's Comet comes back every 76 years). …
Maria Lopez, Mexico City, Mexico

A few months ago I was thinking about an old friend from university. His name was Jung Xiu. He always said that we would get married one day. The next day I checked my email as usual. To my amazement, there was an email from Jung Xiu. He asked me if I was still living in Bejing and he told me what he was doing. …
Hui Zhong, Bejing, China

My friend and I from Thomas Abney Secondary School in South London did a gap year together when we were 18. We went to Australia and found a job in a small insurance office in Melbourne. It was really boring work but quite well paid. One day the manager said he was hiring another worker to help us. …
Liam Bentley, London, UK

Language focus 2
Reported speech

1a Work in pairs. Read the beginnings to the coincidence stories above. How do you think each story ends? Compare your ideas.

b 🎧 6.3 Listen and check. Did you guess correctly?

c Work in pairs and discuss.
- Which coincidence do you find strangest?
- Which one is least strange?

2a Which of the people in the text do you think said the sentences below? Write their names.

1 We'll get married one day.   *Jung Xiu*
2 I don't want to see you anymore.
3 I came in with the comet and I expect to go out with it.
4 I'm hiring another worker to help you.
5 I've just had a dream about you.

b Look at audio script 6.3 on page 171 and find the corresponding sentences in reported speech. Write them next to the quotes above.

He always said that we would get married one day.

GRAMMAR

Tenses in reported speech

1 Underline the verbs in the direct speech sentences in exercise 2a. Then underline the verbs in the reported speech sentences that you wrote. How do the tenses change in reported speech?

2 Complete the table with examples from exercise 2 and a tense.

Direct speech	Reported speech
Present simple: *I don't want to see you anymore.*	**Past simple:** *She said (that) she didn't want to see me anymore.*
Present continuous:	
Present perfect:	
Past simple:	
will:	

Remember the difference between *say* and *tell*.
- say something: *He said he loved her.*
- tell someone something: *He told me he loved her.*

Reported questions

3 Find three reported questions in audio script 6.3 on page 171. Which verb introduces them? Write the actual question for each reported question.

4 What is the difference in the word order of reported and direct questions?

5 In what types of questions do we use *if* and *whether*?

PRACTICE

1 Read the start of a true coincidence story. Then read the conversation below and complete the story with reported speech.

> In the early 1970s, the actor Anthony Hopkins got a part in a film called *The Girl from Petrovka*. It was based on a book by George Feifer. By chance one day, Hopkins found a copy of the book on a bench in a London tube station. It had handwritten notes on the pages. Two years later George Feifer, the author of the book, went to see Hopkins on the set of the film in Vienna.

1 Feifer told Hopkins that *he didn't have a copy of the book anymore* .
2 Hopkins asked him _____ .
3 Feifer said that _____ .
4 _____ .
5 _____ .
6 _____ .
7 _____ .
8 _____ .

F: I don't have a copy of the book anymore.
H: What happened to your copies?
F: I lent my last one to a friend and she lost it.
H: Where did she lose it?
F: She left it on a bench in London.
H: Is this book yours? I found it on a bench in London.
F: Yes, it is mine! That's incredible!
H: I'll give it back to you when filming is finished.

2a Look at the questions for famous people below. Choose four that you want to ask. Then imagine the answers and write them down.

1 Jack Dorsey (founder of Twitter): How many followers have you got on Twitter?
2 Madonna (pop star and actor): Do you think you are a better singer or actor?
3 Duchess of Cambridge (wife of Prince William): Is it better to be a princess or a pop star?
4 Diego Maradona (footballer): What was your best goal?
5 Tim Berners-Lee (inventor of the World Wide Web): Where were you when you had your idea?
6 Carlos Slim (one of the richest people in the world): Does money make you happy?

b Work in pairs. Tell your partner the question you asked and the answer that the famous person gave.

I asked Madonna whether she thought she was a better singer or actor. She told me that …

Unit 6, Study & Practice 2, page 148

Vocabulary

say and *tell*

1a Complete the sentences with *say* or *tell*.

1 Do you often _____ jokes? Can you _____ any jokes in English?
2 Do you have an elder brother or sister? Did he or she _____ you what to do as a child?
3 Can you _____ hello, goodbye and thank you in four different languages?
4 If you hated your friend's hairstyle and she asked your opinion, would you _____ the truth?
5 Can you _____ me something about your last holiday?
6 In your family, do you usually _____ a prayer before meals?
7 Did your teachers in primary school _____ you off a lot?
8 If you had a minor car accident and it was your fault, would you _____ sorry to the other driver?
9 Can you _____ the difference between British and American English?
10 If one of your classmates was cheating in a test, would you _____ something to the teacher?
11 Do you think it's always wrong to _____ lies? When is it acceptable?
12 If a homeless person asks you for money, do you usually _____ *yes* or *no*?

b 🎧 **6.4 Listen and check your answers.**

2 Add the phrases with *say* and *tell* to the diagram.

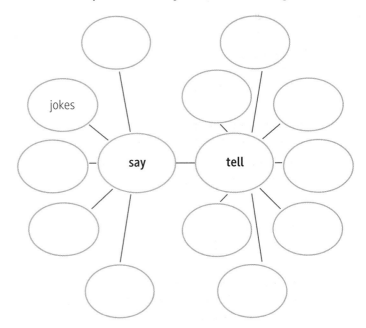

3 Work in pairs. Choose eight questions from exercise 1a. Take turns to ask and answer the questions.

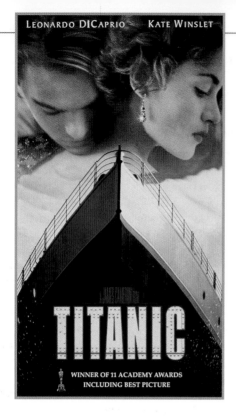

LEONARDO DICAPRIO   KATE WINSLET

TITANIC

WINNER OF 11 ACADEMY AWARDS
INCLUDING BEST PICTURE

Reading and speaking

1 Look at the poster above. Can you think of any other disaster movies based on real events?

2a Work in pairs. You are going to read about Josh Peltz's real-life experience of a plane crash. Before you read the text, look at the photo and answer the questions.

    1 What do you think Josh thought about as the plane was going down?
    2 What do you think he did when he was safe?

b Read the text and compare it with your ideas from exercise 2a.

3 Read the text again and put the events in the correct order, 1–10.

    a Josh read the emergency information.
    b Josh opened the door and got out of the plane.
    c The captain made an announcement.
    d Everyone was silent for a while.
    e Josh cried.
    f An explosion happened not long after they had taken off. *1*
    g The plane crashed into the water.
    h A ferry arrived to rescue the passengers.
    i Some of the passengers screamed.
    j The passengers went out onto the wing of the plane.

4 Work in pairs and discuss.

    • What technique did Josh use to survive the crash?
    • What would do in a situation like this?
    • Read 'It's a fact!' Are you surprised by the fact about plane safety?

5a You are going to read about real-life experiences of a shipwreck and a shark attack. Which experience do you think the phrases in the box below relate to? Write SW (shipwreck) or SA (shark attack).

> to bite   the crew of a boat   a rubber dinghy   a flare
> to feel numb   to hold on   to let go   a life belt
> to paddle   a searchlight   a surfboard

b Work in pairs. Student A: Turn to page 129 to read 'Shipwrecked'. Then answer the questions about it. Student B: Turn to page 131 to read 'Attacked by a shark'. Then answer the questions about it.

IT REALLY HAPPENED TO ME!

Josh Peltz was on US Airways Flight 1549, which crash- landed in the Hudson River in New York in January 2009.

I was in seat 10F next to the emergency exit. A few minutes after take-off there was a loud explosion. Everybody gasped and there were a few screams. Then, surprisingly, it went very quiet – everyone was assessing the situation.

    It soon became obvious we weren't going back to LaGuardia Airport, we were heading for the water. I started thinking this was it. I thought about my wife, Tesa, and our two children. Then I heard the announcement, 'This is the captain, brace for impact,' and everything suddenly got very clear. I had to stop thinking about death and start thinking about what I was going to do once the pilot landed in the water. 'You sat in this seat,' I thought, 'you've got to get this door open.'

6a Take turns to tell your partner about your story. Ask questions to find out the details of your partner's story.

b Read each other's stories. What else did you learn?

7 Discuss the questions.

- What was the worst experience in your opinion?
- What was the worst part of each experience?
- Do you know any stories of experiences like this? What happened?

IT'S A FACT! Air travel is extraordinarily safe. 95 percent of people involved in aviation accidents survive!

At about 300 feet (91.5 metres), I started reading the instructions. There were six steps, and I read them two or three times, testing myself on each step and trying to imagine myself opening the door. Suddenly, we hit the water. It felt like the worst car crash you could imagine. My first thought was, 'This plane is sinking, we have to get everybody off as soon as possible.'

Someone next to me was trying to pull the door in and I said, 'No, it's got to go out.' Fortunately, I'd just read that. I managed to get the door open and I grabbed the hand of a woman sitting next to me. We walked out onto the wing, which was sinking lower and lower. We walked as far along as we could to make room for other people. Everyone was helping each other. It was freezing, and nobody had a jacket. Some people were underwater to their waists.

It felt like half an hour before we saw the first ferry, although it can have been only five or ten minutes. I was fourth onto the ferry, and I started helping people onto the boat. Fortunately, everyone had survived the crash.

I got through it by taking it one step at a time: get the door open, throw the door out, figure out if you're sinking. I just kept on doing that until I reached solid ground. Only then did I go into the men's room and cry for a few minutes.

FIND OUT MORE Go online to find out more about **Josh Peltz** and the story of US Airways Flight 1549.

Vocabulary
Adverbs for telling stories

1 Match the sentences in A and B.

A
1 The audience were completely silent.
2 Mrs Brown was over 80 when she died.
3 The police searched the area for several days.
4 I realised I'd left my purse at home.
5 As the woman came round the corner, she was knocked off her bicycle by a passing car.
6 Robert really loves French food and culture.
7 My sister's family were in a minor car accident yesterday.
8 Hannah found out today that she didn't get that job she applied for.
9 Marianne and Laura were great friends at university.

B
a **Unfortunately**, she never saw her only grandchild, who was born in Australia.
b **Surprisingly**, though, he's never visited France.
c However, they **gradually** lost touch over the years.
d I **immediately** ran over to see if she was alright.
e **Suddenly**, a mobile phone rang and everyone turned and stared.
f **Fortunately**, I had my credit card in my pocket.
g **Obviously**, she was very disappointed.
h **Eventually**, they found the piece of evidence they were looking for.
i **Thankfully**, they were all OK.

2 Complete the sentences in a logical way using both adverbs.

My aunt fell down the stairs the other day.
Thankfully, *she didn't hurt herself.*
Obviously, *she was quite upset.*

1 My dad's been on a strict diet for nearly a month.
   Unfortunately …
   Surprisingly …

2 I first met my wife at a party five years ago.
   Immediately …
   Surprisingly …

3 When I came to live here, I didn't know anybody.
   Gradually …
   Eventually …

4 I spent an hour looking for the missing keys.
   Eventually …
   Fortunately …

5 The room was in complete darkness.
   Eventually …
   Suddenly …

Task

Retell a story

Preparation Listening and vocabulary

1 You are going to listen to a 'classic ghost story'. Look at the picture and information and answer the questions.

1 What kind of writing was Saki famous for?
2 In what century is the story set?
3 Find the three main characters in the picture:
- Frampton Nuttel, a young man who is suffering from a nervous illness.
- Mrs Sappleton, a distant acquaintance of Frampton's sister.
- Vera, her 15-year-old niece.
4 Who can you see in the garden?

2 Check the meaning of the key phrases below.

to find a body	a letter of introduction
a great tragedy	French windows
to go shooting	to go insane with grief
to sink in a bog	a cure for bad nerves
to chase someone	to have a nervous breakdown
snarling dogs	to knock someone off their bicycle
to see a ghost	

The Open Window by Saki

H.H. Munroe (Saki) 1870–1916: British writer who is considered a master of the short story. His stories about Edwardian society were witty, mischievous and sometimes macabre.

3a 🎧 6.5 Listen to the first part of the ghost story. Which questions can you answer? Compare your answers in groups.

1 Why was Frampton staying in the countryside?
2 Why was he visiting Mrs Sappleton?
3 Who entertained him while he was waiting for Mrs Sappleton?
4 What terrible tragedy did Vera tell him about? How did she describe it?
5 What did Mrs Sappleton believe about the tragedy?
6 What did she say when she came into the room?

b Listen again and check. You can also read the audio script on page 172 as you listen.

Task Speaking and listening

1 Work in pairs. Retell the story so far in as much detail as you can.

> Useful language a and b

2a Look back at the picture and the key phrases in exercise 2. Some key phrases are important in the second part of the story. Can you guess what happens next?

b Work in groups and compare your ideas. Whose ideas do you like best?

3a 🎧 6.6 Listen to the second part of the story and answer the questions.

1 Did Mrs Sappleton listen carefully to Frampton? Why / Why not?
2 What exactly did they see in the garden?
3 Why did Frampton run away?
4 What did Mrs Sappleton tell her husband about Frampton Nuttel?
5 How did Vera explain Frampton's behaviour?
6 What was Vera's speciality? Give <u>two</u> examples.

b Did you predict the ending of the story correctly?

4 Work in groups. Retell the second part of the story to your group. Whose version is the best?

> Useful language a, b and c

5 Listen to the story again and discuss the questions.

- Is this really a ghost story? Why / Why not?
- Do you like the story? Why / Why not?

Follow up Writing

1 EITHER write the story of *The Open Window* from the point of view of one of the other characters: Mrs Sappleton, Mr Sappleton or Vera.
OR write a ghost story of your own (either one you know or one you have invented yourself).

Think about:
- when to start the story.
- how to describe the setting and give background information.
- how to describe the main events.
- how people felt.
- what happened in the end.

> Useful language a, b and c

WORLD CULTURE

A STORY THAT ROCKED THE WORLD

Find out first

1a What do you know about Chile? Try to complete the fact file by choosing the correct answers.

FACT FILE CHILE

Population:	Around **17 / 27 / 37** million
Neighbours:	Argentina, Bolivia and **Peru** / **Brazil** / **Paraguay**
Capital:	**La Paz** / **Santiago** / **Tierra del Fuego**
Life expectancy:	**58 / 68 / 78** years
Biggest export:	**fruit** / **copper** / **oil**
Extraordinary fact:	The Atacama Desert is the **driest** / **windiest** / **hottest** place on Earth.

b Go online to check your answers or ask your teacher.

Search: Chile fact file / Chile life expectancy

View

2 Read the newspaper extract below. Do you remember this story? Can you guess/remember what happened? Use the numbers in the box to help you.

700,000-tonne block of rock below ground	33 miners 69 days	700 metres 17 days

Miners trapped below ground

In October 2010, one of the biggest global news stories of the year began in the San José Mine in Copiapo, Chile. The world looked on anxiously as rescue teams worked day and night to free the miners. …

3a ▶ Watch the first part of the video and check your answers to exercise 2. Briefly say what happened in your own words.

b Work in pairs and discuss.

- How do you think the miners survived for the first 17 days?
- What effect do you think the experience had on the miners?

c Watch the second part of the video and check your answers.

4 Watch the video again and tick the two correct sentences. Correct the other four sentences.

1. San José was a copper mine.
2. Angelique was feeding her daughter at home when she heard the news.
3. The news made her feel physically ill.
4. The first proof that the miners were safe was a note.
5. Edison stopped communicating with the other miners.
6. Angelique wants Edison to show her more love.

World view

5 Watch three people talking about a time when the world's eyes were on their country or city. Make notes as you listen to each speaker and complete the table.

	Luis	Eben	Kirsten
What was the event?			
When was it?			
What happened and what made it memorable/important?			

6a Work in groups. Can you think of a time when world attention was focused on your country? What happened? How did you feel about the event?

b Take turns to describe the events to other students.

7a Work in pairs. Do you know where and when the incidents below happened?

- the Three Mile Island accident
- Apollo 13
- US Airways Flight 1549
- asteroid 2012 BX34

b Go online to find out more about some of the incidents. Answer the questions.

1 When and where was it?
2 What caused the incident?
3 What nearly happened?
4 What actually happened?

Search: Three Mile Island / Apollo 13 / US Airways Flight 1549 / asteroid 2012 BX34

▶ Write up your research

8 Write a paragraph about one of the incidents you researched. Use the prompts below to help you.

- This incident happened in ...
- (A nuclear reactor) nearly ...
- People were worried that ...
- In the end ...
- The main reason it didn't happen was that ...

AFTER UNIT 6 YOU CAN ...

Explain the order of events in the past.

Report what is said in a conversation.

Tell a short story.

Report a news story.

07

MUST SEE!

Vocabulary and speaking
Entertainment and television

1a Work in groups and discuss. Which things do/don't you do?

* watch satellite/cable TV
* listen to the radio
* listen to podcasts
* watch TV online

b What are your favourite TV and radio programmes? Which types of show are they? Find them in the box below.

cookery programmes	documentaries	reality shows	sitcoms
sports programmes	travel news	soap operas	phone-ins
nature programmes	weather forecast	drama series	chat shows
murder mysteries	talent shows	quiz shows	game shows

c Can you think of any other types of TV or radio show? Add them to the box.

2 Work in pairs and read the statements below. Which types of TV and radio programmes do they describe in your country? Compare your answers.

* There are too many programmes like this.   *phone-ins*
* There aren't enough programmes like this.
* We don't have programmes like this.

3 Work in groups and discuss. How would you like to change TV and/or radio in your country?

> There should be fewer adverts on cable TV. I find them really annoying.

66

Language focus 1
-ed/-ing adjectives

1 Look at the pictures. What kinds of programmes are the people watching?

2 Complete the descriptions in A with the adjectives in B.

A	B
1 The tennis match is very ...	**a** terrified.
2 The women are very ...	**b** terrifying.
3 The children are ...	**c** exciting.
4 The film is ...	**d** excited.

GRAMMAR

1 Choose the correct answers. Then find example sentences from exercise 2.

1 We use an **-ed** / **-ing** adjective to describe how someone feels:

_____

2 We use an **-ed** / **-ing** adjective to describe the thing that makes the person feel that way:

_____

2 Write four more adjectives that have an **-ed** and an **-ing** form.

PRACTICE

1 Check the meaning of the words in bold. Choose the correct adjective to complete the sentences.

1 Did you see that documentary about corruption last night? It was really **shocked** / **shocking**.

2 The Prime Minister said that he is very **pleased** / **pleasing** with the country's economic progress.

3 The instructions for this DVD player are really **confused** / **confusing**. I'm getting a bit **frustrated** / **frustrating** trying to follow them.

4 I missed the film last night because my boss phoned. I was so **annoyed** / **annoying**.

5 Most chat shows with celebrities are really **embarrassed** / **embarrassing**. The interviewers ask too many personal questions.

6 There was an **amazed** / **amazing** programme about elephants on TV last night – did you see it?

7 We stayed up late on Saturday to watch the Angelina Jolie film, but it wasn't particularly good – we were a bit **disappointed** / **disappointing**.

8 I had a fantastic music teacher at school – we all found her really **inspired** / **inspiring**.

2 Work in pairs. Discuss how you would feel in the following situations. Use -ed/-ing adjectives.

You switch on the TV to watch your favourite drama and discover that there's golf on instead.

> I'd be annoyed. I find golf really boring.

> I wouldn't mind, I quite like it.

1 You find out that your favourite actor / rock star is appearing on a chat show this evening.

2 One of your friends phones you in the middle of your favourite soap.

3 You are at home alone. You have just watched a scary movie and now you have to go to bed.

4 You watch a news item about a war on the other side of the world.

5 You suddenly see one of your friends on TV.

Unit 7, Study & Practice 1, page 150

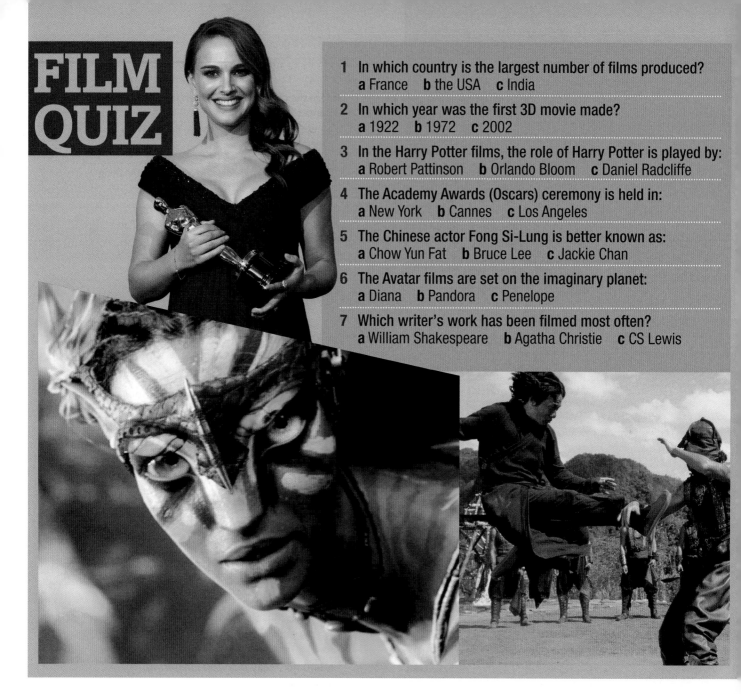

FILM QUIZ

1 In which country is the largest number of films produced?
a France   b the USA   c India

2 In which year was the first 3D movie made?
a 1922   b 1972   c 2002

3 In the Harry Potter films, the role of Harry Potter is played by:
a Robert Pattinson   b Orlando Bloom   c Daniel Radcliffe

4 The Academy Awards (Oscars) ceremony is held in:
a New York   b Cannes   c Los Angeles

5 The Chinese actor Fong Si-Lung is better known as:
a Chow Yun Fat   b Bruce Lee   c Jackie Chan

6 The Avatar films are set on the imaginary planet:
a Diana   b Pandora   c Penelope

7 Which writer's work has been filmed most often?
a William Shakespeare   b Agatha Christie   c CS Lewis

Speaking and listening

1 Work in pairs and discuss.
- What's the most amazing film you've seen recently?
- What's the most disappointing film you've seen recently?
- What is your 'film of the decade'?

2 How much do you know about films? Do the film quiz above to find out.

3 🎧 7.1 Listen and check your answers. How many of the quiz questions did you answer correctly? What else did you learn?

Language focus 2
The passive

1a Read sentences 1–9 about the quiz. Which verbs in bold are active (A) and which are passive (P)?

1 Daniel **was chosen** to play Harry Potter when he was 11.
2 The author, JK Rowling, **chose** Daniel herself.
3 This famous actor **changed** his name to Fong Si-Lung in the late nineties.
4 However, he **is** better **known** as Jackie Chan.
5 Jackie Chan **has appeared** in more than 100 films.
6 More than 400 films of Shakespeare's plays **have been made**.
7 *Avatar* **was directed** by James Cameron.
8 A sequel **is being filmed** at the moment.
9 A third film **will be made** next year.

b Look at the first two sentences in exercise 1a again. In sentence 1, do we know who chose Daniel? And in sentence 2?

GRAMMAR

Active and passive

1 Read the rules and find examples from exercise 1a.

1 In active sentences, the subject is the 'doer' of the verb:

_____

2 In passive sentences, the 'doer' of the verb is not the subject. The main focus is on the action or the person/thing it happened to, not the 'doer':

_____

Form of the passive (*be* + past participle)

2 Find an example of these forms in exercise 1a.

1 Present simple passive: _____
2 Past simple passive: _____
3 Present continuous passive: _____
4 Present perfect passive: _____
5 Future passive: _____

Use of the passive

- In passive sentences, we put the object at the beginning of the sentence to give it more emphasis.
  Four hundred Shakespeare films **have been made**.
  (We are interested in the films, not in who made them.)
- Often, we do not say who did the action in passive sentences because this is unknown, obvious or unimportant.
  He *is known* as Jackie Chan.
  (by people generally – this is obvious)
- However, we can say who did the action, using *by* before their name.
  *Avatar was directed **by James Cameron**.*

PRACTICE

1 Complete the sentences with the correct passive form of the verb in brackets.

1 Around 900 movies _____ (produce) in the USA every year. However, more films _____ (make) in India: over a thousand 'Bollywood' films _____ (release) every year.
2 The world's first 3D movie _____ (show) in Los Angeles on 27th September 1922. Unfortunately, since then the movie _____ (lose).
3 Between 2002 and 2011, eight Harry Potter films _____ (make) and in all eight films the role of Harry _____ (play) by Daniel Radcliffe.
4 No more Harry Potter movies _____ (release) in the future, because all of the books _____ (already make) into films.
5 A sequel to *Avatar* _____ (film) at the moment – it _____ (shoot) ten kilometres under the surface of the ocean!

2 Choose the correct answers in the text.

MOVIE WINNERS ... AND LOSERS

The Chinese action movie *Crouching Tiger, Hidden Dragon* [1]*released* / *was released* in 2000 with a budget of just $17 million dollars. It [2]*won* / *was won* the Academy Award for Best Foreign Language film in the same year, and since then it [3]*has made* / *has been made* more than $200 million. It [4]*has described* / *has been described* as 'the most profitable foreign-language film in American movie history'. Kevin O'Connell [5]*has called* / *has been called* the unluckiest person in the history of the Academy Awards. His job title is Sound Re-recording Mixer and he [6]*holds* / *is held* the record for the most nominations without a win. Since 1983 he [7]*has nominated* / *has been nominated* 20 times but never won! The 2010 romantic comedy *How Do You Know*, starring Owen Wilson and Reese Witherspoon, [8]*cost* / *was cost* $120 million to make, but reviews were bad – one film critic [9]*wrote* / *was written*, 'It starts badly and just gets worse.' It [10]*removed* / *was removed* from US cinemas after just a few weeks. Overall, the movie [11]*lost* / *was lost* more than $100 million.

3a You are going to make your own quiz about media and culture. Write a list of artists, writers, actors and composers that you know.

b Choose three people from your list. Write a question about each person's work using the passive form and the prompts below.

1 When was/were ... made / published / written / first released?
2 How many ... have been made / published / written / released?
3 Who was/were ... directed / painted / composed / written by?
4 Where is/are ... set?

c Write three possible answers to each quiz question. Add background information to each correct answer.

Who was Guernica painted by?
a Dali   b Miro   c Picasso

Guernica was painted by Picasso in 1937. He painted it to show the terrible things that were happening in the Spanish Civil War. It is considered his greatest painting.

4 Work in groups. Ask your quiz questions in teams. After the other teams have answered, read out the correct answer and background information.

> Unit 7, Study & Practice 2, page 150

The newspaper collage (headlines and articles)

And the Wimbledon **A month of rain**

1 A Beijing woman is so furious with a local cinema that she is suing them for wasting her time. Chen Xiaomei is suing the cinema's owners because she was not warned about the 20 minutes of adverts and trailers before the main feature. She is demanding a full refund (35 yuan), compensation for emotional damage and a written apology. In addition, Xiaomei now says that length of advertisements should be published on its website. In total, they should be less than five minutes, she believes.

2 Terrified by the latest horror film? Or in tears at the latest romantic comedy?

Soon advertisers will be able to see your reaction to a film, so that adverts can be changed to make them more effective. Technology is now being developed which can capture how the cinema audience reacts. 'It will give film directors and advertisers useful information about what audiences enjoy and what captures their attention,' says the inventor, Dr Abdul Farooq. The technology will also be used to find pirates who secretly record films and then sell them illegally.

3 A German DJ has broken the record for the world's longest non-stop radio show. Dominik Schollmayer, 26, ran his show for 169 consecutive hours, beating the previous record by one hour.

Schollmayer was observed by doctors all through his broadcast; they said that the DJ had gone 'completely mad' and was dancing 'like a crazy man' in the last few hours. At the end, Schollmayer said he was 'totally exhausted'.

4 Viewers of the Weather Channel thought they were watching a soap opera ... but the drama they saw was 100 percent real. Kim Perez was presenting the weather forecast when her boyfriend, Marty Cunningham, walked onto the set. 'How are you?' Cunningham asked. Kim was astonished when Cunningham went down on one knee ... and so were the viewing public when he said: 'I love you and I want to spend the rest of my life with you. Will you please marry me?' Music began playing, and the weather map behind Kim was changed into a giant 'Will You Marry Me?' graphic.

'I will,' said a delighted Perez. The people in the studio began to applaud and Kim started to cry when Marty put the engagement ring on her finger.

Tuesday, July 3, 2012

Cost of country living
LIVING in the country may be idyllic —
you £39 a week

GOING into the stadium

BRITAIN'S washout summer
magistrates court yesterday.

Reading
News stories

1a Use the prompts below to prepare questions to ask students in your class. Then ask and answer the questions to find students who do these things.

- reads a newspaper every day
- never reads newspapers
- watches 24-hour news channels
- often listens to the news on the radio
- usually checks the news online
- isn't very interested in the news

> Do you read a newspaper every day?
>> No, I never read newspapers.

b Look at your results. Did you find someone for every question? Which ways of finding out the news are most popular? Which way do you think is the best?

2 Read the news headlines below. Can you guess what the articles are about?

A German DJ breaks record

B TV weather presenter gets on air proposal

C Women sues movie theatre

D Who's watching the audience?

3 Read articles 1–4 quickly and match them with headlines A–D. Were your answers to exercise 2 correct?

4 Choose the best answers to complete the article summaries.

1 The woman in Beijing is suing the movie theatre because *she didn't enjoy the film she saw / the tickets were too expensive / she had to wait a long time to see the film*.

2 Dr Farooq is developing new technology which will *ask the audience questions about the film / show pictures of the audience / capture the audience's attention*.

3 The German DJ behaved strangely *after / before / towards* the end of his broadcast because *he wanted to break the record / he wanted people to notice him / he was extremely tired*.

4 Kim Perez was very *worried / surprised / disappointed* because *it was her first time on TV / she didn't want to get engaged / she didn't expect her boyfriend to propose*.

5 Find words in the articles with these meanings:

1 an advertisement for a new TV programme or film: _____ (article 1)
2 a film which tells a love story in an amusing way: _____ (article 2)
3 the people watching a TV programme or film: _____ (article 2)
4 the transmission of a radio or TV programme: _____ (article 3)
5 the place in a studio where a TV show is made: _____ (article 4)
6 a computerised design: _____ (article 4)
7 to clap your hands to show you enjoyed something: _____ (article 4)

6a Choose three questions about the media that you would like to discuss.

1 Should there be fewer adverts and trailers in cinemas or do you like watching them?
2 Do you agree that the maximum length of adverts should be five minutes?
3 Would you mind if you were filmed by advertisers while you were watching movies? Why / Why not?
4 Is it important that people are stopped from making illegal copies of films? Why / Why not?
5 Do you know of any more unusual world record attempts? What did the person do?
6 Has anything unusual (like Marty's proposal) ever happened on live TV in your country?
7 Do you think what Marty did was romantic or embarrassing? Why?

b Work in pairs and discuss the questions you chose.

> I don't want to be filmed by advertisers when I'm in a cinema. I hate being filmed.

Vocabulary
Extreme adjectives

1a Match the extreme adjectives from the news articles with an ordinary adjective.

A	B
1 terrified (line 11)	a very angry
2 astonished (line 36)	b very frightened
3 delighted (line 43)	c very happy
4 exhausted (line 30)	d very surprised
5 furious (line 01)	e very tired

b Why do you think writers use extreme adjectives? Look back at the texts on page 70 for examples.

2 Write definitions for these extreme adjectives using ordinary adjectives. Use a dictionary if necessary.

awful *very bad*
1 hilarious
2 excellent
3 fantastic
4 terrible
5 freezing
6 boiling

3 Read the headlines and replace the words in bold with extreme adjectives.

Manager **very happy** with **very good** performance
Manager ecstatic with fantastic performance

1 Prime Minister **very angry** at criticism
2 'I made a **very bad** mistake,' admits President
3 Players **very tired** after a long season
4 **Very cold** weather causes problems on the roads
5 Joey Spillane stars in **very funny** new comedy
6 Audiences **very frightened** by new horror movie
7 Film star **very surprised** at Oscar nomination

PRONUNCIATION

1 🎧 7.2 Listen and write the words you hear in the correct column according to their stress pattern.

Oo	Ooo	oOoo	oOo

2 Practise saying the words with the correct word stress.

Task

Talk about a show you love or hate

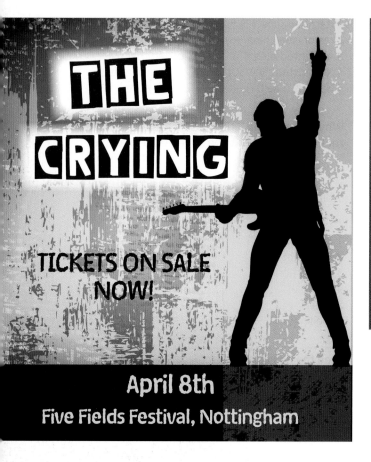

THE CRYING

TICKETS ON SALE NOW!

April 8th
Five Fields Festival, Nottingham

THE HOUSE OF ELIOTT
Tonight at 9 o'clock

Preparation Vocabulary and listening

1a What types of entertainment can you see in the photos? Choose from the words in the box.

musicals	films	plays	classical concerts
pop videos	TV dramas	ballet	comedy shows
rock concerts	opera		

b Write each type of entertainment on the line below.

LOVE ← ♥♥ _____ ♥♥ → HATE

c Work in groups. Talk about your favourite forms of entertainment. How often do you see the things you like? Compare your answers.

> I love musicals, but I only go about once a year because the tickets are really expensive.

2 What are the three most important things for each form of entertainment in exercise 1a? Choose from the box below, then discuss your answers in groups.

scenery	acting	singing	music
special effects	costumes	the set	camera work
characters	music	the cast	lighting
dancing	the plot	lyrics	performances
an orchestra	jokes		

> Acting, special effects and music are the most important things in a film.

3a 🎧 7.3 Listen to four people talking about something they've seen. Which questions does each speaker answer and what do they say?

1 What was the show, film, etc.?
2 Where and when did you see it?
3 Did you like or dislike it?
4 Which aspects of it did you like/dislike?

b Listen again and tick the phases you hear in the Useful language box.

The Fillmore Opera Company
presents

Turandot

by Giacomo Puccini
Lakeside Open-air Theatre
19th–25th September

IT'S A FACT!
The Mousetrap,
a murder mystery
by Agatha Christie,
has been playing
in London since
1952.

USEFUL LANGUAGE

a Giving information
I want to tell you about (the first time I went to a ballet).
A (TV show) that I really like at the moment is …
It stars …
It's written/produced/directed/composed by …
He/She also wrote / directed / appeared in …
It's about …
It's set in …
It's based on …

b Giving your opinion
I thought it was (really amazing/disappointing).
The performances were (great/terrible).
The worst thing about it was (the dancing).
I loved the fact that …
I'd recommend it to anybody!
I wouldn't recommend it at all.
I've never seen a better (movie).

Task Speaking

1a You are going to give a short talk about a film or TV programme that you either loved or hated. Make notes about the questions below.

   1 Is it a TV programme, a flim or a live show?
   2 Who was in it, wrote it, etc.?
   3 What was your overall opinion of it?
   4 What did you particularly like/dislike about it? Think about the things in exercise 2 on page 72.
   5 Who (if anyone) would you recommend it to?

  b Plan what you want to say. Ask your teacher for any words/phrases you need.

> Useful language a and b

2 Work in pairs. Take turns to practise your talks and ask each other questions.

3 Now give your talk to the class and listen to other students' talks. As you listen, make notes about the questions in exercise 1a. Ask your own questions at the end.

SHARE YOUR TASK

Practise your talk about a show you loved or hated until you feel confident.

Film/Record yourself telling your story.

Share your film/recording with other students.

LANGUAGE LIVE

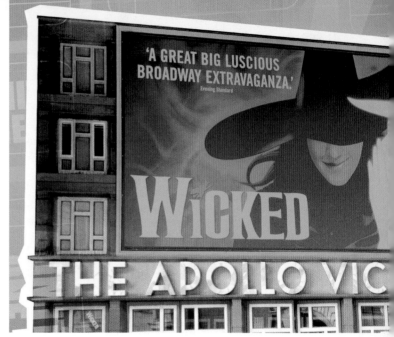

Writing
A review

1 Read about the musical *Wicked* and answer the questions.

   1 Is the musical successful? How do you know?

   2 Would you like to see it? Why / Why not?

**MUST SEE ›› **   'Best Musical of the Decade'

Based on a novel by Gregory Maguire and characters from the flim *The Wizard of Oz*, *Wicked* is the story of two inspiring women, and is the must-see musical of the decade! Now in its eighth year at the Apollo Victoria Theatre in London, *Wicked* has been seen by more than 20 million people worldwide, and it was recently voted 'Best Musical of the Decade' by the magazine *Entertainment Weekly*.

---

2 Read some online reviews of *Wicked*. Put them in order, from most positive to least positive.

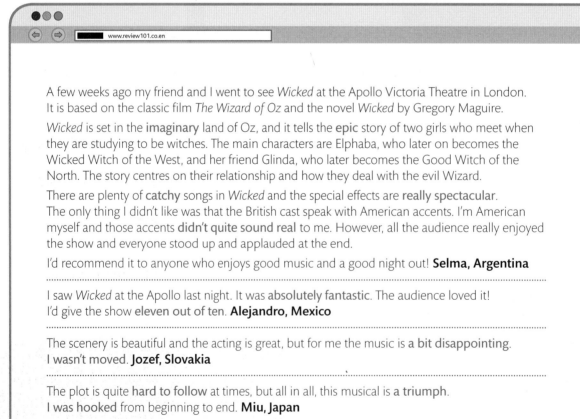

www.review101.co.en

A few weeks ago my friend and I went to see *Wicked* at the Apollo Victoria Theatre in London. It is based on the classic film *The Wizard of Oz* and the novel *Wicked* by Gregory Maguire.

Wicked is set in the **imaginary** land of Oz, and it tells the **epic** story of two girls who meet when they are studying to be witches. The main characters are Elphaba, who later on becomes the Wicked Witch of the West, and her friend Glinda, who later becomes the Good Witch of the North. The story centres on their relationship and how they deal with the evil Wizard.

There are plenty of **catchy** songs in *Wicked* and the special effects are **really spectacular**. The only thing I didn't like was that the British cast speak with American accents. I'm American myself and those accents **didn't quite sound real** to me. However, all the audience really enjoyed the show and everyone stood up and applauded at the end.

I'd recommend it to anyone who enjoys good music and a good night out! **Selma, Argentina**

I saw *Wicked* at the Apollo last night. It was **absolutely fantastic**. The audience loved it! I'd give the show **eleven out of ten**. **Alejandro, Mexico**

The scenery is beautiful and the acting is great, but for me the music is **a bit disappointing**. I wasn't moved. **Jozef, Slovakia**

The plot is quite **hard to follow** at times, but all in all, this musical is **a triumph**. I **was hooked** from beginning to end. **Miu, Japan**

COMMENTS – *Add your own*

See you at 8pm

3a Read Selma's review again. In which paragraph does she answer these questions?

a What did you like and what didn't you like?
b Do you recommend the show? Why / Why not?
c What did you see? Where did you see it? When did you go and who with?
d What is the story about? (Don't tell the ending!)

b What do you learn about the musical *Wicked* in each paragraph?

Paragraph 1 – it's based on the film The Wizard of Oz

4 Look at the words and phrases in blue in the reviews. Write them in the correct column below.

Positive	Negative	Neutral
		imaginary

5a You are going to write a review of a film, musical or concert that you have seen recently. Make notes using the questions in exercise 3a.

b Write your review. Then check what you have written using the checklist below.

- Have you answered the four questions in exercise 3a in four clear paragraphs?
- Have you used some of the vocabulary in exercise 4?
- Have you checked your punctuation and spelling?
- Have you used passive forms and *-ed/-ing* adjectives where appropriate?

Speaking
Making a social arrangement

1 If you had a spare ticket for a show, who would you ask to go with you?

2 ▶ Karina has a spare ticket for a gig tonight. Watch the video and answer the questions.

1 Why isn't Karina going with her boyfriend?
2 Who else can't go? Why not?
3 Who agrees to go with her in the end?

3a How many gaps from the conversations can you complete? Watch again and check.

1 Hello, Josh, _____ Karina. I'm _____ _____ _____ if you'd like to go to a gig with me tonight.
2 When you get this message, will you _____ _____ a _____ ?
3 I've got two tickets to see The Magnetos tonight. _____ you _____ _____ come?
4 _____ , _____ , _____ _____ . I'm going to my mum's.
5 But _____ _____ _____ ?
6 _____ _____ next week instead?
7 Yeah, _____ _____ _____ . Thanks.
8 _____ _____ meet at 8 o'clock?
9 Great. _____ _____ you there.

b Find two useful phrases in exercise 3a for each situation below.

1 inviting: *I'm phoning to ask if you'd like to ...*
2 accepting and refusing invitations:
3 making suggestions:

PRONUNCIATION

1 ▶ Watch and listen to the key phrases. Practise saying the sentences with the same stress.

I'm **phoning** to **ask** if you'd **like** to ...

4 Work in pairs. Turn to page 128 and follow the instructions.

AFTER UNIT 7 YOU CAN ...

Explain how you feel about TV and radio programmes.

Ask general knowledge questions about culture and the media.

Give a short talk about a show.

Write a review.

Make a social arrangement.

08

SOCIAL LIFE

IN THIS UNIT

- **Grammar: Polite requests; *will* and *shall* for instant responses**
- **Vocabulary: Social behaviour; Talking about norms and customs**
- **Task: Give tips on how to behave**
- **World culture: Addicted to games**

MY BIG NIGHT OUT!

The DJ sits in a Bentley in the middle of the dance floor

Jiao Wu is 28 years old and lives in Beijing in China.

The nightlife in Beijing is unbelievable. I usually meet up with my friends around midnight. That's quite early in BPT (Beijing
5 Party Time). First we hit the bars in the Chaoyang Park district. There's a club there called Bling where the DJ sits in a Bentley car in the middle of the dance floor. It's outrageous! Around four in the
10 morning we often head over to Ghost Street, where the restaurants are open all night. By the time I get home the sun is coming up. In the past we rarely went clubbing. We would usually have a long dinner in a restaurant and then go to an all-night karaoke bar. But nowadays there's so much choice and the clubs are always full. In BPT, every night
15 is party night!

Reading and vocabulary

1a Look at the activities in the box. Tick the things that you sometimes do on a night out with your friends. Cross out the things that you never do.

go to the cinema	go out for a coffee	go dancing
go to a private party	have dinner in a restaurant	go to a karaoke bar
watch live music	go to a bar	go for a walk
go clubbing	go driving around town	grab a snack
stay out late	go home early	

b Work in groups and compare your answers.

2 Discuss the questions using phrases from exercise 1a.

- What do you do on a typical Friday/Saturday night out?
- What would you do on your ideal night out?
- Which activities are most popular with young people in your country?
- Which activities do older people prefer?

3 Look at the photos and read the photo captions and quotes, but do not read the full article. Answer the questions.

1 Where do the three people live?
2 Can you guess what they do or don't do on Saturday nights?

From Beijing to Barcelona, from Scotland to Sydney, people everywhere love a big night out. We all want to unwind and have fun with our friends, colleagues or partner. But do we all enjoy ourselves in the same way? We hear from people in three very different places.

We throw little notes from our car windows

Hassan Kashani is 19 years old and lives in Tehran in Iran.

Iranzamin Street in the centre of Tehran is where all the young fashionable
20 Iranians hang out. On Saturday night my friends and I go driving there. We write our mobile numbers on pieces of paper and throw them into girls' cars. But they usually
25 only read the note if they see you're driving a smart car! One night, we were driving around in my friend's car and we drove up beside some girls, trying to give them our numbers. Suddenly we realised that one of the girls in the car was my friend's girlfriend. She was furious! My friend
30 tried to make excuses, but she knew what he was up to. I hate to be alone, so I always surround myself with my friends. We chat and make jokes and have fun. We're just the same as young people all over the world, I guess.

It's a bit like going clubbing with your parents

Ewen Anderson is 22 years old and lives on the tiny Isle of Eigg, off the west coast of Scotland.

There are only 70
35 inhabitants on the Isle of Eigg where I live, so there isn't a lot of choice. We do the same thing
40 most Saturday nights. Around 9 o'clock we all head down to the community hall. By ten the hall is full of people; young and old, friend and foe, we all socialise together. Some people might find it a bit strange – it's a bit like going to a club with your parents – but it's our way.
45 There's usually a folk band from the mainland. When they get going, people start flying round the hall, dancing like crazy and having fun. The older people go home around midnight, but some of the younger ones are still there the next morning.

4a Read the article, then work in pairs. Explain why the things below are important in each person's night out.

Jiao Wu	BPT, Bling, a Bentley, Ghost Street
Hassan	driving, mobile numbers, pieces of paper, a smart car
Ewen	70, the community hall, young and old people, a folk band

b Read the article again, then answer the questions.

1 How has nightlife changed in Beijing?
2 Why was Hassan's friend's girlfriend angry?
3 How is Saturday night on Eigg different for young and old people?

5 Look at these expressions from the text. Can you guess the meaning of the words and phrases in bold?

1 we **hit** the bars in ... (line 05)
2 to be **outrageous** (line 09)
3 to **make excuses** (line 30)
4 what he's **up to** (line 30)
5 we all **head down to** ... (lines 40–1)
6 a **foe** (line 42)
7 **it's our way** (line 44)
8 **the mainland** (line 45)

FACT! GOING OUT

- Pubs have been at the centre of British social life for over a thousand years. The oldest pub is over 1,200 years old.
- Restaurants existed in the city of Kaifeng in China in the 11th century. People ordered from a menu and used paper money to pay.
- The first discos took place in Paris during the Second World War. People danced to records in clubs because live music was banned.
- In Spain and Latin America, many people don't even go out until 11 o'clock or midnight.

6a Work in groups. Choose one of the questions and discuss your ideas.

- What does each account tell you about life in that place?
- Whose night out sounds the most/least fun? Why?
- Is nightlife changing where you live? In what ways?

b Read the fact box above. Which facts didn't you know? Which are surprising?

Language focus 1
Polite requests

1 🎧 8.1 Look at the pictures. Listen and find the person in the pictures who is making each request.

2a 🎧 8.2 Listen to the six conversations. Does the other person say *yes* or *no* to the request in each case? What reason does he/she give when he/she refuses?

b Listen again and complete the questions and answers.

1 **A:** _____ _____ have the bill, _____ ?
  B: Certainly, sir.
2 **A:** _____ _____ , can I get past, please?
  B: _____ .
3 **A:** _____ _____ pass me the water, please?
  B: Here you are.
4 **A:** _____ _____ alright _____ _____ sit here?
  B: Sure, _____ ahead.
5 **A:** _____ _____ _____ _____ _____ leave
  a bit early today?
  B: I'm afraid I need you here at the moment.
6 **A:** _____ _____ _____ _____ my bag while I go
  to the toilet?
  B: _____ _____ not .

PRONUNCIATION

1 🎧 8.3 Listen to the first five requests again. Notice the polite intonation pattern.
  1 Can I have the bill, please?
  2 Excuse me, can I get past, please?
  3 Could you pass me the water, please?
  4 Is it alright if I sit here?
  5 Do you mind if I leave a bit early today?

2 Practise saying the requests.

PRACTICE

1 Work in pairs. Rewrite the conversations to make them sound more polite. Then act them out.

Can I   please
~~I want to~~ speak to Nadia^?

1 **A:** I want to use your pen.
  B: Yes.
2 **A:** Pass me my coat.
  B: Here you are.
3 **A:** Lend me €10 till tomorrow.
  B: I haven't got any money.
4 **A:** Bring me another coffee.
  B: Yes.
5 **A:** Lend me your phone.
  B: The battery is flat.
6 **A:** If you're going into town, give me a lift.
  B: Yes.
7 **A:** Tell me the way to the bus station.
  B: I don't know this area.
8 **A:** Pick up my suit from the dry cleaner's.
  B: I won't be able to. I'll have too much to carry.

2a Think of five real requests to make to students in your class. Use the prompts below.

help (me) to do something	open/close something
turn something on/off/up/down	lend (me) something
pass (me) something	move something
borrow something (for a second)	have a look at something

> I really like your ring. Could I have a look at it?

b Mingle and make / respond to the requests politely. If you say *no*, you must give a reason. How many of your requests were accepted?

Unit 8, Study & Practice 1, page 153

Language focus 2
will and *shall* for instant responses

1 🎧 8.4 Look at the pictures. One person wants to do something. What do you think it is? Listen and check. Which person gets what they want in each case?

2 Listen again and choose the correct answers.

Conversation A
1 *Shall we / We shall* go on the roller coaster?
2 *I'll / I'm going to* go on the big wheel with you, but not the roller coaster.
3 *Shall I / Will I* help you?
4 Alright. *I'll / I'm going to* give it a go.

Conversation B
5 *Shall we / We'll* have a quick coffee?
6 *I'll / I'm going to* try and go to the gym tomorrow morning.
7 *I'll / I'm going to* do some shopping on the way home.
8 *Shall I / I'm going to* take you to the supermarket?

GRAMMAR

1a Look at the sentences in exercise 2. Find:
1 two examples of offers. *Shall I ...*
2 two examples of suggestions.

b Which verb forms are used for each?

2a Look at the other four sentences.
1 In which cases has the speaker already decided what to do?
2 In which cases is he/she deciding as they speak?

b Which verb forms are used in each case?

PRACTICE

1 Work in pairs. Look at the situations on page 127 and decide which response you would give. Why?

2 Which situation on page 127 is the conversation below based on? Complete it with *shall I, shall we, I'll* or *I'm going to*.

A: Have you heard about Johnny's broken leg? He's at home really bored, apparently.
B: Poor Johnny! ¹_____ go round and see him this afternoon?
A: Sorry, I can't. ²_____ do some revision this afternoon for my exam tomorrow morning. Perhaps ³_____ go and see him after the exam if I can.
B: OK, well ⁴_____ go round this afternoon on my own, then. ⁵_____ do some shopping, then I think ⁶_____ go after that.

3 Work in pairs and choose two more situations from page 127. Write conversations similar to the one in exercise 2. Act out your conversations for the class.

Unit 8, Study & Practice 2, page 154

Vocabulary and listening

Social behaviour

1a Work in pairs. Look at the pictures and talk about what 'good manners' and 'bad manners' mean for you. Add three ideas to each column of the table.

Good manners	Bad manners
say thank you when someone helps you	talk on your mobile phone in the cinema

b Work as a class and compare your opinions. Is there any behaviour that you disagree about?

2a Match the verbs in A with the expressions in B to make phrases related to social behaviour.

A	B
1 to offer	a on both cheeks
2 to share	b each other
3 to shake	c to pay
4 to go out on	d paying
5 to kiss someone	e a date
6 to take someone	f the bill
7 to hug	g home
8 to insist on	h an invitation
9 to refuse	i to your house
10 to invite someone	j someone up
11 to pick	k hands

b Find the phrases from exercise 2a in the quiz and underline them. Were your answers correct?

3 Work in pairs. Do the quiz, then explain your answers to each other. Compare your answers with the class.

4a 🎧 8.5 Listen to five excerpts from a conversation about the issues in the quiz. Answer the questions.

  1 How old do you think Florence and Ruth are? What is their relationship?
  2 Which questions from the quiz are they discussing in each excerpt?
  A ___ B ___ C ___ D ___ E ___

b Listen again. Which answers does each speaker choose? If they give more than one answer, in which situation is each answer true?

5 Work in pairs and discuss.

  • Which of Florence and Ruth's answers do you particularly agree/disagree with?
  • Are there differences in manners between generations in your country? If so, give examples.
  • Has the way that men and women treat each other in social situations changed in the last 30 years?

MODERN

1 While you are out, you meet a friend in the street. What do you do?
  a Shake hands.
  b Say hello.
  c Kiss each other on one or both cheeks.
  d Hug each other.

2 You are having a meal with friends in a restaurant. What do you do with your mobile phone?
  a Put it on the table and answer any calls or text messages that you receive.
  b Switch it to vibrate, then check discreetly if you have any important messages which you need to answer.
  c Switch it off until you leave the restaurant.

3 A friend invites you to her house for the evening, together with six other guests. When should you arrive?
  a At exactly the time you were invited, or just before.
  b Ten or 15 minutes after the time you were invited.
  c No more than an hour after you were invited.
  d At least an hour after you were invited.

4 A smoker is visiting friends who don't smoke. What should he do?
  a Ask politely for an ashtray.
  b Ask if it's OK to smoke in the house.
  c Ask if it's OK to smoke in the garden or on the balcony.
  d Wait until he leaves before he has a cigarette.

MANNERS

5 A man and woman go out on a date to a restaurant. What should happen?
  a The man should pay the bill.
  b The woman should offer to pay her half of the bill but accept if the man insists on paying.
  c They should share the bill.
  d Whoever has more money should pay.

6 When a man goes out with a woman, which things below should he do?
  a Pick her up from her house.
  b Open doors for her and help her with her coat.
  c Take her home at the end of the evening.
  d Treat her with respect.

7 You are on a diet on which you cannot eat certain foods. Friends invite you to dinner. What do you do?
  a Refuse the invitation because of your diet.
  b Phone your hosts in advance and explain what you can and cannot eat.
  c Tell your hosts when you arrive.
  d Say nothing and try to avoid those foods in the meal as much as you can.

8 After dinner or a party at a friend's house, what should you do?
  a Say thank you as you leave.
  b Send a text or an email to say thank you.
  c Post a message on your friend's social networking site to say thank you.
  d Send a handwritten letter or card to say thank you.

Vocabulary
Talking about norms and customs

1 Read the tips about customs in Britain. Tick the things that are the same in your country and mark with a cross those that are different. Compare your answers with the rest of the class.

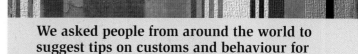

We asked people from around the world to suggest tips on customs and behaviour for visitors to Britain. These were the top seven …

1 **It's good manners to** say please and thank you. You should also say 'excuse me' if you want to get past someone and 'sorry' if you are in someone's way.

2 **It's considered rude to** jump queues.

3 On the whole, **it's OK to** use first names. Young and middle-aged people **don't tend to** use 'Mr' and 'Mrs' very much, although many older people prefer it.

4 **It's unacceptable to** ask people how much they earn.

5 Generally speaking, people only shake hands when they are introduced for the first time. **It isn't usual to** shake hands every time you meet people.

6 When people go out, they **tend to** take turns to buy drinks. **It's important to** take your turn.

7 **It's perfectly normal** for people in shops **to** call you 'love' or 'dear' or 'mate'. Don't be offended!

2 Write the phrases in bold from exercise 1 in the correct category below.

- Phrases for making generalisations:
  It isn't usual to …
- Phrases for saying what is good manners / acceptable:
- Phrases for saying what is bad manners / unacceptable:

3a Look at the customs you marked with a cross in exercise 1. Rewrite them to describe the situation in your country. Use the phrases in bold from the text.

It's quite important to say please and thank you.

b Use the prompts below and the phrases in exercise 2 to make sentences about customs in your country.

It's unacceptable to wear casual clothes in the office.

1 wear casual clothes in the office
2 keep your shoes on in people's houses
3 blow your nose in public
4 take flowers or a bottle of wine when you go to someone's house for dinner
5 leave food on your plate at the end of a meal in someone's house
6 men to kiss women on the hand
7 women to go out in groups on their own

Task

Give tips on how to behave

Preparation Listening

1 🎧 8.6 Listen to seven people giving advice and information about social behaviour. Which topic (B) is each person discussing? There may be more than one possible answer.

A
1 Aleksander, 39, from Poland
2 Mei, 24, from China
3 Lee Kuan, 20, from Singapore
4 Simone, 28, from the USA
5 Rosa, 33, from Peru
6 Ramon, 29, from Spain
7 Khalid, 24, from Bahrain

B
a Tips for foreigners about customs and behaviour in your country
b Advice about going out in your city/country
c How to behave when you first start dating
d How young people behave in your country
e Etiquette for various types of communication (texting, social networking, etc.)

2 Work in pairs. Can you remember what each person said about the topics? Listen again and check.

3 Listen again and tick the phrases you hear in the Useful language box.

> Useful language a and b

USEFUL LANGUAGE

a What to do
You should always/definitely ...
Generally speaking, (people ...)
Most Spanish/young people ...
Always remember to ...
It's important / perfectly OK / uncool (to ...)
People expect you to ...

b What not to do
You should never ...
These days, nobody ...
Nobody cares (about) ...
It might seem strange if you ...
It's not acceptable to ...

Task Speaking

1   Work in groups. You are going to present a list of tips about norms and customs. Choose one of the topics in exercise 1.

2a Make a list of tips on your own. Ask your teacher for any words/phrases you need.

b   Compare your ideas with the rest of the group. Compile a list of the best tips.

3   Read your group's tips to the class. Can they add ideas to your list? Are there any tips that people disagree with?

Follow up Writing

1   EITHER write out the best tips about the topic you chose with your group.
OR choose another topic from exercise 1 and write tips about it.

SHARE YOUR TASK

Practise giving your talk on the topic you wrote about until you feel confident.

Film/Record yourself giving the talk.

Share your film/recording with other students.

WORLD CULTURE

ADDICTED TO GAMES

Find out first

1a What do you know about video games and gaming? Try to guess the missing information in the fact file below.

Video games

The industry
Total revenue: $_____

....

The gamer
Average age: _____ years old
Female gamers: _____%
Average number of hours playing: _____ per week
Most popular game ever: _____

....

The games
Current most popular game: _____
Most popular game ever: _____

---

b Go online to check your answers or ask your teacher

....

Search: video games statistics / average gamer / best-selling video games

View

2a Work in pairs and discuss.
- Do you play video games? If so, which games and how often?
- Do you know anyone who is addicted to gaming?

b ▶ Watch the video about gaming addiction. Choose the best way to complete each sentence.

1 The presenter is interested in ...
  a how to stop children playing video games.
  b why games are so popular.
  c the dangers of video games.
2 Chris reacted violently when ...
  a his mother tried to stop him using the internet.
  b his mother tried to make him go to school.
  c his mother took his copy of *World of Warcraft*.
3 In South Korea, ...
  a a majority of boys are seriously addicted.
  b a small minority of boys are seriously addicted.
  c serious addiction to games is not a problem.
4 The presenter believes that ...
  a parents should stop their children playing games.
  b parents should encourage their children to play games.
  c parents shouldn't ignore their children when they are playing games.

3a What do the numbers in the box refer to? Watch the video again and check your answers.

five years	three billion	20 hours a day	85 percent
ten hours	two percent		

b Work in pairs and discuss.
- What are the main problems experienced by Chris's parents and Sang Wook's parents?
- What would do in their situation?

World view

4a ▶ Watch three people talking about video games. Tick the questions that each person is answering.

	Imogen	Steve	Carol
1 What is an acceptable amount of time to spend playing video games?			
2 Are video games too violent?			
3 Are violent video games a problem for children?			
4 How should parents prevent children becoming addicted?			

b Watch again. Make notes about what each speaker says.

c Work in small groups and discuss the questions above.

FIND OUT MORE

5a How do you feel about the things in the box? Do you think it is possible to be addicted to them?

social networking   mobile phones   junk food
television

b Go online to find out more about one of the possible addictions in exercise 5a. Try to find answers to the questions below.

1 Are there any statistics to show that this is a problem?
2 What, if any, are the signs of addiction?
3 Are there any interesting personal stories relating to this issue?
4 How should you treat someone with this problem?

Search: social networking addiction / mobile phone addiction / junk food addiction / television addiction

Write up your research

6 Write a paragraph about the addiction you researched. Include answers to the questions in exercise 5b and use the prompts below to help you.

- According to statistics ...
- The first signs of addiction are ...
- One person described how ...
- The best way to treat this problem is to ...

AFTER UNIT 8 YOU CAN ...

Make and respond to polite requests.

Describe and discuss customs and social norms.

Give advice about how to behave in social situations.

Research a topical issue online.

09

STUFF!

Reading and speaking

1a Complete the sentences to make them true for you. Use the ideas in the box.

> clothes shoes handbags and jewellery CDs DVDs books electronic gadgets food furniture and things for the house presents

1 I really hate shopping for …
2 I love shopping for …
3 I never go shopping for …

b Work in pairs and discuss. If you could go out and buy anything today, what would it be? Do you ever buy things you don't need?

2 Read the introduction to the article and look at the photos and headings. What do you think the article is about?

3a Work in pairs. Student A: Read text 1. Student B: Read text 2. Make notes about these questions.

1 What do you learn about Louise/Andrew as people? (e.g. age, job, income, where they live, personal life, etc.)
2 Do they have a lot of possessions? Explain what and why.
3 What reasons do Louise/Andrew give for their lifestyle choices?
4 Are there other people like Louise/Andrew, according to the article? What does it say about them?
5 What reasons are given in the article for these trends?

b Tell your partner about what you read.

4 Read the other text, then discuss the meaning of the words and phrases below with your partner.

1 a reward (line 09)   5 a quick-fix solution (line 29)
2 a purchase (line 14)   6 homeless (line 36)
3 to deserve (line 20)   7 to seek (line 46)
4 time-poor (line 27)   8 lack of choice (line 47)

5 Work in groups. Choose at least one question each to ask the group.

1 Would you like to have Louise or Andrew's lifestyle? Why / Why not?
2 Who, if either, are you naturally more similar to? In what way?
3 What do you think it would be like living with or being married to one of these people?
4 Do you think Louise has a problem, or is her shopping just harmless fun? Explain your opinion.
5 Do you think Andrew and Chris will be able to live the way they do permanently? Why / Why not?
6 Which physical possessions do you think will be replaced with digital goods in the future? What are the advantages and disadvantages of this?

 FIND OUT MORE Go online to find out more about shameless shopaholics and extreme minimalists like Andrew Hyde and Chris Yurista.

Consumer CRAZY

We live in a world where there are more and more goods available. More gadgets, more clothes, more furniture, more books than ever before. How should we deal with it all? We look at two extreme responses.

1 The extreme shopper

1 Last Saturday morning Louise Anderson was up early, ready to begin her usual weekend routine. First stop was the shoe department in Selfridges, in London's Oxford Street, then she moved on to other department stores and finally to the designer
5 boutiques along New Bond Street.

When she arrived back in her flat she had three pairs of designer shoes and a matching handbag. She had also picked up two cashmere sweaters, a £200 pot of face cream and another £200 worth of make-up. 'Shopping is my reward to myself for
10 working hard all week,' says 31-year-old Louise, who is single and childless. 'And buying shoes gives me such a high.'

In the last month, Louise has also bought eight designer bikinis and a set of black Gucci luggage.

Louise admits that she doesn't even wear all her purchases.
15 'There is an entire wall of my bedroom which is covered in boxes of shoes, all carefully labelled,' she says. 'Sometimes I don't actually wear them to go out. I just put them on in my bedroom and admire them.' So what drives her to spend so much on things she will never need?
20 Louise believes that she deserves these luxuries in return for the stresses of her highly paid job. 'I see shopping as my main hobby. I don't drink and I don't smoke. Most of my money goes on my shopping habit, but it's my money that I'm spending.'

Consumer psychologist Dr Paul Marsden encounters more
25 and more women like Louise, who are 'addicted to shopping'. He believes that the lifestyle of modern women is to blame. 'Women today are time-poor. If they have busy careers, other parts of their lives are often not very satisfactory, but they want to feel good about themselves. Shopping is a quick-fix
30 solution. It's a way of telling themselves that they matter and are important.'

2 The extreme minimalist

Andrew Hyde is a technology mogul and successful entrepreneur who travels between New York City and Silicon Valley. By rights, he should live in an expensive Manhattan apartment and dine in top restaurants. Instead he has chosen 35 to be homeless.

And he has reduced his possessions to just 15 things. In addition to the clothes on his back, he has two pieces of outerwear, some exercise clothes, a backpack, a pair of socks, 40 some underwear, a pair of sunglasses, a phone, a laptop, an iPhone, a camera and one or two other items.

So what made him sell everything else that he owned? For Andrew it is all about freedom from the responsibility of possessions. Socrates once said, 'Happiness is not found in 45 seeking more, but in learning to enjoy less.' Or as Andrew puts it on his blog, 'Lack of choice helps, not hurts.'

Andrew is not alone. Chris Yurista, a DJ and travel agent from Washington, DC, has also given up his apartment and reduced his possessions to a backpack full of designer clothes, a laptop and a 50 bicycle. For him, like other '21st-century minimalists', technology is the key to it all: digital goods have provided replacements for his physical possessions. 'The internet has replaced my need for an address,' says the 27-year-old, who sleeps on friends' couches. All his bills and letters arrive electronically and his record 55 collection of 2,000 albums has been relocated onto an external hard drive. His only worry is that a hard drive crash or a problem with a server will cause him to lose all his digital possessions.

'My life doesn't feel empty, because I've figured out a way to use digital technology to my advantage,' says Mr Yurista. 60

'Shopping is my reward to myself for working hard all week'

'Happiness is not found in seeking more, but in learning to enjoy less'

Language focus 1
Defining relative clauses

1 Work in pairs. Close your books and think of five things that are common today but which didn't exist, or were uncommon, 20 years ago.

touch screen phones, iPads …

2 Compare your ideas with the words in the box. Then match the words with the correct definitions. There are four extra words.

energy drink	internet addict	podcast
personal trainer	password	tattoo
YouTube clip	blogger	sat-nav
home recycling bin	app store	guyliner
Facebook wall	wi-fi hotspot	

TWENTY YEARS AGO
THEY WEREN'T PART OF OUR LIVES!

1 It's a virtual shop which sells applications for phones, etc.
an app store
2 It's a machine that gives you directions when you are driving.
3 It's a secret word which you use to access computers, bank accounts, etc.
4 It's make-up men put on their eyes.
5 It's a person who writes a kind of online diary for others to read.
6 It's a public area where people can connect their phones and computers to the internet.
7 It's a professional you hire to help you to improve your fitness.
8 It's a person whose life is dominated by the internet.
9 It's a section of your social networking profile where people can leave messages for you.
10 It's a drink which is designed to give you more energy.

GRAMMAR

1 Underline the relative pronouns in the definitions in exercise 2. Two don't have relative pronouns.
It's a drink <u>which</u> is designed to give you more energy.

2 Complete the rules.
1 … and *that* are used to refer to people.
2 … and *that* are used to refer to things.
3 … is used to refer to locations and places.
4 … is used to replace possessives.

3 Choose the correct answers to complete the rules.
1 The relative pronoun in definitions 4 and 7 can be left out because it's the **subject** / **object** of the relative clause.
2 In definition 10, the relative pronoun and the verb *be* can be left out because the sentence is **active** / **passive**.

4 Which other definition in exercise 2 can you write without the relative pronoun?

PRACTICE

1a Complete the definitions below with a word from the box and the correct relative pronoun.

a boiler	a decorator	a cleaner
a cooker	a bodyguard	a plumber
a launderette	a photocopier	a freezer
a stationer's	a vacuum cleaner	a dry cleaner's

1 A _____ is a machine _____ makes copies of documents.
2 A _____ is a person _____ protects important people from being attacked.
3 A _____ is a place with washing machines _____ you can wash your clothes.
4 A _____ is a person _____ job is to mend central heating, taps, etc.
5 A _____ is a machine _____ you use to clean floors and carpets.

b Match the other words in the box with the prompts below. Then write definitions for them using *which, that, who, whose* or *where*.

machine / keep / food very cold
A freezer is a machine which keeps food very cold.
1 machine / cook / food
2 person / you pay / clean your house or office
3 shop / they clean your clothes for you
4 person / job is to paint houses
5 shop / you buy office supplies
6 machine / heat water for baths, etc.

c Look back at the definitions in exercises 1a and 1b. In which definition can you leave out the relative pronoun?

2 Work in pairs. Student A: Close your book. Student B: Read five definitions from exercise 1. Can Student A remember the correct words? Swap roles and repeat.

What do you call a machine which keeps food very cold?

A freezer.

3 Work in groups. Make a vocabulary revision quiz for other students. Group A: Look at the instructions on page 129. Group B: Look at the instructions on page 130.

Unit 9, Study & Practice 1, page 156

Vocabulary and listening
How gadgets work

1 Which of the gadgets in the box do you own? Do they ever go wrong?

a DVD player	a digital camera	a laptop
a games console	an MP3 player	a dishwasher
a tablet computer	a touch screen phone	a photocopier
a vacuum cleaner	an electric cooker	

2 🎧 **9.1** Listen to four conversations and answer the questions.

1 Which gadget in exercise 1 is each person talking about?

2 Which words and phrases tell you this?

3 Listen again and number the phrases in bold in the order you hear them.

1
try **reinstalling the software**
I have to **restart** it
it **crashes**   *1*
the screen **freezes**

2
switch the machine **off** at the wall
the machine **breaks down**
hold down this button
unplug it

3
recharge the battery
touch the icons
scroll down the menu with your finger

4
press this button
it's **switched on**
it **doesn't work**
pause it

4a Choose four gadgets from the box in exercise 1. Which expressions in exercise 3 can you use to talk about each one?

A dishwasher – *You can switch it on/off.*
– *You can pause it.*
– *You can can press buttons on it.*
– *You can unplug it.*

b Work in pairs. Read out your list of verbs without saying the name of the gadget. Can your partner guess which gadget it is?

5 Work in pairs. Choose a gadget that you own. Explain briefly to your partner how it works.

PRONUNCIATION

1 Notice the stress patterns in compound nouns.

noun + noun	adjective + noun
● dishwasher	● ● electric cooker

2 Where is the stress in these compound nouns?

recycling bin	personal trainer
energy drink	instruction manual
bodyguard	digital camera
mobile phone	internet addict
washing machine	personal computer

3 🎧 **9.2** Listen and check. Then practise saying the compound nouns.

Language focus 2
Quantifiers

1a Work in groups. Read about Fadil, Abigail and Joel. Then discuss the questions.

- Have you ever been on a trip into the desert, a climbing trip or to a music festival? When and where?
- Think of four useful things to take on each trip. Explain why.

b Can you guess which trip(s) the objects below are useful for?

- insect repellent
- sleeping bag
- map and compass
- wet wipes
- torch with spare batteries
- swimming gear
- warm clothes
- wellies
- sunscreen
- high-energy food (e.g. raisins, peanuts)

2a 🎧 9.3 Listen to Fadil, Abigail and Joel. Write down six things they say you should take on each trip.

In the desert: *wet wipes*
Climbing:
At a music festival:

b Were your guesses in exercise 1b correct?

3 Listen again and complete the sentences with the quantifiers in the box. Some quantifiers can be used more than once.

too many	too much	a lot of	plenty of	some
enough	several	a bit of	a few	a couple of

Fadil
1 We tell people to bring _____ packs of wet wipes.
2 We bring _____ water with us.
3 It's good to bring _____ plastic bags.
4 _____ people forget that the desert is freezing cold at night, so you need to bring _____ warm clothes.

Abigail
5 They haven't packed _____ warm clothes to deal with a change in the weather.
6 I always advise people to take _____ insect repellent and _____ food.
7 _____ people these days rely on a handheld GPS navigator. ... but they can break.

Joel
8 You need a torch with _____ spare batteries.
9 Often people bring _____ food with them and they always regret it, because they spend _____ time carrying it around and, actually, there are _____ places to buy food.
10 So really ... all you need is _____ money!

GRAMMAR

1 Which words are countable? Which are uncountable?

water   people   food   bag   money   battery

2 Put the quantifiers from exercise 3 in the correct group.
1 Quantifiers used with countable nouns: *a couple of*
2 Quantifiers used with uncountable nouns: *too much*
3 Quantifiers used with both: *a lot of*

3 Are these pairs of sentences the same or different?
1 I took **a lot of** food with me.
   I took **too much** food with me.
2 We had **enough** money with us.
   We had **plenty of** money with us.

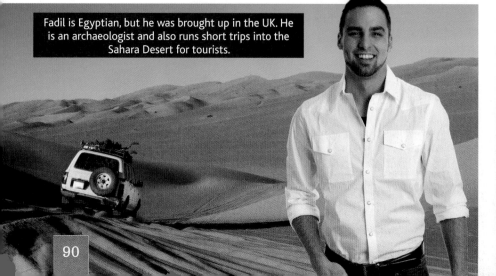

Fadil is Egyptian, but he was brought up in the UK. He is an archaeologist and also runs short trips into the Sahara Desert for tourists.

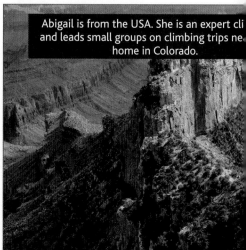

Abigail is from the USA. She is an expert cli[...] and leads small groups on climbing trips ne[...] home in Colorado.

PRACTICE

1 Complete the sentences with an appropriate quantifier and verb.

On camping trips ...
1 there **are** / **aren't** _____ insects.
2 there **is** / **isn't** _____ space in your tent.
3 you **need** / **don't need** _____ equipment.

On trips to big cities ...
4 you **can** / **can't** find _____ cheap places to eat.
5 there **are** / **aren't** _____ people.
6 there **are** / **aren't** usually _____ interesting places to visit.
7 there **are** / **aren't** usually _____ museums and art galleries.

At the beach ...
8 there **is** / **isn't** _____ sand.
9 it's better if there **is** / **isn't** _____ sun.
10 there **are** / **aren't** usually _____ things to do.

2a Work in pairs. Choose three of the trips below and decide what to take. Think about clothes, equipment, food and entertainment.

- a camping trip in autumn
- a city break in Paris
- a beach holiday at a smart hotel
- a holiday on a tropical island
- a business trip to New York
- a walking holiday in the mountains
- a 24-hour coach journey

> I think we need to take a few books.

> Yes, and we mustn't forget a couple of pillows.

b Choose one trip that you've discussed. Tell the class what you are going to take, but do not say which trip it is. Can they guess?

> Unit 9, Study & Practice 2, page 157

Vocabulary
Describing everyday objects

1 Work in pairs and close your books. How many objects from exercise 1b can you remember?

2a Match the descriptions below with the objects in exercise 1b.

They're <u>made of rubber</u> and they're used for keeping your feet dry. *wellies*
1 It's round and it's used for finding your way.
2 It's rectangular and it's made of fabric.
3 They're used for cleaning.
4 It's got batteries inside and it's made of metal.
5 It's used for protecting your skin.
6 It's used for keeping insects away.

b Underline useful words and phrases for describing objects in exercise 2a.

3 Add phrases from exercise 2a to the categories below. Can you think of any more phrases to add?

- It's ...
- It's made of ...
- It's got ...
- It's used for ...

4 Work in groups. Take turns to choose everyday objects, but do not say what they are. The other students ask *Yes/No* questions to find out what the object is.

> Is it used for carrying things?

> Is it made of plastic?

Joel is a British university student. He goes to more than ten festivals every year.

Task

Talk about things you couldn't live without

Preparation Reading

1 A newspaper recently asked some successful people what things they couldn't live without. Read the texts and answer the questions.

  1 What reason does each speaker give for his/her choice?
  2 Which choice do you find the strangest / the most sensible?

2a Read the texts again and underline the phrases that express how strongly the writer feels.

  b Look at the Useful language box. Tick the phrases you have underlined in the text.

Task Speaking

1a Make a list of five things that <u>you</u> couldn't live without. They can be objects, ideas, activities, foods or pets, but not people.

  b You are going to tell other students about the things on your list. Decide what to say about each item. Think about the points below and ask your teacher for any words/phrases you need.

  • why it's so important in your life
  • which people or activities you associate it with
  • the shape, what it's made of, etc.
  • what it feels/sounds/tastes like
  • what you use it for
  • any stories or memories connected to it

  > Useful language a, b and c

2 Work in groups and take turns to talk about the things on your lists. Answer any questions that the other students have about them.

3a Which were the most common things chosen in your group? Compare your answers with the class.

  b Which was the most unusual thing chosen in your group? Tell the class about it.

I couldn't live without ...

Jewellery
Rachel Billington
Novelist

<u>I just couldn't do without</u> my jewellery. The first thing I do when I wake up is put on a necklace. <u>It makes me feel good</u> on a grey morning. I just can't understand why some women save their jewellery for going out.

Lemsip
Shyama Perera
Broadcaster and novelist

They say it can help with colds and flu, but I think it can help with all sorts of problems. I use it for dealing with everything from insomnia to writer's block. The poet Andrew Motion drinks it too – so I'm in good company.

Horror films
Alex Zane
TV presenter and DJ

I love movies. When I was ten years old, while everyone else was out playing football, I was indoors watching films. These days, if I want to feel scared, I turn off all the lights and watch *The Ring*.

Bicycle
Oliver Peyton
Restaurateur

It's the fastest way around London – I completely rely on it. I don't have a lock so I never leave it anywhere it can be stolen. London is much more interesting when you see it as a cyclist.

Spikes
Darren Campbell
100m Olympic gold medallist

I can't do without my Reebok spikes. I've got big size 12 feet and these spikes are incredibly comfortable. I started wearing them last year and then became Olympic champion.

Pavoni coffee machine
Justin Cartwright
Novelist

I am addicted to coffee. My machine is eight years old. It's not an easy machine to use, but it still makes great coffee. I can't do without it. I even take it on holiday.

My cats
Patrick Moore
Astronomer

There are two things that I couldn't bear to live without: one is black and white and the other is dark brown and they both say 'meow'. I love all animals but I've always been a cat person and I've had these two for a long time. They're really special to me.

USEFUL LANGUAGE

a Introducing things
I couldn't (bear to) live without …
I can't do without …
I am addicted to …

b Describing things
It's made of …
They're incredibly comfortable/beautiful/useful.
I use it for …
It used to belong to …
I got it when I was …

c Saying why it's important
Without it, I couldn't …
It makes me feel (good) …
It's special to me (because …)
I (completely) rely on it.
It reminds me of (my grandmother).
I've had them for (a long time).

SHARE YOUR TASK

Choose something from your list and practise talking about it until you feel confident.

Film/Record yourself talking about it.

Share your film/recording with other students.

LANGUAGE LIVE

3a Match the sentences in A with the responses in B.

A
1 Can I help at all?
2 Do you have these in a size 10?
3 How did you get on with those? Did they fit?
4 Can I bring them back if they aren't right?
5 How would you like to pay?
6 I'm trying to place an order on your website, but I'm having some problems.
7 Have you got a product code?
8 Do I have to pay for delivery?
9 Could you confirm the first line of your address?

B
a By debit card, please.
b I'll have a look for you.
c Yes. It's 76b Alton Road.
d Yes, that's fine. Just keep your receipt.
e That's fine. I can take your order over the phone.
f No, I'm just looking, thanks.
g Yes, it's 'I L five nine three nine'.
h No, you don't. Orders over £25 are delivered free.
i Yes, they were OK.

b ▶ Watch and listen to the key phases to check. Practise saying the questions and answers in pairs.

4a Work in pairs. Prepare a conversation about buying one of the things in the box. Use the phrases in exercise 3.

a mobile phone	a pair of shoes
a coffee machine	a bottle of perfume
a puppy	a gold necklace

b Act out your conversation for the class.

Speaking
Buying things

1a Work in pairs. Make a list of typical questions that sales assistants ask in shops.

b ▶ Watch the video of two conversations. Were any of your questions from exercise 1 used?

2 Watch again and complete the table.

	Conversation 1	Conversation 2
Product		
Product code/Brand name		
Cost		
Delivery cost		
Address		
Pay by ...		
Other useful information		

Writing
A short thank-you message

1 Work in pairs and discuss.

- If you receive a present or stay at someone's house, how do you usually say thank you?
- Are you ever offended if other people forget to say thank you?

2a Read the messages. What is the person saying thank you for in each case?

b Complete the messages with the phrases in the box.

I wanted to thank you again for	Cheers
Thank you so much	Thanks for

c Read the messages again and answer the questions.

1 How old do you think each writer is?
2 What is their relationship with the person they are thanking?

3a Which text is the least formal? Which is the most formal? What words and phrases tell you this?

b Complete the table with informal and formal phrases from the texts.

Informal	Neutral	Formal
Cheers	Thanks for … Thank you so much	*I wanted to thank you again for …*
	I had a great time!	
	Hope to hear from you soon	
	Best wishes,	

4 Choose two of the situations below. Write a message to thank the person. One message should be formal and the other informal. Choose an appropriate form for the message (text, card, email, etc.).

- a present you received recently
- a social event you attended
- a favour that someone did for you

A

A message from Ulrika Mitchell

_____ girls. Great evening out. We danced, we sang, we missed the last bus home! See you all in October for the wedding. xx
July 18 at 11.15 a.m.   Like Comment

Charlotte Spence
You're welcome, Ulrika. I had a fab evening and can't wait for October! Speak soon xx
July 18 at 2.05 p.m.

Anouk Van Sighem
I have some great photos of the dancing! I'll post them online later. x
July 18 at 6.33 p.m.

B

Messages

Hi Auntie Jen. _____ the jeans. They're so cool and they fit perfectly!!! I know you're busy but let's meet. Love Carolina x

C

To: martinwallace@manning-barton.co.uk
Subject: Yesterday's interview

Draft: message

Dear Mr Wallace,

_____ taking the time to meet with me regarding the position of Accounts Manager at your company. I very much enjoyed the experience and I enjoyed talking to you and the other members of the interview panel.

After our conversation, I am confident that my skills and experience are ideal for your needs. I hope that you feel the same and if you have any further questions, please do not hesitate to get in touch with me.

Thank you once again for your time. I look forward to hearing from you soon.

Yours sincerely,
Felipe Marcos Covas

D

Dear Julie and Max,

_____ for having us to stay at the weekend. We had a great time. Your new flat is lovely and it was really nice to have a walk by the river on Sunday morning. You must come and stay with us in the summer. Let's arrange a date.
Hope to hear from you soon.
Best wishes,
Rosa and Martin

AFTER UNIT 9 YOU CAN …

Explain how a machine works.

Talk about objects that are important to you.

Go shopping in different contexts.

Write different types of thank-you notes.

10

SOCIETY AND CHANGE

IN THIS UNIT

- **Grammar: Making predictions; Hypothetical possibilities with *if***
- **Vocabulary: Numbers and statistics; Society and change; Society and social issues**
- **Task: Balance the budget**
- **World culture: In orbit**

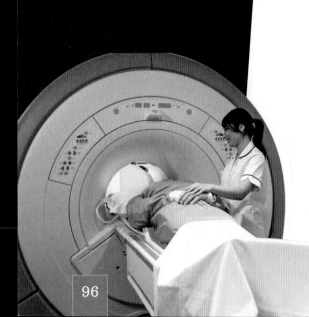

The **future** will surprise us

The future is coming and some people believe it will be more surprising and more incredible than we can imagine. Read the ideas of three scientists in their own words and decide for yourself.

Dr Aubrey de Grey
Gerontologist, Chief Science Officer, SENS Foundation

❝ We will be able to live to 1,000 years old

Doctor Aubrey de Grey is a gerontologist at the SENS Foundation in California. He believes that people will soon be able to live to 1,000. In fact, he thinks that most people who are alive today, and that includes you, will be able to reach that age.

'The human body is a machine that can be fixed. As medicine becomes better and better, we will almost certainly be able to beat ageing, just as we can beat many diseases today. I think we are already close to that point. As we get older, our cells become damaged through natural processes. Along with scientists around the world, I am working on a detailed plan to repair all types of damage to human cells. The project might be ready for humans in just 20 years. And then we will no longer die of old age. We will probably live to be 1,000 or more in excellent health. In fact, I think the first person to live to 1,000 might be 60 already. And I think we're unlikely to get bored if we live that long. People with a good education and time to use it never get bored.'

Reading

1 Work in pairs and discuss the questions. Think about films and TV programmes you have seen and books and articles you have read.

- Have you found any predictions about the future in these areas?
  - robots and computers
  - space travel
  - life expectancy
- What do you think will happen?

2 Read the article and find the answers to the questions below.

1 What does each scientist predict?
2 When does each scientist think it will happen?

Dr Michio Kaku
Physicist and professor

' 40,000 people will work in space

Dr Michio Kaku is a professor at the City College of New York and a graduate of Harvard University. His book, *The Physics of the Impossible*, is about how science fiction technology may be possible in the future.

'By 2030, space tourism will almost certainly be common and around 40,000 people will work in space. A company called the Space Island Group is planning to build an international space station with hotels, research facilities, restaurants and sports arenas (for new zero-gravity sports). Other companies are working on similar projects. And what language will people speak in space? Well, it probably won't matter because there is likely to be a tiny computer that fits in your ear and translates what you hear into your own language.'

Ray Kurzweil
Scientist, inventor, author and entrepreneur

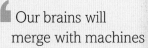

' Our brains will merge with machines

Many of Ray Kurzweil's predictions about the future have come true. For example, in the early 1990s he predicted the incredible growth of the internet. Now Kurzweil believes that robots and humans will one day merge.

'The future will be far more surprising than most people realise. By the end of the 2030s, robots will be more intelligent than humans. Before that time, humans and machines will start to merge. We have 100 trillion very slow connections in our brain. Tiny robots (nanobots) will be implanted in our brains to improve our memory and our thinking skills. These nanobots will allow our brains to talk directly to computers, and they will also allow our brains to communicate wirelessly with other brains. We will become telepathic. Billions of nanobots will also travel through our bodies. They will keep us healthy. As a result, we will be able to live forever.'

3 Check the meaning of the words in bold, then read the article again. Are the ideas below the same or different from what the experts say? Write S or D.

1 We will soon be able to **cure** many **diseases**.
2 We will soon be able to mend **damaged human cells**.
3 Some people who are middle-aged now will live to 1,000.
4 People will get bored if they live to be 1,000.
5 In 20 years, people will go into space for holidays.
6 We will invent new sports to play in space, because there is no **gravity**.
7 Everyone at **space stations** will speak the same language.
8 In about 25 years' time, robots will be just as intelligent as human beings.
9 Humans will have robots **implanted** in their **brains**.
10 **Telepathic communication** between humans will be possible.

4 Work in groups. Read the article again and discuss.

- Which ideas in the text do/don't you think will come true?
- Which would/wouldn't you like to come true?
- What are your top three predictions for the future? When do you think they will happen?

Vocabulary
Numbers and statistics

1 🎧 **10.1 How do you say the following figures? Listen and practise saying them.**

1	71%	6	300,000 km/sec
2	2030	7	199,859
3	892,000 m²	8	17%
4	8.2 billion	9	127,000,000
5	55,680,000 km	10	-89°C

2a Work in pairs. Use the numbers in exercise 1 to guess the answers to the questions below.

1 What percentage of the world's surface is covered in water?
2 What is the lowest temperature ever recorded?
3 In which year will the football World Cup be 100 years old?
4 What is the closest distance between Earth and the planet Mars?
5 What will the world population be in 2029?
6 What is the speed of light?
7 What is the population of Japan?
8 What is the area of the world's largest shopping mall?
9 What percentage of British people are over 65?
10 What was the largest crowd ever for a sporting event?

b 🎧 **10.2 Listen and check.**

3 Write down eight statistics. Show them to your partner. Can he/she say the numbers correctly?

4a Work in pairs. Student A: Look at the information about China on page 128. Student B: Look at the information about the United Arab Emirates on page 130.

b Ask and answer questions to complete the information about the other country. Do not show each other the numbers – say them!

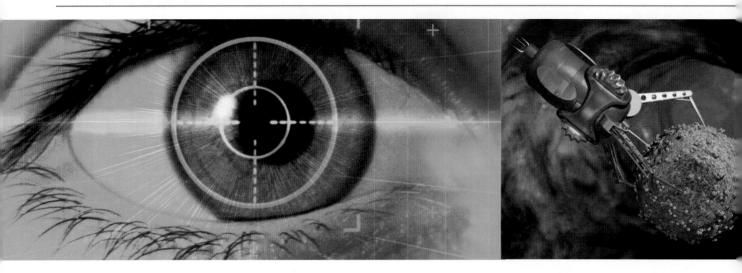

Language focus 1
Making predictions

1 Read five more of Ray Kurzweil's predictions for things that will happen by 2029. Which do you think will happen?

a There will be intelligent roads and driverless cars. Human beings will not be allowed to drive without computer assistance.

b Tiny cameras implanted in our eyes will record everything we see.

c Most communication will be between humans and machines, not between humans.

d Poverty and disease will be almost non-existent.

e Robots will say they are alive and demand the same rights as humans.

2 🎧 **10.3** Listen to five people giving their reaction to the predictions. Complete the table below.

Prediction being discussed	Do they think it will happen? (yes/no/maybe)	Reasons
1 c	no	
2		
3		
4		
5		

3 Which phrases did the speakers use to talk about the predictions? Choose the correct answers, then listen again and check.

1 Machines **may well / might not** sound like humans in the future.

2 We're **likely to / unlikely to** have a cup of coffee and chat with them.

3 By 2029, cameras **will almost certainly be / definitely won't be** small enough to fit inside a human eye.

4 Poverty **will probably disappear / probably won't disappear** by 2099.

5 **It's very likely / It's very unlikely** that we'll have driverless cars one day.

GRAMMAR

When you make predictions there are different ways of showing how sure you are.

1 Adverbs with **will/won't** (notice the word order)
It'**ll probably** happen before then.
Computers **definitely won't** become smarter than humans.

2 Modals
Machines **may well** look like humans soon.
Change **might not** come as fast as we think.

3 is (un)likely to
It **is(n't) very likely** that we'll have driverless cars.
We'**re (un)likely to** have a cup of coffee with a robot.

1 Put the words/phrases in the best place on the line to show how sure we are that the prediction will happen.

will probably	probably won't
will almost certainly	almost certainly won't
is/are likely to	is/are unlikely to
could / may well	may/might not

100%   will definitely

1 _____
2 _____
3 _____
4 _____
5 _____
6 _____
7 _____
8 _____

0%   definitely won't

PRACTICE

1a Look at the predictions below and give your opinion on each one. Use phrases from the Grammar box and add *by* + a year if you think it will happen.

Tablet computers will replace books.
I think tablet computers will almost certainly replace books by 2030.

1 We will buy everything online.
2 People will live to the age of 150.
3 Computers will become more intelligent than humans.
4 We'll spend more time online than in the real world.
5 All housework will be done by robots.
6 There will be a cure for most diseases.
7 People will say that their best friend is a robot.

b Work in groups and compare your opinions.

2 Write five predictions of your own for the things below.

- famous people
- your friends or family
- sporting events
- yourself
- technology
- television

> **Unit 10, Study & Practice 1, page 159**

Vocabulary and listening
Society and change

1a Check the meaning of any words or phrases that you don't understand.

In the last 50 years:

1 Life expectancy
    a has increased.
    b has decreased.

2 Average income
    a has risen.
    b has fallen.

3 The amount of free time we have
    a has gone up.
    b has gone down.

4 Health care and education
    a have got better.
    b have got worse.

5 Living standards
    a have improved.
    b have deteriorated.

6 Our levels of happiness
    a have increased.
    b have stayed the same.

b You are going to hear a radio programme about how these things are changing. Work in pairs and predict whether the speakers will say a or b.

2a 🎧 10.4 Listen to the first part of the programme. Were your predictions correct?

b Listen again. What is the 'big question' that experts have been asking? What do you think the answer is?

3 🎧 10.5 Listen to the second part of the programme. Were your answers the same?

4 Complete the sentences using an appropriate phrase from exercise 1a. Change the tense as necessary.

1 The number of very happy people is ...
2 Our trust in other people is ...
3 Inequality is ...

5 Work as a class. Discuss the current trends for these issues in your country. Give reasons for your opinions.

- life expectancy
- national diet
- health care
- education
- living standards
- unemployment

> I think life expectancy is going down because we are all eating so much junk food!

PRONUNCIATION

1 Complete the table.

Noun	Verb	Adjective
1 _____	to decrease	_____
2 _____		economic
3 education	_____	
4 _____		equal
5 _____	to improve	
6 _____	to increase	

2 🎧 10.6 Listen and check. Then mark the stressed syllables. Is the stress the same in each form of the word?

3 Practise saying the words, paying attention to the stress.

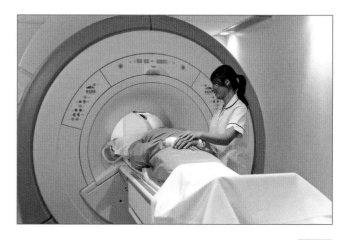

What would you do if you were invisible for a day?

According to news this week, scientists have made an important breakthrough in inventing a material that would make us invisible. An invisibility cloak like Harry Potter's won't be ready any time soon, but we asked people on the street …

1 I'd get on a first-class flight to Cuba if I was invisible. I've always wanted to go there … but I've got no idea how I'd get back.

2 If I was invisible, I'd follow my boyfriend around all day and I'd check that he doesn't flirt with anyone. I'd also listen to what my friends say about me when I'm not there.

Language focus 2
Hypothetical possibilities with *if*

1 Work in pairs and discuss. What would you do if you were invisible for a day?

2 Read what six people said they would do if they were invisible. Which answer is most similar to yours? Which do you think is the most interesting?

3 Read the comments again. Are the speakers describing real or imaginary situations?

GRAMMAR

1a Which sentence below describes:
- a real situation?
- an imaginary situation?
1 I'd get a first class ticket to Cuba.
2 I'll definitely go to Cuba one day.

b Which verb forms are used in each? Underline other examples of *would* + verb in the quotes in exercise 2.

2 We often talk about hypothetical situations using *if*. Find two examples in the quotes. Which tense is used after *if*? Does this describe things that happened in the past?

3 Cross out the sentence that is incorrect.
1 If I were invisible, I would rob a bank.
2 I might rob a bank if I were invisible.
3 If I would be invisible, I would rob a bank.

PRACTICE

1a Complete the conversations with the correct form o the verb in brackets.

1 A: If you _____ (have) the opportunity, _____ (you / listen) to what other people said about you behind your back?
B: I don't think so. I _____ (be) too worried about what I might hear.

2 A: _____ (you / ever steal) money, if no one _____ (can) find out?
B: No, I _____ (never / steal) money. Even if no one _____ (know), I _____ (feel) guilty.

3 A: If someone _____ (do) something really unkind to you, _____ (you / take) revenge?
B: I don't think so. I _____ (try) to forget abou it and focus on other things.
A: Mmm. If someone _____ (be) really horrible to one of my family, I _____ (do) something horrible back to them.

4 A: If you _____ (be) suspicious of your partner _____ (you / ever / follow) him?
B: No, I think that _____ (be) a really stupid thing to do. If I _____ (think) he was doing something wrong, I _____ (ask) him about it.

5 A: _____ (you / ever / travel) first class without a ticket?
B: I'm a real coward, so no, I _____ (not dare). If someone _____ (catch) me, I _____ (feel) so embarrassed.

b 10.7 Listen and check. Which sentences do you agree with? Which sentences don't you agree with? What would you do instead in those situations?

3 I would definitely play a few tricks on my friends if they couldn't see me – it would be really fun! Then who knows? Maybe I'd rob a bank and run away with the money … just joking!!!

4 I'd follow round someone mega-famous, like the President or a Hollywood star, and I'd find out what their life is really like.

5 Mmm, I don't know. I wouldn't cross the road, that's for sure. If I were invisible, someone might run me over!

6 If I were invisible for a day, I'd take my revenge on a girl from school who used to bully me. I would stand next to her and every five minutes I'd do something weird to scare her.

2a Read the moral dilemmas below and decide what you would do.

NEVER say never

Would you ever …

1 travel on a train without a ticket?

2 lie to someone close to you?

3 pretend to be ill to get the day off work or college?

4 lend a large sum of money to a friend?

5 drive above the speed limit?

6 hit someone?

7 give a lift in your car to a complete stranger?

8 keep some money that you found in the street?

9 walk out of a restaurant without paying?

Under what circumstances?

b Work in groups and compare your answers.

3a Decide if the prompts refer to real possibilities in the future (RP) or imaginary situations (IS). Then make questions using the pronoun *you*.

If / go on holiday / next year / where / go? *RP*
If you go on holiday next year, where will you go?

1 If / have the chance to travel in space / you do it?
2 If / live to be 1,000 / how / your life be different?
3 If / live to be old / what / do in your retirement?
4 If / buy a new computer / what type / buy?
5 If / invent your own personal robot / what / it be able to do?
6 If / have more money next year / how / spend it?
7 If / be a billionaire / what / do with your life?
8 If / move house in the next few years / where / you move to?
9 If / can live anywhere in the world / where / live?

b Choose five questions from exercise 3a to ask another student. Work in pairs and take turns to ask and answer the questions.

PRONUNCIATION

1 🎧 10.8 Listen to eight sentences. Write 1 if you hear *'ll* (= *will*) and 2 if you hear *'d* (= *would*).

2 Look at audio script 10.8 on page 174. Practise saying the sentences, paying attention to the form.

4 Choose two imaginary situations in exercise 3a and write three or four sentences about each one. Compare your ideas with other students.

Unit 10, Study & Practice 2, page 160

Vocabulary
Society and social issues

1 Work in groups and discuss.

- Would you like to be the president or prime minister of your country. Why / Why not?
- Think of <u>one</u> thing that you would change if you were prime minister.

2a Write the words in the box in the correct category below.

the wealthy	crime
corruption	education
health care	the poor
racism	the government
unemployment	ordinary people
homelessness	pollution
defence	transport
tax payers	poverty
the opposition parties	balancing the budget

1 Groups in society: *the wealthy*
2 Social problems: *crime*
3 Government responsibilities: *education*

b Can you add more words to each category?

3a Check the meaning of the words and phrases in bold. Then complete the sentences for your country. Use words from the box in exercise 2a.

1 The government should **increase taxes** for _____ .

2 The government should **reduce taxes** for _____ .

3 The government's **priority** should be _____ .

4 The government shouldn't **waste money on** _____ .

5 The government should **increase spending on** _____ .

6 The government should **reduce spending on** _____ .

b Work in pairs and compare your answers.

4 Which of the things in exercise 2a do you think are a problem in your country at the moment? Why?

> I think homelessness is a problem because …

Task
Balance the budget

Republic of Peakoilia

Population:	329,000
Capital city:	Moza (population 100,000)
Language:	English
Currency:	dollars ($1 Peak Oilian = $1 US)
Main industries:	oil, tourism
Army:	2,500 soldiers

The Republic of Peakoilia is a small island. The south of the island is developed, but in the north there is a lot of poverty and unemployment. Many businesses on the island are closing because people do not have much money to spend. Peakoilia's main industry is oil, but the current oil wells are starting to run out. Peakoilia's schools and hospitals are becoming old and the opposition parties are complaining about the condition that they are in. Traditionally, Peakoilia has made a lot of money from tourism, but at the moment the number of tourists is falling. The government of Expandia, Peakoilia's nearest neighbour, recently said that Peakoilia was 'one of our islands'. These are difficult times for Peakoilia and the government has to make some important decisions.

Preparation Listening

1 Read about the Republic of Peakoilia and answer the questions.

1 What are its six main problems?
2 Which problems do you think are the most serious?

2a 🎧 10.9 Listen to four people from Peakoilia and answer the questions about each person.

1 What do they think are the country's biggest problems?
2 What solutions do they suggest? Why?

b Listen again and tick the phrases you hear in the Useful language box.

Peakoilia's choices

Increase spending: Each of the following options would cost $250 million.

Health care	• build a new hospital
Education	• repair schools and buy new equipment • build a new university in the north
Tourism	• build a new airport in the north • promote Peakoilia as a holiday destination
Defence	• increase the army to 5,000
Transport	• build a motorway between north and south
Industry	• explore new oilfields to the north of the island
Tax	• reduce tax on ordinary people by 2% • reduce tax on the wealthy by 15%

Reduce spending: Each of the following options would save/make $250 million.

Health care	• close one of the seven hospitals
Education	• reduce the number of teachers
Tourism	• cancel plans to build a golf resort in the north
Defence	• reduce the army to 1,000
Transport	• cancel plans for more roads in the north
Industry	• close down two older oil wells which employ 500 people each
Tax	• increase income tax on ordinary people by 2% • increase tax on the wealthy by 20% (they currently pay 35% of their income in tax)

USEFUL LANGUAGE

a Giving and discussing opinions
To me, the biggest problem is …
I think the government should … to pay for …
I agree with … because …
Yes, but what about (unemployment)?
First we have to …

b Proposing ideas
I'd suggest that we spend more/less on …
The best option is to (build a new …)

c Explaining advantages/disadvantages
… will definitely create more jobs.
If we spent more/less on … we'd (create more jobs).
This would help to …
The problem is (that …)
… would be very (un)popular.

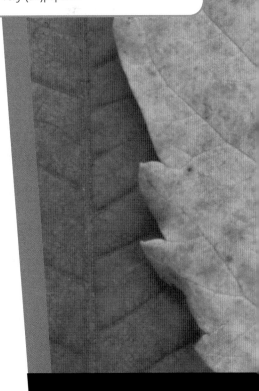

Task Speaking

1a Work on your own. Imagine you are a member of the Peakoilian government. You want to improve the situation, but you must also balance the overall budget. Choose four changes in spending that you would like to make from the list above.

b What will be the result of each choice you make? Make notes about how to justify the results. Ask your teacher for any words/phrases you need.

> Useful language a, b and c

2 Work in groups. Take turns to put forward your proposals, giving reasons. Try to agree on the best four changes to make while balancing the budget.

3 Present your group's proposals to the class, explaining your decisions. Which choices were the most/least popular? What differences were there between the budgets?

SHARE YOUR TASK

Practise presenting your proposals until you feel confident.

Film/Record yourself giving your talk.

Share your film/recording with other students.

WORLD CULTURE

IN ORBIT

Find out first

1a What do you know about satellites? Try to complete the text below by choosing the correct answers.

Satellites

The first man-made satellite to orbit Earth, *Sputnik 1*, was launched in 1957 / 1967 / 1977 by the Soviet Union. There are now around 35 / 350 / 3,500 working satellites orbiting the Earth. Those in 'low Earth orbit' can be as close as 20 / 200 / 2,000 kilometres away, while those in 'high Earth orbit' are more than 400 / 4,000 / 40,000 kilometres from Earth. Nearer satellites travel much faster than further ones. For example, the Space Shuttle, when it was in orbit, travelled at around 3,000 / 30,000 / 300,000 kilometres per hour.

b Go online to check your answers or ask your teacher

Search: how many functioning satellites in orbit / low Earth orbit / high Earth orbit / space shuttle speed

View

2 ▶ Watch the video and answer the questions.

1 What is Maggie Aderin-Pocock's job?
2 What food and drink is mentioned in the video?
3 How many satellites has Maggie used before 9 a.m.?

3a Match the verb(s) in A with the phrases in B to create things that satellites do or help to do.

A
1 keep
2 send and receive
3 orbit
4 deliver
5 take
6 harvest
7 beam
8 forecast

B
a a signal to the television
b the weather
c an eye on us from space
d data
e the Earth
f milk
g the wheat
h photographs for military use

b Watch the video again. Which phrases from exercise 3a does the presenter mention?

4 Which facts from the video do you find most interesting or surprising? Why?

World view

5a ▶ Watch four people talking about technology that has changed their lives. Which technology is each person talking about? Complete column 1 of the table.

- high-speed broadband
- smartphones
- tablet computers
- Wikipedia
- online social networks
- digital music
- e-books (Kindle)

	Which technology?	How does it change their life?
Stephanie		
Sion		
Steve		
James		

b Watch again and complete column 2.

6a Work in pairs. Choose what you think is the most important new technology in exercise 5. List the ways in which it has changed your life.

b Change partners and talk about how it has changed your life.

FIND OUT MORE

7a Look at the items below. What do you know about each one? Are you interested in them? Why / why not?

- the digital divide
- e-commerce
- e-waste
- smartphone ownership
- social media

b Go online to find out about issues and ideas related to the items.

Search: digital divide / e-waste / e-commerce / smartphone ownership / social media

Write up your research

8 Choose one of the issues or ideas you researched in exercise 7 and write a short paragraph about it. Talk about the positive and negative facts, figures and trends. Use the prompts below to help you.

- Surprisingly, ...
- Amazingly, ...
- It's unfortunately true that ...
- Most people would be shocked to learn that ...
- It's not all bad/good news, however.

AFTER UNIT 10 YOU CAN ...

Describe social changes.

Talk about social and moral problems.

Discuss and decide a budget.

Research technology online.

11

RULES

IN THIS UNIT

- Grammar: Obligation and permission in the present; Obligation and permission in the past

- Vocabulary: Linking words; Crime and punishment

- Task: Discuss new laws

- Language live: Expressing and responding to opinions; An opinion essay

Listening
Annoying rules

1 Work in groups. Think of at least one rule that you would find in these places.

motorways	classrooms	libraries	swimming pools
airports	websites	nightclubs	parks and open spaces

2 🎧 11.1 Listen to five people complaining about a rule they find annoying. Answer the questions.

  1 Which place in exercise 1 is each person talking about?
  2 Find the photos that the rules refer to.

3 Listen again. Why exactly do they find these rules annoying? Which rules (if any) do they agree with?

4 Work in groups and discuss.

- Which speakers do you agree with?
- Which other rules and laws do you find annoying?
- Do you ever break rules? If so, which rules and in which circumstances?

Caution
Slippery surface

NO HATS OR HOODIES
PLEASE REMOVE YOUR HOOD, CAP OR HELMET BEFORE ENTERING THESE PREMISES

Language focus 1
Obligation and permission in the present

1 Read the sentences about rules shown in the photos. Cross out the incorrect sentence in each group.

You **have to** read the terms and conditions.
You **should** read the terms and conditions.
~~You **can't** read the terms and conditions.~~

1 You **can** play ball games here.
   You**'re not allowed to** play ball games here.
   You **mustn't** play ball games here.
2 You**'re not allowed to** use your phone in this lesson.
   You **can't** use your phone in this lesson.
   You **ought to** use your phone in this lesson.
3 You**'re allowed to** drive at 120 kph on most motorways.
   You **have to** drive at 120 kph on most motorways.
   You **don't have to** drive at 120 kph on motorways.
4 You **have to** show ID to prove your age.
   You **must** show ID to prove your age.
   You **shouldn't** show ID to prove your age.

GRAMMAR

Put the verbs in bold from exercise 1 in the correct category.
1 It is necessary: *have (got) to*
2 It is not necessary (it's optional):
3 It is OK/permitted:
4 It is not OK / not permitted:
5 It is a good idea / the correct thing to do:
6 It is not a good idea / not the correct thing to do:

PRACTICE

1 Find the signs that these sentences refer to. Complete the sentences with the correct form of the verb in brackets.

1 The public _____ (allow) to come in here.
2 Cyclists _____ (allow) to use this path.
3 You _____ (have) to cycle on this path; you _____ (allow) to walk, if you prefer.
4 You _____ (have) to show your passport or indentity card. You _____ (should) have them ready.
5 You _____ (ought) to be careful walking here.
6 You _____ (must) wear a hat or hoodie. You _____ (should) remove them before entering.

PRONUNCIATION

1 🎧 11.2 Listen to the pronunciation of each of the verbs in exercise 1.

aren't allowed to ... the public aren't allowed to ...
the public aren't allowed to come in here

2 Practise saying the verbs separately, then practise the complete sentences.

2 Complete the sentences with a suitable verb to make them true for your city/country.

In city centres ...
1 You _____ park in the city centre.
2 Lorries _____ drive through the centre.
3 You _____ pay to drive your car into the city.
4 Cars _____ stop at pedestrian crossings.

On roads ...
5 You _____ wear a seat belt.
6 You _____ pay to use the motorways.
7 You _____ drive at 180 kph.
8 You _____ take your driving test if you're 17 years old.

On trains ...
9 You _____ buy your ticket in advance.
10 You _____ buy your ticket on the train.
11 You _____ pay a fine if you're caught without a ticket.
12 You _____ smoke.

3a Think of a place that has a lot of rules. Use your own ideas or the ones in exercise 1 on page 106. Write a list of rules for the place, but don't say where it is.

b Work in groups. Read out your rules. Can the other students guess the place?

You have to get there two hours in advance.

Unit 11, Study & Practice 1, page 162

Reading

1 **Work in groups and discuss.**

- Are you a member of any clubs or societies?
- Think of three different clubs and societies. What rules do they have?
- Do you know of any exclusive clubs? Who do/ don't they accept as a member?

2 **You are going to read about three unusual societies. Read the first few lines of each text and then answer the questions.**

1 What kind of people are members?
2 What is the main activity of each society?

3 **Which society do you think these words and phrases relate to?**

a murder case	to cause damage	to surrender
to vandalise	to solve a crime	a new recruit
an aristocrat	a battle	to smash

4 **Work in pairs and have a reading race. As quickly as you can, find out from the text which club has the rules below.**

They have to be specially qualified professionals.
the Vidocq Society

1 They have to have a lot of money.
2 They aren't allowed to leave before their contract has finished.
3 They have to change their names.
4 They have to pay for everything they break.
5 They can't contact friends or family for several months.
6 They have to have a strong stomach.
7 They have to wear an expensive uniform.
8 They aren't allowed to give up.
9 They are allowed to change their nationality.

5a **Read the article again and underline at least two unusual things about each society. Compare your answers with the class.**

b **Work as a class and discuss.**

- Which, if any, of these societies would you like to join? Why?
- Are any of them controversial? Why?
- Do you know of any societies with strange rules? What are they?

> **FIND OUT MORE** Go online to find out more about the Vidocq Society, French Foreign Legion and Bullingdon Club.

Exclusive clubs

These are some of the world's most exclusive clubs. But even if you could join them, you might not want to!

The Vidocq Society

The Vidocq Society was set up in 1990 and its motto is 'Cuisine and crime-solving'. To become a member of the society you have to be a crime specialist. Members meet every month in a restaurant in Philadelphia to discuss a 'cold case': a murder that has never been solved. But first they have a large lunch. While they are eating, they hear details of the case and use their skills to try and solve it. The photographs that they see and the stories that they hear during the presentation of the murder case would stop most people from eating. However, the members of the society don't mind. They are professionals.

The society is named after Eugène François Vidocq, the 18th-century criminal who became the world's first private detective. Only 82 people are allowed to be members of the club (Vidocq was 82 when he died) and new members have to be invited by a committee. Two new cases come in every week and members use their experience to think of new ways to solve each case. Their first success was in 1991. A man called Huey Cox had been murdered. Cox's family believed that the wrong person had been arrested and when the society looked at the case, they agreed. They helped the family and as a result the suspect was quickly set free. The society estimates that so far it has helped to solve around 300 murders.

The French Foreign Legion

There are about 7,500 members of the French Foreign Legion, which was set up in 1831. The Legionnaires are part of the French army, although most of them are not French. Legionnaires come from lots of different countries around the world. They join because they want a new life or a new challenge, and once they have joined, they must stay for five years. They are not allowed to leave before that for any reason, and for the first two months they are not allowed to write to or phone anyone.

New recruits don't have to speak French, but they have to learn while they are training. They are not even allowed to keep their real name: they take a new French name when they join.

Training is extremely hard. For example, new recruits have to run 8 km with a 13 kg backpack in less than an hour. What is more, they are not allowed to surrender or lose their gun in battle – they have to fight to the death. For their hard work they get £1,000 a month and after three years they can become French citizens. Since 1990, the French Foreign Legion has fought battles and wars in at least 14 different countries.

The Bullingdon Club

The Bullingdon Club is an exclusive 'dining club' for upper-class male students at Oxford University. The club is over 200 years old and is famous for the destruction and chaos that its members cause. Members meet twice a year, usually in a restaurant. They eat and drink all evening and then, for fun, they start to fight and cause damage. In 2004, all 17 members of the club were arrested for vandalising a 15th-century pub. On another occasion, the club hired a group of classical musicians and then smashed all their instruments, including a Stradivarius violin. However, after they have finished destroying things, it is a strict rule that members have to politely pay for all the damage in cash.

Obviously, members have to be extremely wealthy. The uniform alone costs about £3,500 and then there is all the damage to pay for. New members have to be invited to join and if they are accepted their college room will be vandalised by the other members. Previous members have included a mayor of London, a British finance minister and even British Prime Minister, David Cameron. When questioned about his membership of the club, Cameron said, 'We do things when we are young that we deeply regret.'

Vocabulary
Linking words

1 Look at the words in the box used to join sentences and link ideas. Reread the article and underline five examples of these. Which ideas are they linking?

also	although	besides
despite this	for that reason	however
as a result	therefore	what is more

2 Write the linkers in exercise 1 in the correct category below.

  1 similar meaning to *and*:
  2 similar meaning to *but*:
  3 similar meaning to *so*:

3 Complete the sentences in <u>two different</u> ways, using a suitable linker from exercise 2 each time. Add punctuation if necessary.

Everyone knows that smoking is bad for you.
  a *What's more*, it can be very expensive.
  b *Despite this*, many young people start every year.

1 Regular exercise can prevent heart disease.
  a _____ experts recommend exercising three times a week.
  b _____ it can help to control your weight.
2 Many people nowadays believe that it is wrong to kill animals for food.
  a _____ they think eating meat is unhealthy.
  b _____ more and more people are becoming vegetarians.
3 Doctors agree that too much alcohol is bad for your health.
  a _____ a small amount of alcohol may actually be good for you.
  b _____ it can make you depressed.
4 Doctors have found cures for many serious diseases in the last 100 years.
  a _____ the average person is living longer.
  b _____ there is still no cure for the common cold.

> **Unit 11, Study & Practice 2, page 163**

The harsh world of 18th-century justice

Criminal justice in the 18th century was a harsh business – there was no **community service** and few **criminals were** even **sent to prison**! If you **committed a crime** and **were arrested**, for many crimes you could expect **the death penalty**.

At the end of the 18th century, there were over 200 crimes that could **be punished** by **hanging**. As well as serious crimes like **murder** and **kidnapping**, these included **burglary**, **robbery**, **shoplifting** and **mugging**. Even if you **were caught** cutting down a tree or stealing a rabbit, it could result in death.

If the **judge** was more lenient, the **defendant** might **be sentenced** to transportation instead. This meant travelling by ship to Australia. Conditions on the ships were terrible and many **prisoners** died on the way. If they lived, they had to do at least seven years' hard labour before they could **be released** for good behaviour.

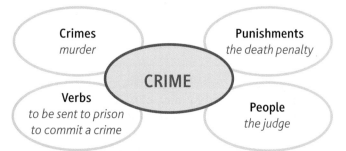

Vocabulary
Crime and punishment

1 Work in groups and discuss.

- What was the criminal justice system like in your country 200 years ago?
- Was it harsher or more lenient than it is today?

2 Read the text above about criminal justice in Britain 200 years ago. Answer the questions.

1 What crimes resulted in capital punishment?
2 What was considered a more lenient option?

3a The words in bold in the text are connected to crime and punishment. Write them in the correct category below. Can you add any more words?

- **Crimes** *murder*
- **Punishments** *the death penalty*
- **CRIME**
- **Verbs** *to be sent to prison* *to commit a crime*
- **People** *the judge*

b Look at the crimes in the diagram. For each one write the verb and the person.

a murder, to murder, a murderer

A famous criminal from the 18th century

Jack Sheppard was born into a very poor family in 1702. When he was six he started to work and at the age of 15 he became an apprentice carpenter. In the spring of 1723, he ¹_____ his first _____ : he stole two silver spoons from a shop. He wasn't caught and he soon moved from ²_____ to burglary: he usually stole from the houses where he was working as a carpenter.

Sheppard ³_____ first _____ in February 1724, but he escaped within three hours and continued ⁴_____ houses. He ⁵_____ three more times in 1724, but each time he escaped. Then on 31st October, Sheppard ⁶_____ a shop and stole a black silk suit. He was arrested the next day for the final time. Two weeks later, he ⁷_____. Two hundred thousand people – one-third of London's population – attended his funeral. Sheppard had become a celebrity ⁸_____.

JACK SHEPPARD.
In Special Irons.

4a Read the story of a famous 18th-century British criminal. Complete the text with the words in the box.

was ... arrested   was hanged   committed ... crime
got caught   burgling   shoplifting   robbed   criminal

b Work in pairs. Take turns to remember facts about Jack Sheppard using vocabulary from exercise 4a.

Sheppard stole two silver spoons from a shop.

5 Work in groups and discuss.

- Do you know of any 'celebrity criminals'?
- What crimes did they commit?
- Why do you think some criminals become famous?

Language focus 2
Obligation and permission in the past

1 Read the text below and answer the questions.

    1 Why were people in the 18th century sent to prison?

    2 Why did some people never leave?

    3 What is the connection between prison and the British novelist Charles Dickens?

2 Complete the text with the verbs below to express obligation. There may be more than one possibility.

had to / didn't have to   could/couldn't
were allowed to / weren't allowed to

A prison 200 years ago

In Britain in the 18th century, people were often sent to prison if they had debts. However, even though they were there because they were in debt, they ¹_____ pay for everything while they were in prison! If they had some money, they ²_____ use the prison restaurant and they ³_____ wear the heavy metal chains that other prisoners wore. Some better-off prisoners ⁴_____ live outside the prison, and they ⁵_____ get married and even work. This meant they could earn money to repay their debts and eventually leave prison.

Most prisoners, however, had no money. Even if they paid their original debt, they ⁶_____ leave until they had paid for staying in prison. Some prisoners spent years and years in prison and many starved to death. Men often brought their families into prison with them. Their children ⁷_____ work just to keep their family alive. The English novelist Charles Dickens ⁸_____ leave school at the age of 12 for this reason. His father was in prison for a debt to a baker and the young Dickens ⁹_____ get a job in a factory to help support his family. Debtors prisons were not abolished until 1868.

GRAMMAR

Write the past forms of the following verbs, where possible. Which three verbs do not have past forms? Which form is used instead?

    1 can   2 is/are allowed to   3 isn't/aren't allowed to
    4 can't   5 don't have to   6 have got to
    7 must   8 mustn't   9 have to

PRACTICE

1 Complete the descriptions with the past form of a verb from the Grammar box. There may be more than one possible answer.

Strange laws from the past!

Under Peter the Great of Russia, noblemen ¹_____ have beards! If they wanted to keep their beard, they ²_____ pay a special tax to the government.

    In the USA in the 19th century, female teachers ³_____ get married. If they got engaged, they ⁴_____ resign from their job immediately.

    In 19th-century Britain, if you travelled in a motor vehicle, someone ⁵_____ walk in front of you waving a red flag. However, you ⁶_____ take a driving test in order to drive a car … so perhaps this law was a good thing!

    During the French Revolution, you ⁷_____ use the polite form of you (*vous*) because this was the word that servants used to their masters. Instead everyone ⁸_____ use the familiar form (*tu*).

    In Switzerland, women ⁹_____ vote until 1971. In New Zealand, on the other hand, women ¹⁰_____ vote from 1893, making it the first country in the world to give women the vote.

2 Write down five laws or rules from your country's past. Think about the groups of people in the box below. Compare your answers with other students.

poor people   women/girls   children   criminals   everyone

Women weren't allowed to vote.

Unit 11, Study & Practice 3, page 163

Task

Discuss new laws

Preparation Reading and listening

1 Read the suggestions for laws that should exist and answer the questions as a class.

    1 Which suggestions do the photos relate to?
    2 Do any of these laws already exist in your country?
    3 Think of one argument for and one argument against each law.

2 🎧 11.3 Listen to people talking about four of the laws suggested on the website. Which ones are they? What reasons and examples do they give?

3 Listen again and tick the phrases you hear in the Useful language box.

Task Speaking

1 What laws would you suggest on the website? Think of your own ideas, then make a list with the rest of class.

> Useful language a

2a Choose two suggested laws that you would like to discuss, either from the website or from the list your class made.

  b Make notes for each law. Use the headings below and ask your teacher for any words/phrases you need.

    • Your opinion (for or against):
    • Reason(s):
    • Examples or cases that support your opinion:

> Useful language b

3 Work in groups. Tell the other students which laws you would like to discuss and give your opinion and reasons. Find out what they think.

4 Work as a class. Tell the class which laws your group discussed and what your opinions were. Find out what the rest of the class think.

> Useful language c

 WIFI

SHARE YOUR VIEW

Q: What laws do you think should exist?

A: I think everyone should have to do a short test on current affairs before they are allowed to vote.
political_harry, 2 hours ago

A: I would ban smoking in all public places, even outside.
e=mc3, 4 hours ago

A: I would make a law saying people who beat or hurt animals should receive the same treatment themselves.
Tiffin, 4 hours ago

A: The long-term unemployed should have to do voluntary work to get unemployment benefit from the government.
Martin, 5 hours ago

A: I think speed limits on motorways should be abolished.
2cool4school, 5 hours ago

A: I would make it the law that if you go and live in a foreign country, it should be compulsory to learn the language of that country.
Beverley, 6 hours ago

A: I think adverts should only be allowed to give information which is true.
10den, 8 hours ago

A: Drivers should have a trial driving licence for a couple of years before they are allowed to have a full licence. They should only get a full licence if they have shown that they are safe on the road.
Hui, 10 hours ago

A: People who do dangerous sports shouldn't have the right to free medical care if they hurt themselves.
Raymond, 1 day ago

A: I think that hunting and harming animals for sport should be banned.
Hui, 2 days ago

A: I would change the law so that young people have the right to vote at 16.
birdsong, 3 days ago

75%

a Describing the new law
I think there should be a (new) law that …
It should be compulsory to (have a trial licence).
I (don't) think it should be banned.
(Young people) should (not) be allowed to (vote).
(Animals) should have the right to (live).
It should be legal/illegal to (smoke in public).

b Giving your opinion
I (don't) think this is a good idea because …
I'm (not) against (hunting).
I agree / don't agree with this idea because …
I think this law would be fair/unfair because …
What I don't agree with is (hunting for sport).
To me, it/that doesn't make (a lot of) sense.

c Presenting your opinions to the class
We discussed …
We all / Most of us agree that …
We all had different opinions about this …

IT'S A FACT!
In most countries the voting age is 18, but in Austria and Brazil it is 16. In Malaysia and Oman it is 21.

SHARE YOUR TASK

Choose one law to talk about for 30 seconds.

Practise what you want to say until you feel confident.

Film/Record yourself giving your talk.

Share your film/recording with other students.

LANGUAGE LIVE

Speaking
Expressing and responding to opinions

1 Read the newspaper article. What do you think is an appropriate punishment for the boy?

Local boy sentenced for robbery

Mark Forest from West Kirby has been sentenced to 25 hours' community service for robbing a local newsagent. Mark, who is 16, walked into the shop on Broad Street and stole £75 from the till. He also threatened the shop owner, Mr Keith Perry.

2a ▶ Watch the video of two conversations about the crime. What's the relationship between the people in each conversation? What does each person think about the crime?

b Read the extracts below. Then watch again and number the phrases in the order you hear them.

Conversation 1
a That may be so, but …
b In my opinion …
c I don't know about you, but I don't think …
d What do you mean?
e Really? Why do you say that?
f I don't know about that.

Conversation 2
a You have to remember that …
b Terrible, isn't it?
c But to be honest, I don't really agree.
d I take your point.

3 Write the phrases from exercise 2b in the correct category below.

Expressing an opinion	Responding to an opinion
Terrible, isn't it?	That may be so, but … But to be honest, I don't really agree.

PRONUNCIATION

1 ▶ Watch and listen to the key phases. Notice how the speaker uses intonation to remain polite, even when disagreeing.

4a Work in pairs. Student A: Use a phrase from the table in exercise 3 to express an opinion about the statements below. Student B: Respond to Student A's opinion with a phrase from the table. Try to give a reason for the opinion you express.

1 It's acceptable to send children to prison.
2 Avoiding tax is not a crime.
3 All forms of hunting should be banned.
4 Military service should be compulsory.
5 The main aim of prison should be to re-educate criminals, not punish them.

> I don't know about you, but I think that it's OK to send children to prison sometimes.

> Really? I'm not so sure. In my opinion …

b What are your own opinions about the statements in exercise 4a? Compare your ideas with the rest of the class. Use phrases from exercise 3.

Writing
An opinion essay

1a Read the opinions and check the meanings of the phrases in bold. What topic is being discussed?

> ❝ Where I live in the USA, if you commit three crimes then you automatically get a **life sentence**. I think it's a really **good deterrent**.

> ❝ I'm **against** sending people to prison for **minor** crimes. If people go to prison they are more likely to commit **serious crimes** in the future.

> ❝ Long prison sentences just aren't **effective**. Punishments like **community service** are much better.

> ❝ I'm **in favour of** much **tougher punishments**. I think criminals are treated too **leniently** and the victim is just forgotten.

b Read the opinions again. Who supports tougher punishments for criminals? Who is against them? Which argument(s) do you agree with?

2 Read the opinion essay below. Is the writer in favour of tougher punishments for criminals? Which opinions from exercise 1a are mentioned?

Most prison sentences are too short. Discuss.

a What is the appropriate punishment for a crime? This is a difficult and controversial issue in many societies. Some people argue that crime is high because prison sentences are low. However, in my opinion, we should not make prison sentences longer than they are now.

b Firstly, it is important to remember that the best place to learn how to commit crime is in prison. Criminals only talk to other criminals in prison and as a result they learn new ways to commit crimes. For that reason, if a young person is sent to prison for a minor crime, he or she is much more likely to commit more crimes in the future.

c What is more, prison is expensive. In the UK, it costs over £40,000 a year to keep a person in prison. There are other cheaper ways to punish criminals, and a lot of these other methods are more effective. For example, criminals can be 'tagged'. This means that they have to wear an electronic tag at all times which shows police where they are.

d However, there are some important arguments in favour of increasing prison sentences. Many people argue that longer prison sentences are an important deterrent. They also argue that the victims of crime are often forgotten. And, of course, some criminals are so dangerous that they have to remain in prison.

e Despite this, I strongly believe that in most cases the disadvantages of long prison sentences outweigh the advantages. I am therefore convinced that courts should choose alternatives to prison if possible.

3a In which paragraph(s) does the writer:

1 give a final opinion?
2 give the opposite point of view?
3 give an initial opinion?
4 give reasons for his/her opinion?

b Underline the phrases that the writer uses to introduce the ideas in exercise 3a.

1 _I strongly believe that ..._

c Underline the linking words that the writer uses to join ideas.

Paragraph a – However

4a You are going to write an opinion essay. Read the topic below and mark the statements + (for) or - (against). Think of arguments to support each statement.

The aim of prison should be to re-educate rather than punish. Discuss.

1 Most people who end up in prison have had a difficult life and few opportunities.
2 Criminals do not learn their lesson unless life in prison is hard.
3 It is unfair to their victims if criminals are not punished.
4 Education will help prisoners to get a job and make a better contribution to society in the future.

b Can you think of any more arguments for or against? What is your own opinion?

5 Write a first draft of your essay. Use the checklist to help you.

- Have you used the paragraph structure in exercise 3a?
- Have you introduced each paragraph with an appropriate phrase?
- Have you used linkers correctly? (see page 109)

6 Work in pairs. Swap essays and suggest ways to improve your partner's essay. Write the final draft.

AFTER UNIT 11 YOU CAN ...

Describe and discuss laws and crimes.

Give arguments for and against controversial issues.

Write an essay giving your opinion.

12

YOUR CHOICE

How do you respond when things *go wrong?*

Some people blow their top, some people blame themselves. *What do you do? Do the quiz and find out.*

1 You've been working really hard and you start to feel ill. You have a headache and you feel nauseous. You think:

a I'll take a couple of painkillers and it will pass.
b I shouldn't have worked so hard recently.
c Oh no! This is the start of something really serious.
d Why do these things ALWAYS happen to me????

2 You have a meeting with your boss. She tells you that you need to improve your performance. After the meeting you think:

a How can I show her I'm better than she thinks?
b I shouldn't have taken this job.
c I'd better start looking for a new job. I'm going to lose this one.
d She was completely wrong. I should have given my point of view!

3 You are driving your car and you make a mistake. You nearly hit a car coming the other way. You think:

a That was unusual! I'm normally a really good driver.
b I wasn't concentrating. I'll have to drive more carefully.
c I could have died!
d That driver shouldn't be on the road!

4 After an argument, your partner storms out of the house. You think:

a He/She will calm down. We can work it out.
b I wouldn't have walked out like that. It's a bit silly.
c I've lost him/her for ever.
d He/She's such an idiot!

5 Your best friend is driving alone. She stops to help someone by the side of the road. That person takes her money and steals her car. The next day your friend is crying as she tells you the story. You say:

a It's not your fault. You couldn't have known it was a trick.
b I hope you've learnt a lesson.
c I wouldn't have stopped to help a stranger. Never!
d People like that should be shot!

Language focus 1
could have, should have, would have

1a Read the title and introduction to the quiz. How do you cope with problems?

b Do the quiz. Count up the number of a's, b's, c's and d's that you have. Then check your profile on page 130.

c Work in pairs. Compare your answers and profile with your partner. Which conclusions do you agree/disagree with?

2 Think of a problem that you have experienced recently. How did you react? Tell your partner.

3 Look at the quiz again and underline the examples of *could(n't) have*, *should(n't) have* and *would(n't) have*.

GRAMMAR

Choose the correct answers.

1 I could have died.

This sentence refers to the **past / present**. It means:
a I died.
b I didn't die.
c It was possible for me to die, but I didn't.

2 I shouldn't have taken this job.

This sentence refers to the **past / present**. The speaker thinks:
a I took the job, but now I think it was a mistake.
b I didn't take the job and now I think it was a mistake.
c I took the job and now I think it was the right decision.

3 I wouldn't have stopped to help a stranger.

This sentence refers to the **past / present**. The speaker:
a was in this situation – it really happened to him/her.
b wasn't in this situation – he/she is imagining a situation in the past.
c was possibly in this situation but can't remember.

PRONUNCIATION

1 🎧 12.1 In speech, past modal forms often sound like one word. Listen to the verbs on their own:

could have	/kʊdəv/	couldn't have	/kʊdntəv/
should have	/ʃʊdəv/	shouldn't have	/ʃʊdntəv/
would have	/wʊdəv/	wouldn't have	/wʊdntəv/

2 🎧 12.2 Listen to the verbs in full sentences. Practise, paying attention to the pronunciation of the modals.

PRACTICE

1 Complete the conversations with *could(n't) have*, *should(n't) have* or *would(n't) have*.

1 **A:** I gave up football when I was a teenager.
B: But you were great. You _____ played for Barcelona.

2 **A:** It's a shame the concert was cancelled.
B: Yeah, it _____ been great.

3 **A:** Congratulations. You did really well.
B: Thanks. I _____ done it without you.

4 **A:** My boyfriend went on holiday with his friends last month.
B: Really! I _____ allowed my boyfriend to do that. No way!

5 **A:** Are you still in bed? I've just done all the housework.
B: You _____ woken me up. I _____ helped you.

6 **A:** How annoying! My evening class was cancelled at the last minute.
B: The school _____ called you. You _____ stayed at home.

7 **A:** I was really sleepy in the car.
B: You _____ driven. You _____ had an accident.

8 **A:** When he said he wanted a divorce, she cut holes in all his clothes.
B: She _____ done that. I _____ said 'Great! Goodbye!'

2a Read about Olivia and her husband. What was the problem? How did Olivia deal with it?

Olivia and her husband were asleep in bed one night when they heard someone downstairs burgling their house. Olivia's husband went downstairs and, after listening to their conversation for a few minutes, Olivia realised that the burglar had a gun. There was a phone by the bed, but Olivia decided to go downstairs herself. She managed to hit the burglar over the head with a vase. He was later arrested.

b Write some sentences about Olivia's story.

In my opinion, she should/shouldn't have …
The burglar could have …
In her position, I would have …

3a Work in pairs. Student A: Read the story of Gill and George on page 127. Student B: Read the story of Jackie and her children on page 129. You are going to summarise the story for your partner.

b Tell each other your story. Discuss what the characters could/should have done and what you would have done in their position.

Unit 12, Study & Practice 1, page 165

Listening

1 Work in pairs. Read the introduction below about a journey Andrew and Debra Veal decided to make. How would you feel in that situation? What problems might you have?

2 Something went wrong for the couple after a few days of the race. Look at the key words from the story. Can you guess what happened?

an experienced rower	a collision	a violent storm
to abandon the race	a phobia	an oil tanker
to support someone	loneliness	a rescue boat
to shake with fear	sharks	a motivational speaker

3 🎧 12.3 Listen to the first part of the story and answer the questions.

1 What experience did Debra and Andrew each have of rowing?
2 How did they each react to life on the ocean?
3 What happened a few days into the trip? How did Andrew react?

4 🎧 12.4 What do you think they decided to do? Listen to the rest of the story and answer the questions.

1 Did they agree about what to do?
2 What physical dangers did Debra face?
3 Why was day 74 of her trip a particularly good one?
4 How long had she been at sea when she arrived in Barbados?
5 Who was waiting to meet her?
6 How many days behind the winner was she?
7 In what ways has her life changed since then?

5 Work in groups and discuss.

- What do you think Debra and Andrew's behaviour shows about their characters?
- Do you think they made the right decision?
- If not, what do you think they should have done instead?

The toughest decision of their lives

In October 2002, Debra and Andrew Veal, a couple from south-west London, entered the Ward Evans Atlantic Rowing Challenge. They would race 34 other crews, rowing 5,000 km from Tenerife in the Canary Islands to Barbados in the Caribbean – a journey expected to take 60 days. To do this, each team of two people rows 24 hours a day, in shifts of two hours.

Language focus 2
Hypothetical situations in the past with *if*

1 🎧 **12.5** Match the sentence halves about Debra and Andrew Veal. Then listen and check.

A
1 If Andrew <u>had known</u> about his phobia,
2 If Andrew had stayed on the boat,
3 If Debra's boat had hit an oil tanker,
4 If they had continued the race together,
5 If Debra hadn't had this experience,

B
a it would have sunk.
b she wouldn't be a successful motivational speaker now.
c his phobia would have got worse.
d he <u>wouldn't have entered</u> the race.
e the couple might still be married now.

2 Underline the verb in each half of the five sentences.

2a Complete the sentences with the correct form of the verb in brackets. Use *might* where appropriate.

1 If Erin _____ (not have) a baby, she _____ (continue) working.
2 If she _____ (not leave) her job, she _____ (spend) a lot of time away from her children.
3 The family _____ (have) a lot more money now if she _____ (stay) in her old job, but she _____ (not be) happy with the situation.
4 Kieron _____ (become) a top-class footballer if he _____ (not break) his leg.
5 If he _____ (be able) to play for a big club, he _____ (not become) a coach.
6 He _____ (be) happier now if he _____ (fulfil) his ambitions.
7 If Margot _____ (not go) to Greece for her holidays that year, she _____ (not meet) Nikos.
8 She _____ (forget) about Nikos if he _____ (not follow) her home.
9 If she _____ (not marry) Nikos, she _____ (still live) in England.
10 If she _____ (not move) to Greece, she _____ (still be) a nurse now.

b Work in pairs and discuss. Would you have made the same decisions in their position?

3a Complete the sentences below to make them true for you.

1 I wouldn't have met ... if ...
2 I would have studied ... if ...
3 I wouldn't have studied ... if ...
4 I wouldn't have gone to ... if ...
5 I would have more money now if ...
6 I'd feel better now if ...

b Work in pairs and compare your sentences. Ask questions to find out more information.

> I wouldn't have met my wife if I hadn't taken a job that I didn't want.
>
> Really? What was the job? Why didn't you want it?

GRAMMAR

1 Answer the questions.
1 Are the sentences in exercise 1 above true or hypothetical?
2 Look at the 'conditions' in A. Do they refer to the present or the past? What form of the verb is used to talk about past conditions?
3 Look at the hypothetical situations in B. Which ones refer to the past? Which refer to the present? What verb forms are used in each case?

2 Notice the verb forms in patterns A and B. Find another example of each pattern in exercise 1.

A Past condition	Past result
*If Andrew **had stayed** on the boat,*	*his phobia **would have got** worse.*

B Past condition	Present/general result
*If Debra **hadn't had** this experience,*	*she **wouldn't be** a successful motivational speaker.*

PRACTICE

1 🎧 **12.6** Listen to three people describe a big decision in their lives. Answer the questions about each person.

1 What was the decision?
2 Why did they make it?
3 How are their lives different now?

Unit 12, Study & Practice 2, page 166

119

Vocabulary
Problems and solutions

1 Read about a problem that Frank had in his life. Check the meaning of the words in bold. Then put the sentences in the correct order.

- **a** Until one day, he realised he **had a problem with** his marriage.
- **b** The friend was **sympathetic** and told him to **trust his intuition**.
- **c** Frank was happy. He **didn't have a care in the world**.
- **d** But it didn't **go away** and he began to **lose sleep over it**.
- **e** Together they **sorted the problem out**.
- **f** Finally, Frank **made a decision**. He talked to his wife about his **concerns**.
- **g** At first, Frank tried to **ignore** the problem.
- **h** So Frank **talked it over** with a friend and asked his advice.

2 Match the words and phrases in bold in exercise 1 with the definitions below.

1 to disappear *go away*
2 to have nothing to worry about
3 to solve (a problem)
4 to discuss a problem
5 to pretend you can't see or notice something
6 to decide
7 to not like something
8 to be kind and willing to listen
9 things you worry about
10 to believe in your feelings
11 to be unable to sleep at night because of something

3a Work in pairs. Choose a problem from the list to write about. Decide whether to make the story sad, funny or just awkward.

- Frank is very worried about a member of his family who is behaving strangely.
- Frank has a secret in his past and he is worried that his wife/friends will find out.
- Frank is having problems with his colleague/boss.
- Frank is very worried because ... (your ideas)

b Decide the details of the problem. Write the story of the new problem together, using at least five phrases from exercise 1.

Frank was happy. He didn't have a care in the world. Until one day he realised he had a problem with his job. The problem was he didn't trust his boss, because he suspected him of stealing.

4 Read your story to the class. Whose story do you like best? Why?

Reading

1 Work in groups. Have you ever found any of these decisions difficult? Discuss how you make decisions in these situations.

- what to wear
- what to eat in a restaurant
- whether or not to apply for a job, do a course, etc.
- which car to buy
- whether to start or end a relationship

2 Read the text about making decisions and answer the questions.

1 Which decision in paragragh 1 is the writer making?
2 What decision does she make in the end?
3 Match headings a–c with paragraphs 1–3.
   - **a** Be intuitive
   - **b** Be logical
   - **c** Take a chance

3 Read the text again and find the answers to the questions below.

1 Which car in the introductory paragraph:
   - **a** uses a lot of petrol?
   - **b** breaks down a lot?
   - **c** hasn't been driven much?

2 Which type of decision-maker (rational, intuitive or fatalistic):
   - **a** doesn't learn to make better decisions?
   - **b** doesn't make quick decisions?
   - **c** doesn't understand why he/she makes a particular decision?

3 Who (Goizueta, Gladwell or Rhinehart):
   - **a** made a bad decision?
   - **b** made the right decision?

4 What were the decisions in 3a and b above? Why were they good/bad?

4 Work in groups and discuss.

- What do you think of Luke Rhinehart's method of making decisions?
- Why do you think he chose to live his life in this way?
- Have you ever made a decision by:
   - making a list of pros and cons?
   - following your intuition?
   - rolling a dice or tossing a coin?
- Which method in the text is best for making decisions, in your opinion?

How to make decisions
by Adriana Nesbit

I'm standing in a used car showroom feeling a bit confused – I don't know which car to buy. Should I buy the boring blue car with low mileage? Should I buy the sporty black car that isn't very economical? Or should I buy the older red car that has lots of character but isn't very reliable? It's not easy. A hundred years ago, Henry Ford said that his customers could have 'any colour they want as long as it's black'. These days, there's much more choice, but that can be confusing. So what's the best way to decide?

1 ___

Rational decision-makers think about each decision carefully. They look at the information and make a list of pros and cons to help them sort the problem out. The trouble is, it can take a long time to analyse all the information and even when you've done that, rational decisions aren't always the best decisions. In 1985 Roberto Goizueta, CEO of Coca-Cola ® decided to change the taste of his company's famous drink. Tests on 200,000 people showed that they preferred the new taste. But when 'New Coke' was launched, customers were angry and the company quickly returned to the old recipe. Taste wasn't the most important factor. People were emotionally attached to the old drink.

2 ___

Some people don't look for logical reasons, they look for a feeling. Do you believe in love at first sight?

If so, then you probably trust your intuition to make some of your decisions. Malcolm Gladwell, author of *Blink: The Power of Thinking Without Thinking*, says that our intuition often makes the best decisions because it ignores extra, confusing information. But our intuition can also lead us to the wrong decision. For example, if you had to close your eyes and try to pull out a red jelly bean from a jar of mostly white jelly beans, which jar would you use: a big jar with 100 beans of which seven are red or a small jar of ten beans of which one is red? Most people chose the big jar because their intuition tells them they have more chance of success with seven red beans in the jar. However, in reality your chances are almost 50 percent higher with the small jar.

3 ___

Fatalistic decision-makers leave the decision to chance or fate. In Luke Rhinehart's novel, *The Dice Man*, the main character makes his decisions by throwing a dice. The novel is based on Rhinehart's own life. When he was at college he started using a dice to make decisions and it certainly helped him to make some good decisions. When he was 21, he saw two pretty nurses walking along the road. He threw a dice to decide whether to offer them a lift and the dice said yes. Now in his 70s, Rhinehart is still married to one of those nurses ... and he still throws

a dice to make decisions! Throwing dice makes decisions nice and simple, but it doesn't help us to make better ones. It just stops us worrying.

How to make good decisions

So here is my advice for making good decisions:

1 Try not to ignore a problem and hope it will go away. Usually, it doesn't.

2 Weigh up the pros and cons, but trust your instincts. It's OK to say 'because it feels right'.

3 Don't lose sleep over a wrong decision. You can learn from it.

So back to my car dilemma. Rationally, I should choose the blue car, but my intuition says the red car. I throw the dice and it says the black car. But I still can't make a decision. Finally, I realise that the question is wrong. It's not *Which car should I buy?* but *Should I buy a car at all?*

Task

Discuss dilemmas

Preparation Reading

1a Read the introduction to the problem page. Do you ever read problem pages? How is this one different?

b Work in pairs. Read the title of each problem and guess what each problem is about.

c Read the problems and check your answers. Do not look at page 131 yet.

2a Work in groups of three. Each student reads one of the problems again to find the answers to the questions.

  1 Which people are mentioned in each case?
  2 What exactly has each person done?
  3 What exactly was the situation at the time that the letter was written and why was the writer worried?

b Close your books and summarise the problem to the other students.

Task Speaking

1 Make notes about the people listed below, thinking about questions 1–3. Ask your teacher for any words/phrases you need.

  1 What did they do right/wrong?
  2 What other options did they have?
  3 What would you have done in their position?

  - Larry
  - Vanessa
  - Vanessa's parents
  - Oscar
  - His parents
  - Astrid
  - Astrid's husband
  - The mother-in-law

  > Useful language a, b and c

2a Work in groups and compare your answers to the questions in exercise 1. Try to reach an agreement as a group about what you would have done.

b Present your ideas to the class. Do other groups agree with you?

Dilemmas revisited
What did they do next?

Every month we feature readers' letters on our problem page and try to give out good advice! But what do readers actually do? This month, we have tracked down three readers whose problems were featured two years ago. Read their original problems, then read what they decided to do on page 131.

1 Should I choose the job or my girlfriend?

I'm 23 and recently I celebrated three years together with my girlfriend Vanessa (she's 22). I asked her parents if I could propose to her – I'm a bit old-fashioned, I guess. Her parents were really pleased and supported me. But when I asked her to marry me, she was angry because I had talked to her parents and said 'not at the moment'. This really upset me, but we didn't talk about it any more.

A month ago I was offered a great new job in a town 300 miles away. I said yes immediately. When I told Vanessa and asked her to move to the new town with me, she was really angry. She said that I should have asked her first. She says she wants to stay together, but she doesn't want to move and she still says that she doesn't want to get married yet. She's the love of my life, but I'm really confused about what to do. Some of my friends say I should split up with her and take the job, but what if I never meet another person like her? **Larry**

3 Read what each person actually did on page 131 and answer the questions.

  1 What did they decide? Was it what you expected?
  2 How do they feel about the situation now?
  3 Do you think they made the right decision?
  4 What do you think they should do now?
  5 Which was the most difficult problem?

2 Professional football or accountancy?

I've played football since I could walk and I've always dreamt of becoming a professional footballer. A couple of years ago, when I was 15, I had a trial with a local football club. They're just a small club in the third division, but I've always supported them. Unfortunately, the club said I wasn't good enough so I decided to concentrate on my studies. I worked hard and last year I was accepted on an accountancy course at a good university. I was really happy about this and ready to start my course.

A couple of weeks ago the club contacted me and asked me to try again. This time they offered me a two-year professional contract, which they will renew if I do well. Now I don't know what to do. My parents say I should go to university, but I've been having dreams at night of playing for the club and for my country. I really think I'm good enough to do that, but I feel really confused. **Oscar**

3 It's my mother-in-law or me!

I've been married for ten years. Last year my husband's father died. His mother was 69 and she quickly became lonely and depressed. We tried to help her as much as possible, but it wasn't easy. We live 80 miles away, we have two children of six and four and we both work. A few months ago my husband asked his mother to come and live with us. I was really angry because he didn't ask me first. He said he had no choice.

My mother-in-law has been living with us for three months now and she is driving me crazy. I know she has never liked me, but now she criticises me in front of the children and says that the house isn't clean enough. She tells me that I shouldn't work and that I should spend more time with my family. My husband says I shouldn't get upset. I've tried to accept it and carry on as normal, but it's very, very hard. Last month I told my husband that it's either her or me. I said we have to find a care home for her. He refuses to talk about it. **Astrid**

USEFUL LANGUAGE

a Discussing options
He/She could have …
On the other hand, he/she could have …
Of course, it depends (what kind of person his girlfriend is).

b Saying what you would have done
In his/her position, I wouldn't have … because …
Personally, I would have …

c Commenting
Personally, I think he/she was right/wrong to …
I think he/she put her in a really difficult situation.
I (don't) think they should have …
He/She definitely shouldn't have …
I can understand why he/she …
You just can't do things like that!

SHARE YOUR TASK

Choose one of the problems.

Practise explaining what you would/wouldn't have done and why until you feel confident.

Film/Record yourself giving your talk.

Share your film/recording with other students.

Follow up Writing

1 EITHER write a letter to Larry, Oscar or Astrid. Tell them what they should do now, two years after their original problem.
OR work in pairs and imagine you are writing a TV drama about one of these stories. Write a scene between two of the characters. Practise the scene and act it out for the class.

WORLD CULTURE

LIFE IN A NEW COUNTRY

Find out first

1 Look at the photos of London and New Zealand and answer the questions.

1 What do you think are the advantages/disadvantages of living in each place?

2 In what ways do you think life is similar/different?

2a Discuss in pairs. What do you know about New Zealand? How much of the information in the table can you complete from your general knowledge?

	New Zealand	UK
Population		
Area		
Capital		
Offcial language(s)		
Climate		
Scenery/ landscape		

b Go online to complete the table or ask your teacher.

Search: New Zealand / UK geographical facts

View

3a You are going to watch a video about Imogen and Charlie, a British couple who are thinking of moving to New Zealand. Before you watch, check you understand the meaning of the words and phrases in the glossary.

Glossary

down under	colloquial phrase used by British people to refer to Australia and New Zealand
outdoor pursuits	things you do outside (e.g. walking, climbing, camping)
a big pull	very attractive
to emigrate	to move permanently to another country

b ▶ Watch the first part of the video. What do you find out about these things? Make notes.

1 Imogen and Charlie's life in the UK
2 the lifestyle in New Zealand
3 their family situations
4 job prospects in New Zealand

c Watch again and complete your notes. Which things attract Imogen and Charlie to New Zealand? Which things do not attract them?

4a At the end of the video, the couple vote where they want to live. How do you think they will each vote? Watch the second part of the video and check you answer.

b Work in groups and discuss.

- Were you surprised at the decision each of them made?
- Why do you think they made that decision?
- What would you have decided in their situation?

World view

5 Watch four people talking about living in a foreign country. Answer the questions for each speaker.

- Anna
- Carol
- Denise
- Bethan

1 Where is she from originally?
2 Which country did she move to and why?
3 What are/were the best things about living there?
4 What are/were the disadvantages of living there?

6 Work in groups and discuss.

- Do you know anyone who has moved to another country? How have they got on?
- Would you ever move to another country permanently? If so, where?
- What would be the most difficult things about living in another country? What would you enjoy?

7a What do you know about worldwide emigration/immigration? Do you think it is increasing or decreasing?

b Go online to answer the questions about emigration/immigration.

Search: emigration/immigration statistics + worldwide/US/UK, etc. / brain drain definition

1 How many immigrants in total are there in the world?
2 How many people approximately go to live in the UK every year?
3 What is the most common reason for people going to live in the UK?
4 How many people approximately leave the UK to live in other countries?
5 Approximately how many people come to live in your country every year?
6 Approximately how many people leave your country to live in other countries?
7 What is a 'brain drain' and why is it a problem?
8 What is one advantage and one disadvantage of immigration?

Write up your research

8 Write a paragraph about going to live in another country. Include some of the information about immigration that you have found out.

AFTER UNIT 12 YOU CAN ...

Describe personal problems and reactions to them.

Discuss and suggest alternative solutions to problems.

Research geographical information online.

Communication activities

Unit 3: Vocabulary
Exercise 2, page 31

Unit 4: Vocabulary
Exercise 2, page 40

Life events quiz

1 Which three phrases need the word *a*? **(3 points)**

get promotion	buy house	get job	start school
go to university	leave home	move house	

2 Which word isn't preceded by *get*? **(2 points)**

children	divorced	engaged

3 Match the verbs with the noun/adjective they were used with on page 40. **(7 points)**

1	move	**a**	an exam
2	bring up	**b**	in love
3	fall	**c**	children
4	lose	**d**	a house
5	make	**e**	money
6	pass	**f**	your job
7	rent	**g**	house

4 Complete the sentences with *to*, *with* or *from*.

1 He got married ___ his brother's ex-wife!
2 Unfortunately, he's just split up ___ his girlfriend.
3 She's been engaged ___ her boyfriend for over four years.
4 She got divorced ___ her husband after just six months.

Unit 4: Language focus 1
Practice, Exercise 3, page 37

- meet a famous person
- see a famous singer/group perform live
- play in a group
- sing in a choir
- learn a musical instrument
- be on TV / in the newspaper / in a play
- win a prize / a competition / money
- go to the ballet / the opera / a classical concert
- visit a country / a city / a famous monument
- climb a high mountain/building
- go parachuting/skiing/sailing
- drive a bus / a lorry / a sports car
- ride a horse / a camel / a motorbike
- break your arm / leg / something very valuable
- lose a lot of money / a credit card / an important document / your mobile phone
- steal something!

Unit 5: Vocabulary
Exercise 2a, page 47

1 Imagination
2 success, failure
3 Knowledge
4 profit

Communication activities

Unit 5: Language focus 1
Exercise 1b, page 48

Quiz conclusions

Mostly a: You are certainly ambitious, and no one can say that you don't have a positive attitude. But make sure your personal relationships don't suffer because of work – one day you'll need your friends and family!

Mostly b: You have a balanced, practical attitude towards your career. You are reasonably ambitious, but you will never become a workaholic. Just make sure that you actually do what you say you are going to do!

Mostly c: You are very sensitive to other people's feelings and put personal relationships before work. However, if you want to be successful, you need to be more determined. Perhaps you haven't found a job that motivates you yet?

Unit 5: Language focus 1
Practice, Exercise 3a, page 49

1 Write down three arrangements or appointments that you have got for the next week or two.
2 Tell your partner about your hopes or plans for your next holiday.
3 Write down how you think you'll spend next Sunday morning.
4 Tell your partner two domestic tasks you are planning to do this weekend.
5 Write down where you are due to be after this lesson.
6 Write down one good intention you have for this week.
7 Tell your partner about two things that you are hoping to buy in the next few months.
8 Tell your partner about your family's plans for the next year or so.
9 Write down two ambitions you have that are not connected with work.
10 Tell your partner what you think your teacher is about to do.
11 Guess your partner's plans for this evening.
12 Predict two things you'll do in your next lesson.

Unit 8: Language focus 2
Practice, Exercise 1, page 79

1 Someone tells you that your friend has broken his leg and is bored at home with nothing to do. What do you say?

  • Shall we go and see him this afternoon?
  • I'll send him a get-well card.
  • I'll try and call him some time.

2 A colleague is complaining that she hasn't got enough money to buy lunch today. What do you say?

  • I'll buy you lunch, don't worry.
  • Shall I lend you some money?
  • Shall we share my sandwiches?

3 Your friend has just started learning English. He calls you to say he is stuck with his English homework and can't come out with you tonight. What do you say?

  • Shall I come round and help you?
  • I'll do your homework for you, if you like.
  • Shall we meet another night instead?

4 You and some friends are visiting a friend for the evening. No one seems to be enjoying themselves very much. What do you say?

  • Shall we put some music on and dance?
  • I'll go and buy some drinks and snacks.
  • I think I'll go home and have an early night.

Unit 12: Language focus 1
Practice, Exercise 3a, page 117
Student A

Gill and George

Gill, a widow in her fifties, was devoted to her seven-year-old cat, George. However, one day George was run over by a car. When she took him to the vet, she was told that the operation to save him would cost €2,000 but that it might not be successful. As Gill did not have much money, her 25-year-old daughter agreed to pay with her credit card. Gill said she would pay her daughter back month by month. Unfortunately, George died.

Communication activities

Unit 3: Language focus 1
Practice, Exercise 3a, page 27

	France	Ireland	UK
How big is the country?	550,000 km²	69,000 km²	241,000 km²
How crowded is the country?	107 people per km²	52 people per km²	241 people per km²
How many tourists are there per year?	75 million	6.5 million	30 million
What is the population of the main city?	Paris 2.2 million	Dublin 1.2 million	London 7.5 million
How busy is the main airport?	Paris Charles de Gaulle Airport: 61 million	Dublin Airport: 18 million	London Heathrow Airport: 69 million

Unit 10: Vocabulary
Exercise 4a, page 97
Student A

	China	United Arab Emirates
Area	9,326,410 km²	
Population	1.4 billion	
Average number of visitors (per year)	55.7 million	
Minimum/ maximum temperatures	-25°C / 33°C	
Ethnic groups	93% Han Chinese 7% other	
Kilometres of road	3,860,800 km	
Airports	562	
Kilometres of coastline	14,500 km	

Unit 7: Language live, Speaking
Exercise 4, page 75

4a Read the instructions on the cards below and invent a telephone or face-to-face conversation for the situations. Act out your conversations.

Student A
You are going to invite Student B to see a show with you. Decide the details before you start.

1 Choose the type of show: **a rock concert / a film / a ballet / a play / a musical.**
2 Decide how to invite him/her: **by phone / in person.**
3 Choose three or four dates when you are available.

NB You are very persistent and make a lot of alternative suggestions if B says that he/she can't come.

Student B
Student A is going to invite you to see a show. Decide the details before you speak.

1 Circle the shows you want to see and cross out the ones you don't: **a rock concert / a film / a ballet / a play / a musical.**
2 Think of some excuses in case you don't want to go (you are revising for an exam / your cousin needs you to babysit, etc.).

NB You don't really have the same taste in shows as A and aren't too keen on going, but you don't want to offend A.

b Swap roles and repeat the activity. Act out your conversations for the class.

Unit 5: Language live, Speaking
Exercise 3, page 55
Student A

You are calling Travel Direct to find out about some airline tickets you ordered. You want to speak to Sandi Elliott.

(Student B answers the phone.)
1 Ask to speak to Sandi Elliott.
2 Give your name.
3 Explain what the call is about.
4 Ask if she can call you back.
5 Give your phone number: 07881 334811.
6 Say goodbye.

Communication activities

Unit 9: Language focus 1
Practice, Exercise 3, page 88
Group A

3a Choose eight words or phrases from the box and write questions for them using relative clauses.

What do you call a person who … ?

possessions	a minimalist	a designer boutique
a hobby	an inhabitant	an audience
a sitcom	a lie	knowledge
an actor	ancient ruins	

b Take turns to test Group B. Your teacher will give you two points for a good question and two points for a correct answer to Group B's questions. The team with the most points at the end wins.

Unit 12: Language focus 1
Practice, Exercise 3a, page 117
Student B

Jackie and her children

Jackie and her three children (eight-year-old Lucas and 18-month-old twins) were driving to visit a friend on a remote country farm. In the middle of nowhere, Jackie's car broke down. Her mobile had run out and she had not brought the twins' pushchair with her. She knew that she had passed a pub less than a kilometre before. After waiting half an hour for someone to go past, she locked the car and left Lucas to look after the sleeping twins while she ran to get help. When she returned 30 minutes later, all three children were crying but they were perfectly safe.

Unit 3: Vocabulary
Exercise 2, page 31

   A: Los Angeles, USA
   B: Mumbai, India
   C: Prague, the Czech Republic

Unit 6: Reading and speaking
Exercise 5b, page 60
Student A

Read the text and answer the questions.

  1 Where were Thomas Sheridan and his wife?
  2 When did they first start to worry?
  3 What was Thomas's first thought when he came to the surface?
  4 How did they survive the first two hours?
  5 How did they finally get rescued?
  6 What does Thomas feel about it now?

Shipwrecked

Thomas Sheridan is a retired professor at MIT in Boston, USA. He was shipwrecked on a boat tour of the Galapagos Islands in 1998.

One warm, clear evening we were on the upper deck watching the sunset when we noticed that the boat was moving one way then the other. At first it didn't worry us, but as the boat began rocking violently, my wife and I had to hold on for dear life. Then the boat rolled to the right, paused and then rolled into the ocean. A wall of water came at us. There was just no way that we could hold on.

We all went over the side into the water. As I tried to come up, I struck my head and went down again. When I managed to get to the surface, my first thought was that I had to find my wife. It was almost dark and I couldn't see her, but I heard her calling me.

I told my wife not to go near the boat as it might pull us down. The water, thankfully, wasn't very cold. We found a life belt, which we held onto until we came across a rubber dinghy holding five passengers. It was dark now. After two hours we found the ship's crew in a larger dinghy, and we all got into it. We found a few flares and when we saw lights on the horizon, we tried two of the flares, but they didn't work.

Eventually, another distant ship passed and we used our last flares, which worked. A searchlight blinked back at us. It was a fantastic moment – people finally knew we were there.

Looking back, I feel like it didn't really happen to me. It's more like a kind of movie, but I have a tremendous feeling of good fortune.

Study, Practice & Remember
Practice
Exercise 1b, page 164

1 to commit a crime	**5** to be sentenced
2 to be arrested	**6** to go to prison
3 to get caught	**7** to be released
4 to go to court	

Communication activities

Unit 5: Language live, Speaking

Exercise 3, page 55
Student B

You work at Travel Direct answering the telephones.
Sandi Elliott, your boss, is in a meeting at the moment.

(Student A calls you.)
1 Answer the phone.
2 Ask who is calling.
3 Ask what the call is about.
4 Explain that Sandi is in a meeting. Ask if you can take a message.
5 Ask for the caller's number.
6 Say you will tell Sandi. End the conversation politely.

Unit 12: Language focus 1

Exercise 1b, page 117

How do you respond when things go wrong?

Mostly a: you are CONFIDENT
You are confident and optimistic. When things go wrong, you try to resolve the problem. You look to the future, not the past, but you sometimes find it difficult to accept your mistakes and to learn from them.

Mostly b: you are LOGICAL
You are logical and sensible. You're always calm in a crisis and you never panic. You accept your mistakes and you try to learn from them. You are not at all emotional. Sometimes you want to feel more passionate.

Mostly c: you are FEARFUL
You are a bit of a worrier. You think about the future a lot and you worry about what might go wrong. You tend to panic when things go wrong. You sometimes wish that you were more adventurous.

Mostly d: you are EMOTIONAL
When things go wrong, you sometimes blow your top. You don't believe that you are ever wrong or make mistakes. You tend to blame other people for problems. You sometimes have big arguments with your friends.

Unit 10: Vocabulary

Exercise 4a, page 97
Student B

	China	United Arab Emirates
Area		83,600 km²
Population		5 million
Average number of visitors (per year)		15 million
Minimum/ maximum temperatures		15°C / 40°C
Ethnic groups		50% Asian 42% Arab 8% other
Kilometres of road		4,080 km
Airports		41
Kilometres of coastline		1,318 km

Unit 9: Language focus 1

Practice, Exercise 3, page 88
Group B

3a Choose eight words or phrases and write questions for them using relative clauses.

What do you call a person who … ?

a colleague	the cast	a joke
a distraction	a well-paid job	qualifications
a leader	an athlete	an award
a palace	a reward	

b Take turns to test Group A. Your teacher will give you two points for a good question and two points for a correct answer to Group A's questions. The team with the most points at the end wins.

Communication activities

Unit 12: Task, Speaking
Exercise 3, page 122

Larry
I got hundreds of letters and emails from readers of the magazine after my problem was printed. Most of them said that I should choose the job, although some people said that I should follow my heart and stay with my girlfriend. In the end, I decided to split up with her. I just felt that the job was a really good opportunity for me.

Since then I've moved to the new city and I've done well in my job. I'm earning good money now, but I still really miss my ex-girlfriend and I haven't met anyone else yet. She's with another guy now, I think. I've emailed her a few times and even left messages on her voicemail, but she doesn't reply.

Oscar
Almost everyone agreed with the advice my parents gave me. They said that football was too insecure to be a career. I decided not to listen and I took the two-year contract with the local football club. It's been a really exciting two years and I've really developed as a player, but I haven't managed to get a regular place in the first team.

My contract comes to an end soon and I don't think they will give me another one. I'm trying to get a contract with another club at the moment. I still dream of playing for my country.

Astrid
Advice from the readers was quite mixed. Some of them thought I should just accept the situation and stop complaining. Others advised me to leave my husband. About a month after I wrote the letter, I blew my top with my husband. He finally listened to me and agreed to look for a care home for his mother. She was very, very upset.

She's been in the care home for about 18 months now. Our family life is back to normal – and that's great– but my mother-in-law hates the home. She's become depressed and she doesn't like the other residents. I don't know if I did the right thing, but something had to change.

Unit 4: Language focus 1
Exercise 2a, page 36

From left to right the photos show:

- Brad Pitt (Hollywood actor)
- The Duchess of Cambridge (Kate Middleton), wife of Prince William, grandson of the British Queen
- Shakira (Columbian pop star)
- Barack Obama (President of the United States)
- Winston Churchill (Prime Minister of Britain and a world leader during World War II)

Unit 6: Reading and speaking
Exercise 5b, page 60
Student B

Read the text and answer the questions.

1 Where was Dunstan when the attack happened?
2 How many times did the shark attack?
3 What was the worst part of the attack?
4 Who helped Dunstan?
5 How long was he in hospital?
6 How has he changed?

Attacked by a shark

Dunstan Hogan, 49, was attacked by a great white shark off the coast of Cape St Francis, South Africa, in 2001.

I went for a surf around seven in the morning before work at Seal Point – a famous surf spot. It was cloudy, but visibility was good. I surfed for about an hour and a half before heading back towards the beach.

The attack came without warning. I was lying on my surfboard when I saw this huge grey shark approaching. The shark caught me and the surfboard in its mouth and lifted me out of the water. Then it let go and took another bite. This time it pulled me under the water.

I opened my eyes under the water and saw this giant shark moving about. I let go of the surfboard and returned to the surface. I couldn't see where the shark had gone. I got back on the surfboard and paddled towards the shore. By then, I knew I'd been badly bitten. Part of my body felt numb.

Suddenly, the shark appeared in front of me again. It came straight at me and hit the surfboard, throwing me into the air. I felt no pain, I just held onto the board as firmly as I could. Then the shark went under the water. This was the worst part. I was 50 metres from the beach and I didn't know where the shark was.

But for some reason, the shark didn't attack again. Perhaps it didn't like the surfboard. Two guys were watching all this and ran down. One guy went to call the doctor. I was in hospital for a week.

I've surfed a lot more since then. I've been given a second chance, so I'm enjoying it. But I'm also more careful, and when the water is the same colour as that day, I get a strange feeling. And I'm no longer the first to catch a wave.

STUDY 1

Questions and short answers

1 Auxiliary verbs

We use *be, have* and *do* to form tenses, questions and negative forms, and we use them in short answers, question tags, etc. In all these cases they are called **auxiliary verbs**.

- We use *be* (+ verb + *-ing*) to form **continuous** tenses.
  Present continuous: *He's studying to become a doctor.*
  Past continuous: *I was talking to Charles the other day.*
- We use *have* (+ past participle) to form **perfect** tenses.
  Present perfect: *We've been here for three months.*
  Past perfect: *The film had started when we got there.*
- We use *do* in **simple** tenses (in the question and negative forms).
  Present simple: *Do all your family live round here?*
  Past simple: *I didn't get your email.*

2 Auxiliary verbs in questions

- In continuous and perfect tenses, **questions** are formed by inverting the subject and auxiliary verb.
  Is he studying to become a doctor?
  How long have your brother and sister lived here?
- In simple tenses, we add *do/does* or *did* (see above).

3 Wh- questions

- We form many questions with *wh-* words and phrases.

When ...?	*Where ...?*	*What ...?*
Which ...?	*Why ...?*	*Who ...?*
Whose ...?	*How ...?*	*What kind of ...?*
What sort of ...?	*What time ...?*	*What colour ...?*
Which book/school/woman, etc. ...?		*How many ...?*
How much ...?	*How often ...?*	*How old ...?*
What exactly ...?	*Where exactly ...?*	*Why exactly ...?*

- Notice the word order after most *Wh-* questions.

(*wh-* word)	Auxiliary verb	Subject	Main verb, etc.
What time	are	your friends	arriving?
Where	do	the other students in your class	live?
What kind of music	does	your boyfriend	listen to?

4 Auxiliaries used on their own

SHORT ANSWERS

- These can make the speaker sound more polite/interested.
  A: Have you been here before?
  B: Yes, I have.
- We also use auxiliaries to avoid repeating long sentences.
  A: Does your family live in Paris?
  B: My father does, but my mother doesn't.

SHORT QUESTIONS AND QUESTION TAGS

A: My brother's gone to live in Australia.
B: Has he?
You were at home last night, weren't you?

PRACTICE 1

1 Choose the correct auxiliary verb.

1 Where **are / do** your parents come from?
2 Johnny **is / has** got 16 cousins!
3 I really enjoyed the concert, but the others **weren't / didn't**.
4 A: Have you got any money with you?
   B: No, I **don't / haven't**.
5 Where **were / did** you born?
6 My boyfriend likes my new hairstyle, but my mother **isn't / doesn't**.
7 How **is / does** your course going?

2 Complete the questions with suitable words.

1 _____ were your parents born, in China or in America?
2 _____'s your new car going?
3 _____ _____ do you have lunch normally?
4 What _____ you studying at university?
5 _____ _____ do you want: red or blue?
6 _____ _____ _____ books do you like?
7 _____ bag is this?
8 _____ _____ do you go to the gym?

3 Put the words in the correct order to make questions.

1 the rest of your family / speak / do / English ?
2 your aunt and uncle / children / have / many / how / do ?
3 your brother / which / go / gym / to / does ?
4 go / what / out / you and your friends / do / time ?
5 born / were / where / your brothers and sisters?
6 applying / you / which / to / are / university ?

STUDY 2

Present simple and Present continuous

1 Present simple

+	I/You/We/They **work**.	
	He/She/It **works**.	
−	I/You/We/They **don't** (= do not) **work**.	
	He/She/It **doesn't** (= does not) **work**.	
?	**Do** I/you/we/they **work**?	
	Does he/she/it **work**?	

We use the Present simple for:

- repeated actions or habits. *We go out every Saturday night.*
- something we see as permanent. *My sister works in a bank.*
- describing a state that doesn't change. *I look like my mother.*

2 Present continuous

+	I'm (= am) working.
	You/We/They**'re** (= **are**) working.
	He/She/It**'s** (= **is**) working.
−	I'm not (= am not) working.
	You/We/They **aren't** (= **are not**) working.
	He/She/It **isn't** (= **is not**) working.
?	**Am** I working?
	Are you/we/they **working**?
	Is he/she/it **working**?

We use the Present continuous for:
- things in progress now, at the moment of speaking.
  *The sun **is shining** and it's a beautiful day!*
- actions that are happening 'around now'.
  *I**'m reading** a very good book at the moment.*
  (= I'm in the middle of reading it.)
- situations we see as temporary.
  *My brother**'s staying** with my aunt until he finds a flat.*
- describing a situation which is gradually changing.
  *People **are working** longer hours nowadays.*

3 Present simple versus Present continuous

Sometimes either form is possible. Compare the following pairs of sentences.
*Paola is the student who **sits** at the back of the class.*
(= she always does this)
*Paola is the student who **is sitting** at the back of the class.*
(= she is there now)
*My parents **stay** at the Metropole Hotel.*
(= every time they visit the town)
*My parents **are staying** at the Metropole Hotel.*
(= in the present period)
*He**'s working** in a café.*
(a temporary job)
*He **works** for a big electrical company.*
(his permanent job)

4 'State' versus 'action' verbs

Some verbs are rarely found in continuous forms. These are verbs which describe 'states' (things which stay the same) rather than 'actions' (things which can change). Some of the most common are verbs:
- connected with emotions: *hate, like, love, want.*
- connected with understanding: *believe, know, prefer, understand.*
- connected with the senses: *hear, smell, sound, taste.*
- connected with possession and unchanging qualities: *belong, cost, weigh.*

PRACTICE 2

1 Which verbs are not correct in the Present continuous? Write the correct Present simple form.

1 Tomas isn't usually speaking much in class.
2 Paula says she'll call you back – she's making a cake.
3 Shh! The children are having a little rest.
4 Look, it's getting dark already!
5 I'm not knowing your brother.
6 Harry's having six older sisters.
7 This city is becoming very expensive.
8 I'm understanding the Present continuous perfectly.

2 Complete the sentences with the correct form of the verb in brackets.

1 Her husband is a taxi driver so he _____ (get) home late.
2 _____ (you like) my new shoes?
3 You can't use the bathroom. Alice _____ (have) a shower.
4 I must go to the hairdresser's. My hair _____ (get) very long.
5 Sorry, but I _____ (think) you're wrong.
6 In my job, I _____ (spend) a lot of time on the phone.

3 Read the text and choose the correct answers.

Hurray for Hollywood

In 1911, the small, peaceful village of Hollywood voted to become part of Los Angeles. Today, over a hundred years later, millions of people around the world [1] *dream / are dreaming* about becoming a star in this town.

Everyone [2] *knows / is knowing* the symbols of Hollywood. There is the famous Hollywood sign which [3] *stands / is standing* above the hills of the town. And [4] *don't forget / don't be forgetting* Grauman's Chinese Theatre, where great actors and actresses [5] *leave / are leaving* their hand and footprints. But most famous of all is the Academy Awards ceremony, better known as the 'Oscars'. In March every year, actors and actresses still [6] *wait / are waiting* nervously to find out if they have won an award.

Nowadays it [7] *becomes / is becoming* more and more common for films to be made away from Hollywood, but it [8] *remains / is remaining* the home of film, and also broken dreams. As one actress said: 'Hollywood is a place where they [9] *pay / are paying* $500 for a kiss, and 50 cents for your soul.'

REMEMBER THESE WORDS

PEOPLE AROUND YOU

an acquaintance	grandparents
a best friend	a half-brother
a boss	a mother-in-law
a classmate	a neighbour
a colleague	a niece
a cousin	an old school friend
an employee	an older sister
an ex-girlfriend	a relative
a flatmate	a stepmother
a grandchild	a stranger

EVERYDAY ACTIVITIES

chatting to friends and colleagues	going to the gym
commuting	hanging out with friends
doing nothing	looking after children
doing paperwork	playing video games
doing the ironing	putting on make-up
doing your hair	relaxing
going on social networking sites	texting
going shopping	tidying up

OTHER

to apply for a course	to multitask
to be home for the holidays	productive
a digital native	to pull a face
to exercise intensively	a social worker
grumpy	to spend time + -ing
I'm really into ...	to train to be a doctor
an internet addict	to waste time + -ing

PRACTICE

1 Replace the underlined phrases with a word or phrase that has the same meaning.

She's my big sister. *older sister*

1 She's my girlfriend from the past. We're not together now.
2 She's my father's new wife.
3 He's not someone that I know.
4 She's my sister's daughter.
5 He's my husband's father.
6 She's my manager.
7 He's my friend I share a flat with.
8 He's someone who works in the company I own.
9 She's my aunt's daughter.
10 He's someone who lives in the house next to mine.
11 She's someone in my English class.
12 He's someone in my family.

2 Complete the sentences with a suitable verb in the correct form.

1 Where do you _____ out with your friends?
2 You look fit. Have you been _____ to the gym?
3 I spend two hours a day _____ to and from work.
4 I spent last night _____ paperwork.
5 How long does it take her to _____ on her make-up and _____ her hair?
6 Who _____ after your children when you go out?
7 Sometimes I like to stay at home and _____ nothing at the weekend.
8 Could you please _____ up your room? It's a real mess.
9 Come round, I'm really bored – I'm _____ the ironing.
10 My children spend too much time _____ video games.
11 I've had such a busy week, I just want to _____ this weekend.
12 Our boss has told us to stop _____ on social networking sites at work.

STUDY TIPS

Using English in class

1 Which statement best describes you? (Be honest!)

a I try to use English in class all the time, even when it's very difficult for me. ☐
b I try to use English in class when I remember. ☐
c I'm a bit lazy and let other people do the talking! ☐

2 Which of these things do/don't you normally do?

a Ask your teacher questions in English rather than in your own language.
b Try to understand the teacher's explanations in English rather than asking for translations.
c Speak as much as you can during pair and group work.
d Answer as many questions as you can, even if you are not sure of the answer.
e Use a monolingual dictionary.
f Explain things to your partner or group in English.

3 Why are the tips in exercise 2 useful? Choose two which you don't normally do. Copy them onto a piece of paper and stick it on the cover of your book so that you read it every lesson!

4 On page 7, you learnt eight useful classroom questions. How many can you remember? Test yourself, then check your answers in audio script 1.3 on page 168.

STUDY 1

Past simple and Past continuous

1 Past simple

+	I/You/He/She/It/We/They **worked**.
	I/You/He/She/It/We/They **left**.
	Regular verbs: base form + **-ed**
	Irregular verbs: see list of irregular verbs on page 175.
−	I/You/He/She/It/We/They **didn't work**.
	I/You/He/She/It/We/They **didn't** (= **did not**) **leave**.
	Regular and irregular verbs: subject + **didn't** (= **did not**) + base form
?	**Did** I/you/he/she/it/we/they **work**?
	Did I/you/he/she/it/we/they **leave**?
	Regular and irregular verbs: did + subject + base form

- We use the Past simple for states and actions which happened in the past. We often say **when** the action happened.
  *I **saw** someone famous **yesterday**.*
- The action can be short or long, single or repeated.
  *I **dropped** the glass and it **broke** on the floor.*
  *He **took** the train to work **every day**.*
- We also use the Past simple to talk about states in the past.
  *When I **was** young, I **loved** playing with my toys.*

2 Past continuous

+	I/He/She/It **was working**.
	You/We/They **were working**.
−	I/He/She/It **wasn't working**.
	You/We/They **weren't** (= **were not**) **working**.
?	**Was** I/he/she/it **working**?
	Were you/we/they **working**?

- We use the Past continuous for actions in progress at a time in the past.
  *I **was living** in London then.*
- Sometimes this includes a specific time or another (completed) past action.
  *We **were having** breakfast at 8 o'clock.*
  *I **heard** the news on the radio while I **was driving** home.*
- The Past continuous often describes the situation or the background to a story. We use the Past simple for the main events.
  *The sun **was shining** and I **was walking** along the road. Suddenly, someone **shouted** to me ...*

- Sometimes the Past continuous action is interrupted.
  *They **were talking** about me when I **walked** in the room, then they stopped.*
- We use the Past continuous for actions we see as incomplete.
  *I **read** a book about Italy on the plane.* (= I read it all)
  *I **was reading** a book about Italy on the plane.* (= I probably didn't read it all)
- The Past continuous has the same characteristics as other continuous forms.
  – Continuous forms describe activities in progress.
    *He's **reading** the newspaper.* (= he's in the middle of it)
    *He was **reading** the newspaper.* (= he was in the middle of it)
  – We use continuous forms to emphasise that situations are temporary.
    *She's **staying** with us at the moment.* (= temporary in the present)
    *I **was sleeping** on a friend's sofa.* (= temporary in the past)
  – We do not use continuous forms with state verbs.
    *I **hated** vegetables when I was young.*
    NOT *I was hating vegetables when I was young.*

PRACTICE 1

1 Match the Past simple sentences in A with the uses in B.

A
1 He put the money on the table.
2 They got back from holiday last night.
3 I often walked to school as a child.
4 It rained for three days without stopping.
5 I felt very homesick at first.

B
a an action which happened at a specific time
b a state
c a short, single action in the past
d a repeated action in the past
e a long action in the past

2 Which verbs are not correct in the Past continuous? Write the correct Past simple form.

1 At 7.30 a.m. I was having breakfast in the kitchen.
2 It was raining hard when we were arriving at the station.
3 I was sitting at home when the doorbell was ringing.
4 We were having such a great time we weren't wanting to go home.
5 I was driving home when I was hearing the news on the radio.
6 At the age of 18, I was liking all kinds of sports.

3 Complete the sentences with the Past simple or Past continuous form of the verb in brackets.

1 The last time I _____ (see) them, they _____ (play) football in the park.
2 I couldn't sleep because my neighbours _____ (argue) very loudly last night.
3 When I _____ (walk) in the room, everyone _____ (stop) talking.
4 The exam _____ (last) nearly three hours.

4 Match the sentence halves. Then write out the sentences, putting the verb in brackets in the correct past form.

A

1 My sister (break) her leg while ...
2 I (meet) my best friend when ...
3 The sun (shine) when ...
4 It (rain) this morning so ...
5 The police (stop) him because ...

B

a my husband (give) me a lift to work.
b he (drive) too fast.
c I (wake up) this morning.
d we (both work) in a sandwich bar.
e she (ski).

STUDY 2

Contrasting past and present

1 *used to* and *would*

+	I/You/He/She/It/We/They **used to work.**
	I/You/He/She/It/We/They **would work.**
–	I/You/He/She/It/We/They **didn't use to work.**
	I/You/He/She/It/We/They **wouldn't work.**
?	**Did** I/you/he/she/it/we/they **use to work?**
	Would I/you/he/she/it/we/they **work?**

• We use *used to* and *would* for habits in the past.
*I **would go** to the gym every day.*
*My sister **used to have** really long hair.*
There is no equivalent form of *used to* or *would* in the present.
*I **usually go** to my parents' house on Sundays.*
NOT *I use to go to my parents' house on Sundays.*
• *Would* is common when we are telling a story or remembering an event.
*Those were the best years of my life. I **would spend** all day on the beach and **go out** every night.*
• For states in the past, we only use *used to*, not *would*.
*I **used to live** in Dubai.*
NOT *I would live in Dubai.*
• We can always use the Past simple instead of *used to* or *would*.
*I **went** to the gym every day.*
*My sister **had** really long hair.*

2 *not ... any longer / not ... anymore*

These phrases mean that an action or state was true in the past, but is not true now.
*I used to play volleyball every Friday, but I **don't any longer**.*
*Andrew **doesn't** drink coffee **anymore** – it gives him a headache.*

3 *still*

We use *still* when we want to emphasise that an action or state has not stopped or changed, but continues up to the present.
*I **still** remember how frightened I was.*

1 Cross out the forms that are not possible or not correct.

1 I *believed* / *used to believe* / *would believe* in ghosts when I was young.
2 *Did you would* / *Did you use to* / *Did you* get into trouble a lot when you were a child?
3 Our parents *use to encourage* / *encouraged* / *would encourage* us to try new sports and activities.
4 She was a difficult child. She *didn't would do* / *didn't use to do* / *didn't do* what she was told.
5 *Would you* / *Did you* / *Did you use to* like eating sweets when you were a child?

2 Complete the sentences with the words in the box.

any   more   still   use   used

1 We _____ to have such a lot of fun when we went out together.
2 I didn't _____ to like Thai food, but I do now.
3 Mr Franks doesn't work here _____ longer.
4 Once there was a huge factory here, but there isn't any _____ .
5 There are _____ some beautiful old buildings in the town centre.

3 Put the words in the correct order to make sentences.

1 time / spend / I / used / playing video games / a lot of / to
_____
2 any exercise / to / never / as a / do / Ali / used / child
_____
3 to / use / did / in art / interested / Phil / be ?
_____
4 any / it / to / quiet here / but / it / be / isn't / longer / used
_____
5 didn't / to / have / relax / use / to / enough time / I
_____
6 on / use / where / you / to / go / holiday / did ?
_____
7 used / any / to / a beard / he / but / he / have / doesn't / more
_____
8 I / frightened of spiders / am / I / be / and / used / to / still
_____

REMEMBER THESE WORDS

CHILDHOOD AND UPBRINGING

to argue	to give someone confidence
ashamed	pocket money
to behave badly	to praise
to criticise	to punish
to encourage	to respect
to get angry	strict
to get into trouble	to tell off

REMEMBERING AND FORGETTING

to remember
– meeting someone for the
  first time
– a person / a word /
  an appointment
– to phone someone
– when something happened

to remind
– someone about a message
– someone of another person
– someone to phone you

to forget
– about something
– a birthday, a message,
  an appointment, etc.
– to do something
– that you did something

to recognise
– a piece of music, a painting, etc.
– someone / someone's face

TELLING A STORY

after a while	in the end
eventually	suddenly

OTHER

accurate	to get tangled
to be tame	lack of (sleep)
the brain	memory
a branch	oxygen
caffeine	(a piece of) research
challenging	to rescue
to concentrate	scientific
emotional	to store something
to fall off	a swing
to float	

PRACTICE

1 Choose the words and phrases that could complete each sentence. There may be more than one possible answer.

1 My parents were very strict, but I still _____ .
    a) got into trouble   b) respected them
    c) behaved badly

2 I think teachers should _____ children and not criticise them.
    a) argue   b) praise   c) encourage

3 How much _____ did your parents give you?
    a) confidence   b) pocket money   c) strict

4 When your parents told you off, did you feel _____ ?
    a) badly   b) angry   c) ashamed

5 Her parents weren't strict at all. They never _____ her.
    a) punished   b) got into trouble   c) got angry

2 Choose the correct answer(s).

1 Did you *forget* / *remind* / *remember* to phone your sister?

2 Florence always *recognises* / *reminds* / *remembers* me of her father.

3 I'm trying to *forget* / *remember* / *remind* the words of the song by heart.

4 I didn't *forget* / *recognise* / *remind* her – she's really changed!

5 I can't *remember* / *forget* / *remind* where I left my glasses.

6 I *remind* / *recognise* / *remember* the painting, but I don't know the name of the artist.

7 I feel terrible – I totally *remembered* / *forgot* / *recognised* about Jennifer's birthday last week!

8 Please *forget* / *remember* / *remind* me to call Jing before I leave the office tonight.

9 I can't *remember* / *forget* / *recognise* seeing her before, but apparently we met at Max's party a few months ago.

10 Don't *remember* / *forget* / *remind* the lesson is cancelled next week, so I'll see you in two weeks' time.

STUDY TIPS

Remember new words

1 If you actively study 'Remember these words' when you finish each unit of this book, it will help to improve your vocabulary. Tick the tips that you already follow.

1 Check that you remember what each word or phrase means. You can use a monolingual English dictionary, a good bilingual dictionary or ask your teacher. ☐

2 Listen to the words and practise saying them. ☐

3 Record yourself saying the words and phrases. ☐

4 Underline the stressed syllable in the new words like this: re<u>mem</u>ber ☐

5 Write sentences using the words and phrases to help you remember them. ☐

6 Write a translation next to the phrases, but make sure it is correct. ☐

7 Cover up your translations and test yourself to see if you can remember the meaning. ☐

8 Cover the English words and see if you can remember them, using your translations as prompts. (Divide the list into sections of ten or 15 words and study one each day, to make this task more manageable.) ☐

9 Select ten words that you really want to remember. Write them on a mini-poster and stick it on your wall. ☐

10 Ask another student or a friend to test you on the words. ☐

2 Now highlight the things that you would like to try. Compare your answers with other students.

STUDY 1

Comparative and superlative adjectives

1 One-syllable adjectives and two-syllable adjectives ending in -y

Adjective	Comparative adjective + -er	Superlative the + adjective + -est
old	older	the oldest
big	bigger	the biggest
large	larger	the largest
friendly	friendlier	the friendliest

2 Other two-syllable adjectives and longer adjectives

crowded	more crowded	the most crowded
boring	more boring	the most boring
interesting	more interesting	the most interesting
polluted	more polluted	the most polluted

3 Irregular forms

bad	worse	the worst
good	better	the best
far	further	the furthest

REMEMBER!

- With short vowels we double the final consonant.
  thin → thinner → the thinnest
- If the adjective ends in -e, we only add -r or -st.
  fine → finer → the finest
- -y changes to -ier and -iest.
  busy → busier → the busiest

4 Big and small differences

If there is a large difference between two objects, we can use *much* and *a lot*.

Russia is	a lot	bigger than Belgium.
	much	

For small differences, we can use *a little* (*bit*) or *slightly*.

France is	a little	bigger than Spain.
	a little bit	
	slightly	

5 Common phrases with superlatives

- *by far the most ... / -est*
  Brazil is **by far the largest** country in South America.
- *one of the most ... / -est*
  Baghdad is **one of the oldest cities** in the world.
- *the second/third most ... / -est*
  Birmingham is **the second biggest** city in England.
- *the least*
  The coach is **the least expensive** way to get to the airport.

REMEMBER!

These superlative phrases are often followed by *in* + place.
Buenos Aires is the biggest city in Argentina.

PRACTICE 1

1 Rewrite the sentences so that they have the opposite meaning. Use the adjectives in brackets.

It's the most polluted place I know. (clean)
It's the cleanest place I know.

1 The bus stop is nearer than the station. (far)
2 It's the cleanest part of the city. (dirty)
3 The traffic's better than I expected. (bad)
4 It's the most interesting museum I know. (boring)
5 Trains are more expensive than buses here. (cheap)
6 He parked in the nearest car park from here. (far)
7 It's the most enormous beach I've ever seen. (tiny)
8 It's the best restaurant I know. (bad)
9 It's colder in the south of the country. (hot)
10 The north of the island is prettier than the south. (ugly)

2 Rewrite the incorrect sentences to make them correct.

China is slightly bigger than the UK.
China is a lot bigger than the UK.

1 New Zealand is slightly smaller than Australia.
2 London is much further north than Paris.
3 Cairo is slightly hotter than Moscow.
4 France is a bit larger than Spain.
5 Hong Kong is slightly more populated than Canada.
6 Chile is much narrower than Argentina.
7 Brazil is slightly larger than the USA.

3 Complete the sentences with the words in the box. Use each word once.

one   more   lot   slightly   of   second   least   in (x2)
little

1 Michael is _____ of the best young musicians _____ the country.
2 Surprisingly, the ticket is only _____ more expensive if you travel first class.
3 Since they moved house, Mark and Melanie have been a _____ happier.
4 Tomorrow's weather will be a _____ bit cooler than today's.
5 All the restaurants around here are expensive, but I chose the _____ expensive one.
6 Marianne is much _____ relaxed since her holiday.
7 Melbourne is the _____ biggest city _____ Australia.
8 Andy is one _____ the nicest people I know.

4 Choose the correct answers.

1 *The baddest / By far worst / By far the worst* earthquake of all time happened in Chile in 1960.
2 The World Financial Centre in Shanghai is *one of tallest / tallest / one of the tallest* buildings in the world.
3 Mount Wycheproof is *smaller / by far smaller / by far the smallest* mountain in the world.
4 India is *the second more populated / second most populated / the second most populated* country in the world.
5 Antarctica is *least populated / the less populated / the least populated* continent in the world.

STUDY 2

Different ways of comparing

* *not as ... as*
  Silver **isn't as** expensive **as** gold.
* Comparing two things which are the same:
  Susan is **as tall as** her mother.
* *less* and *fewer*
  Less and fewer are the opposite of *more*. Use *less* with adjectives and uncountable nouns. Use *fewer* with countable nouns.
  Petrol is **less expensive than** it is in Europe.
  You should spend **less money** on going out.
  Fewer people went to the match than we expected.
* Other useful expressions for comparing things:
  – if two things are nearly the same.
    Their new car is **very similar** to their old one.
    The train times are **about the same as** before.
  – if there is no difference between two things.
    His watch is **exactly the same as** mine.
  – if there is a small difference between two things.
    The new timetable is **slightly different from** the previous one.
  – if there is a big difference between two things.
    The new stadium is **completely different from** the old one.

PRACTICE 2

1 Choose the correct answers.

1 A 'big' city is *exactly the same as / similar to* a 'large' city.
2 A 'boss' is *different from / about the same as* a 'manager'.
3 A 'modern' building is *completely different from / slightly different from* an 'old-fashioned' building.
4 A 'town' is *as big as / not as big as* a 'city'.
5 A 'stranger' is *slightly different from / very different from* a 'friend'.

2 Replace the word that is crossed out with the correct word.

Matt is not as intelligent ~~like~~ his sister.   *as*

1 People seem to have ~~fewer~~ time than they used to.
2 Ukraine is the biggest country ~~of~~ Europe.
3 Nadia is very different ~~of~~ her sister.
4 Your T-shirt is the same ~~like~~ mine.
5 Life here is ~~least~~ expensive than in the city.
6 Alexis is the ~~worse~~ driver I know.
7 There are ~~less~~ students in this class than in my other class.
8 Their car is ~~exact~~ the same as ours.
9 Ali looks very similar ~~with~~ his cousin.
10 The new house looks very different ~~than~~ the old one.
11 It's much colder here in winter ~~as~~ in summer.
12 Oliver lives ~~far~~ from university than Claudia.

REMEMBER THESE WORDS

FEATURES AND SIGHTS

ancient ruins	an island
a bay	a lake
a (sandy) beach	a market
a bridge	a (historic) monument
a canal	a mosque
a cathedral	a museum
a cliff	a palace
docks	a shopping mall
a factory	a skyscraper
farmland	a temple
a festival	a view
a (rain)forest	a village
a harbour	a waterfall
a hill	

ADJECTIVES FOR DESCRIBING PLACES

arty	lively
colourful	modern
cosmopolitan	old-fashioned
crowded	peaceful
dangerous	polluted
dirty	poor
expensive	romantic
friendly	smart
historic	spectacular
industrial	touristy

OTHER

it's famous for (its beaches/shops, etc.)	it's worth (seeing/
it's in the north / it's on the coast	visiting, etc.)

PRACTICE

1 Choose the odd one out in each group.

1	bridge	canal	lake	waterfall
2	cathedral	mosque	palace	temple
3	bay	cliff	beach	docks
4	apartment block	ancient ruins	shopping mall	
	skyscraper			

2 Cover the word list. Write the adjective form of these nouns to describe a place.

romance   *romantic*

1 colour   _____
2 peace   _____
3 tourist   _____
4 art   _____
5 history   _____
6 crowd   _____
7 pollution   _____
8 industry   _____

3 Match the sentence halves.

A
1 There's an industrial
2 Some of the views are
3 The city has a very
4 The market gets
5 The local people are
6 There are some very modern

B
a crowded at weekends.
b spectacular.
c skyscrapers in the centre.
d area just outside the city.
e lively atmosphere.
f usually friendly.

4 Cover the word list and choose the correct answers.

1 The old town is worth *see / seeing / to see*.
2 The ruins are *in / on / at* the north of the country.
3 Paris is *in / on / at* the River Seine.
4 Dubai is famous *about / of / for* its shops.

STUDY TIPS

Make the most of speaking tasks

1 The tasks in Cutting Edge are designed to improve your speaking, but it is important to work actively in these lessons. Tick the tips that you already follow.

1 Before doing the task, spend a few minutes thinking about what you are going to say and how you're going to say it. ☐
2 You can make some short notes to help you, but don't write out every word! ☐
3 If you can, use language you already know, but if you really need any new words, ask your teacher. ☐
4 Look at the Useful language box and see if there are any phrases that you could use. (You do not need to use all or most of these phrases, though – they are just there to use if you need them.) ☐
5 Before you start, practise 'saying it in your head' or whispering it to yourself so that you feel more confident. ☐
6 Concentrate on expressing what you want to say and don't worry about making mistakes! Everyone makes mistakes when they are learning a language – it's how you learn. ☐
7 Listen to and be supportive of other students. Remember, they may feel nervous about speaking in English, too! ☐

2 Highlight the tips that you think will most help to improve your speaking. Compare your answers with other students.

STUDY 1

Present perfect simple and Past simple

+	I/You/We/They**'ve** (= **have**) worked.
	He/She/It**'s** (= **has**) worked.
	subject + have/has + past participle
−	I/You/We/They **haven't** (= **have not**) worked.
	He/She/It **hasn't** (= **has not**) worked.
	subject + haven't/hasn't + past participle
?	**Have** I/you/we/they **worked**?
	Has he/she/it **worked**?
	Have/Has + subject + **past participle**

1 Uses of the Present perfect simple

We use the Present perfect to talk about the relationship between **the past and the present**. The past action or situation is connected to the present in various ways.

* The state or action continues from the past to the present.
  I've known her for many years. (= I still know her now)
* The results of the past action are relevant in the present.
  He's lost his key. (= he doesn't have it now)
* The action takes place in a present time period.
  He's been ill all this week. (= this week isn't finished)
* When we mean 'in my whole life', we do not give a specific time.
  I've been to Spain lots of times. (= in my whole life)

2 Present perfect simple versus Past simple

* We use the Past simple for actions that happened in past time periods which are now finished or completed. Compare these Present perfect and Past simple sentences.
  Marilyn Monroe was married three times.
  (= during her life, now she is dead)
  My friend has been married three times, and she's only 30!
  (= her life is not finished)
  As a child, I spent a lot of time with my grandparents.
  (= I am no longer a child)
  I've spent a lot of time abroad this year.
  (= this year is not finished)
* Whether or not we use the Present perfect or Past simple often depends on **how we see the action**. If we see it as related to the present, we use the Present perfect.
  John's had an accident. They've taken him to hospital!
  If we see it as finished and in the past, we use the Past simple, even if we do not mention the time.
  John had an accident, but he's OK now.

3 Time words with the Present perfect and Past simple

* Time phrases often found with the Past simple:
  – *ago*: *five minutes ago, three months ago, a thousand years ago*
  – questions with *when*: **When** did you see him?
  – specific times in the past: *yesterday, last night, last week, in 1999*
  – narrative time phrases like *then, after that, in the end*
* Time phrases often found with the Present perfect:
  – periods of time which are still in progress: *all my life, this week, this year, so far*
  – *for* and *since*
  – *ever* (= any time in the past before now)
    Have you **ever met** anyone famous?
  – *already, yet* (= before now)

REMEMBER!

We use *yet* in questions and negatives to talk about actions that haven't happened in the past but we think could happen in the future.
Maria hasn't phoned. (= and maybe she won't)
Maria hasn't phoned yet. (= but she probably will later)

* Many time phrases can occur with either the Present perfect or the Past simple, according to the context.
  I've spoken to Robert this morning. (= it's still the morning)
  I spoke to Robert this morning. (= it's afternoon/evening now)
  He's been in prison for many years. (= he's still in prison now)
  He was in prison for many years. (= he is not in prison now)
  I've never been to China. (= in my life until now)
  I never met my grandfather. (= he's dead now)

PRACTICE 1

1 What are the Past simple and Past participle forms of these regular and irregular verbs?

		Past simple	Past participle
1	achieve	_____	_____
2	build	_____	_____
3	bring	_____	_____
4	choose	_____	_____
5	design	_____	_____
6	hear	_____	_____
7	inspire	_____	_____
8	produce	_____	_____
9	read	_____	_____
10	teach	_____	_____
11	think	_____	_____
12	win	_____	_____

2 Look at the irregular verb list on page 175. Cover the Past simple and Past participle forms and test yourself or a partner.

3 Complete the texts with the correct Present perfect or Past simple form of the verb in brackets.

1 In 1965, Paul McCartney _____ (write) the most popular song of all time, 'Yesterday'. Since then, there _____ (be) over 2,500 cover versions.

2 Since he _____ (die) in 1977, Elvis Presley _____ (have) 31 hit singles. During his lifetime, he _____ (produce) over 60 hits, including 18 number ones.

3 Jack Nicholson _____ (have) one of the longest careers in Hollywood – he _____ (work) in the film industry for more than 50 years. Over his career, he _____ (receive) more award nominations than any other actor, and he _____ (win) three Oscars. He _____ (win) Best Actor Award in 1975 and 1997 and he _____ (receive) the Best Supporting Actor Award in 1983.

4 Which movie _____ (be) the most successful of all time? It is difficult to say. *Avatar* _____ (make) the most money since it _____ (appear) in 2009, but it only _____ (win) three Oscars. *Titanic*, which _____ (come) out in 1997, _____ (win) 11 Oscars, and it _____ (make) nearly $2 billion since its release.

STUDY 2

Present perfect continuous

+	I/You/We/They**'ve been** (= **have been**) **working.**	
	He/She/It**'s been** (= **has been**) **working.**	
	subject + **have/has** + **been** + **-ing**	
–	I/You/We/They **haven't been** (= **have not been**) **working.**	
	He/She/It **hasn't** (= **has not been**) **working.**	
	subject + **haven't/hasn't** + **been** + **-ing**	
?	**Have** I/You/We/They **been working?**	
	Has he/she/it **been working?**	
	Have/Has + subject + **been** + **-ing**	

1 Uses of the Present perfect continuous

The Present perfect continuous is like the Present perfect simple in all the ways mentioned in section 1 on page 141. However, we use the Present perfect continuous if:

• we want to emphasise that the action is long or repeated.
  She's **been trying** to pass her driving test for years.
  (Notice that we often use *for* and *since* with the Present perfect continuous.)

• the action is in progress / not complete.
  I've **been doing** my homework. (= perhaps it is not finished)
  I've **done** my homework. (= it is finished)

• we are more interested in the activity than the result.
  I'm really hot – I've **been running.** (the activity that made me hot)
  I've just **run** ten kilometres. (that's what I have achieved)

REMEMBER!

• If we say how often the action happened, we always use the Present perfect simple, because the focus is on the result.
  I've **written** ten / lots of emails today.
  NOT I've been writing ten emails.

• Like other continuous forms, we do not use the Present perfect continuous with 'state' verbs.
  I've **known** Anne for years.
  NOT I've been knowing Anne for years.

2 *for*, *since* and *how long?*

• We use *for* with periods of time.
  I've been learning to drive **for three months.**

• We use *since* with points in time.
  I've lived in this house since **2007 / I was born.**

• Sentences with *for* and *since* answer the question *How long?*
  How long have you been learning to drive?

PRACTICE 2

1 Write the phrases in the correct column.

~~five minutes~~   ages and ages   6 o'clock   months
2009   I was born   30 years   ten seconds
last summer   three weeks

for	since
five minutes	

2 Choose the best answers. Can you explain your decisions?

1 I've **finished / been finishing my essay** and I've **emailed / been emailing** it to my teacher.

2 My cousin has **stayed / been staying** with us for a few weeks.

3 I'm exhausted. I've **worked / been working** really hard since 6 o'clock this morning.

4 I'm really pleased with myself – I've **written / been writing** ten pages of that report today.

5 Why don't we stop and have a coffee? You've **driven / been driving** for ages.

6 A: I like your dress!
  B: Oh, thanks, I've **had / been having** it for ages.

7 We've **gone / been going** to the same hotel for the last five years – we love it!

8 The children have **made / been making** loads of biscuits. Would you like to take some home with you?

REMEMBER THESE WORDS

LIFE EVENTS

to bring up your children	to have children
to change job	to leave home
to fall in love	to lose your job
to get a job	to make a lot of money
to get a promotion	to move house
to get divorced	to pass/fail your exams
to get engaged	to quit your job
to get married	to rent or buy a house
to go to university	to retire
to graduate	to start/leave school

PERSONAL QUALITIES

charming	inspiring
courageous	obsessive
creative	original
dedicated	ruthless
determined	self-confident
egotistical	talented

OTHER WORDS AND PHRASES

to achieve	to have strong principles
to admire	to hit
to be a strong leader	to inspire
to beat	publicity
to care about other people	a racket
to chase	respect
a court	a role model
to deserve	to win an award
to do a lot for	to yell

PRACTICE

1 Match the sentence halves.

A		B	
1	They fell	a	engaged.
2	He cares	b	with a degree in chemistry.
3	My brother has just got	c	house.
4	She's passed	d	a lovely apartment
5	The company has made	e	in love.
6	Do you want to get	f	your job?
7	Her parents are getting	g	principles.
8	He's got strong	h	my apartment last week.
9	My aunt brought me	i	her exams.
10	We've just moved	j	divorced next year.
11	She graduated	k	about me.
12	I left	l	a lot of money.
13	Why did you quit	m	model for children.
14	We're renting	n	up.
15	He's a good role	o	married?

2 Use a dictionary to complete the tables.

Verb	Noun	Adjective
to admire		
to inspire		
	respect	

Adjective	Noun
charming	
courageous	
determined	
dedicated	
self-confident	
talented	

3 Choose the best answers.

1 A: Why do you *admire* / *inspire* / *award* her?
   B: Because she's so courageous.
2 A: Why did you yell at him?
   B: Because he *achieved* / *beat* / *deserved* it.
3 A: Is she famous?
   B: Yes, she is. She's *respected* / *achieved* / *won* lots of awards.
4 A: Why do you think he's lazy?
   B: He's a professional footballer but he doesn't *achieve* / *chase* / *beat* the ball.
5 A: Tell me why you admire her.
   B: Because she *respects* / *does a lot* / *deserves* for the poor and the elderly.
6 A: He's really happy.
   B: Did he *win* / *get* / *find* a promotion at work?

STUDY TIPS

Read the grammar summaries actively

1 When you read grammar summaries in your coursebook, it is important to check what you don't understand. Tick the tips below that you already follow.

1 Think of your own example for each rule.	☐
2 Highlight the grammar rules that are different in your language.	☐
4 Ask your teacher to explain rules that you don't understand.	☐
3 Reread the grammar summary before a test to remind yourself of the rules.	☐
5 Check the summaries again when you make mistakes in a test.	☐

2 Work in pairs. Which ideas from exercise 1 might you use in the future? Tell your partner and explain why.

STUDY 1

Future forms for plans and intentions

1 *going to*

	am/is/are + going to + verb
+	I**'m**/You**'re**/He**'s**/She**'s**/It**'s**/We**'re**/They**'re** going to help.
–	I**'m not**/You **aren't**/He **isn't**/She **isn't**/It **isn't**/We **aren't**/They **aren't** going to help.
?	**Am** I/**Are** you/**Is** he/**Is** she/**Is** it/**Are** we/**Are** they going to help?

We use *going to* to talk about present intentions about the future. This can be the near future or the more distant future.
I'm going to have a bath in a few minutes. (= the near future)
Lucy says she's going to be a ballet dancer one day.
(= the distant future)

2 Present continuous

- We use the Present continuous to talk about things we have already arranged for the future.
I'm meeting Tony this weekend. (= I've arranged this)
What are you doing tonight? (= asking about your plans)
- In some cases, it doesn't matter whether we use the Present continuous or *going to*.
I'm playing football this evening.
I'm going to play football this evening.
I'm going shopping this afternoon.
I'm going (to go)* shopping this afternoon.
- In other cases, there is a clear difference in meaning.
We're going to get married one day. (= an intention)
We're getting married soon. (= the wedding is arranged)

3 *will*

+	I/You/He/She/It/We/They**'ll** (= will) + verb
	I**'ll see** her.
–	I/You/He/She/It/We/They **won't** (= will not) + verb
	I **won't see** her.
?	**Will** I/you/he/she/it/we they + verb?
	Will I **see** her?

We use *will* for talking about things that we think will happen **without** any special plan or arrangement. We predict they will happen or see them as a future fact.
I can give it to her – I'll see her at work.
(= I don't need to arrange this)
I know I'll forget if I don't write it down.
(= this is a future fact / I predict this will happen)

* Some people think it is bad English to repeat *go* like this.

REMEMBER!

We can use *shall* with *I* and *we*. We normally use this in the question form to make offers or suggestions.

Compare the following pairs of sentences.
Will I meet you at the station? (= asking about a future fact)
Shall I meet you at the station? (= an offer)

Will we have dinner at the hotel? (= asking about a future fact)
Shall we have dinner at the hotel? (= a suggestion)

4 Other ways to talk about the future

VERBS
- *hope*: *We're hoping to buy a flat later this year.*
- *plan*: *I'm planning to sell my scooter.*
- *think*: *We're thinking of having a party soon.*

PHRASES
- *due to:* We use *due to* for something that is formally arranged.
The plane's due to take off in about 20 minutes.
- *(be) about to:* when something will happen very soon or immediately.
Gemma's about to have a baby.

PRACTICE 1

1 Choose the correct meaning a–c.

1 I'm going to think about it.
   a a present intention about the future
   b a future prediction
   c a future definite arrangement
2 She'll be 25 next month.
   a a future prediction
   b a future fact
   c a present intention about the future
3 We're taking the train to Vancouver.
   a a present intention about the future
   b a future definite arrangement
   c a future prediction
4 I'll probably work for my father.
   a a present intention about the future
   b a future fact
   c a future prediction
5 I'm seeing my doctor on Thursday.
   a a future definite arrangement
   b a future fact
   c a present intention about the future
6 We're going to try and find a new flat.
   a a future prediction
   b a present intention about the future
   c a future definite arrangement
7 Your books will be delivered on Thursday.
   a a present intention about the future
   b a future definite arrangement
   c a future fact

2 Choose the best verb form in the context.

1 Sorry but I'm busy this afternoon – *I'll meet / I'm meeting* my new boss.
2 I'm really tired. *I'm going to have / I'll have* an early night tonight.
3 You should try that new Italian restaurant – I'm sure *you'll like it / you're liking it*.
4 We haven't got much money at the moment, so we've decided *we won't have / we're not going to have* a holiday this year.
5 Hannah and Tom are a great couple. I think *they'll get married one day / they're getting married one day*.

3 Correct the word that has been crossed out in these sentences. You may need to add an extra word.

1 The course is due ~~starting~~ in September.
2 Are you ~~plan~~ to take your holidays soon?
3 We're thinking of ~~go~~ to Greece for our holidays this year.
4 Olivia is about ~~start~~ her exams.
5 We're hoping ~~buy~~ a new car this year.

4 Use the prompts to make future sentences.

1 I / plan / study engineering.
2 My sister / think / join the army.
3 I / due / take my driving test next week.
4 Alex says he / not going / apply to university.
5 I know I / will not / get the job.
6 My boss / about / retire.
7 I / probably / will not / see you before next week.

STUDY 2

Future clauses with *if, when, unless*, etc.

Even when we are talking about the future, we use a present verb form after *if, unless, when, before, after, as soon as, until, once, next time*, etc.
*If she **fails** her exam again, she'll be really upset.*
*I won't do anything **unless** you **phone**.*
***When** I **find** it, I'll bring it for you.*
*Remember to turn off the lights **before** you **leave**.*
***As soon as** we **get** home, I'm going to have a shower.*
*I'm going to stay here **until** I **find** somewhere to live.*
***Once** we **finish** the decorating, we'll invite you round for dinner.*
Notice that in the other part of the sentence, a future verb form is used (*will, going to*, etc.).

1 Complete the sentences with the words in the box.

as soon as   before   if   until   unless

1 She'll be delighted _____ she gets the job.
2 I want to finish my homework _____ I go out.
3 _____ he gets home, I'll tell him the good news.
4 We're going cycling, _____ it rains of course!
5 I'm not having driving lessons _____ after my exams finish.

2 Choose the best answers.

1 You should stop taking the tablets immediately *if / when / unless* they make you feel sick.
2 Can I borrow your book *if / when / until* you finish it?
3 Sarah is going on holiday for a week *after / as soon as / before* she starts her exams.
4 Come on! We'll be late *if / unless / when* you hurry up!
5 You'll feel better *after / before / until* you have a rest.
6 Go straight on *until / if / unless* you get to the traffic lights. Then you'll see the bank on your left.
7 Jim will earn a bigger salary *when / unless / until* he gets promoted.
8 I'll text you *unless / until / as soon as* I hear any news about Linda.
9 *When / If / Unless* it rains tomorrow, I don't think we should go to the beach.
10 What are you planning to do *after / if / unless* the lesson ends?

3 Cross out the ending that cannot complete the sentence.

1 I'll phone David as soon as *I get home / I will get home / I can*.
2 If I go to university, *I won't live at home / I don't live at home / I won't be able to live at home*.
3 Can you text me before *6 o'clock / you will leave / you leave*.
4 We'll have a barbeque *if it doesn't rain / unless it rains / unless it will rain*.
5 When the baby's born, *they move house / they'll move house / they'll have to move house*.
6 I'll leave my job if *I find another one / I will find another one / I can find another one*.

4 Complete the conversations with the correct form the verb in brackets.

1 **A:** Hello, Martine. I need to speak to Greg.
   B: Hi, Jane. I _____ (ask) him to call you as soon as he _____ (get) back.
2 **A:** Can you call me when the taxi _____ (arrive)?
   B: Sure.
3 **A:** I'm really nervous about my driving test.
   B: Don't worry. I'm sure you _____ (pass) if you just _____ (remember) everything I told you.
4 **A:** _____ (you / visit) Carrie when you _____ (be) in London?
   B: I hope so.

REMEMBER THESE WORDS

WORD FAMILIES

a distraction	knowledge
an experience	productive
a failure	profitable
imagination	a success
improvement	

WORK

badly paid	qualifications
challenging	responsibility
competitive	secure
creative	special training
good communication skills	stressful
good with money/numbers	well-organised
opportunities (to travel)	well-paid
physically fit	to work long hours

OTHER

ambitious	to have experience
assertive	to have potential
business sense	to make decisions
a candidate	maternity leave
clear thinking	to run a course
to deal with a problem	a strength
determined	to take responsibility
disciplined	talent
to enrol for a course	to volunteer
an executive	a weakness
focused	to work for a charity
to get promotion	to work well in a team
hardworking	

PRACTICE

1 Match the words in A and B to make phrases connected with work. Can you remember any other phrases connected with work?

A		B	
1	well	a	-paid
2	work	b	to travel
3	opportunities	c	money
4	badly	d	training
5	communication	e	long hours
6	physically	f	skills
7	good with	g	fit
8	special	h	organised

2 In each list, one word is not an adjective. Underline it and make the necessary changes to make it into an adjective.

1 fit / assertive / success / intelligent
2 ambitious / creative / talent / stressful
3 disciplined / challenging / focus / secure
4 confident / determination / experienced / productive

3 Complete the sentences with the correct form of the word in brackets.

She's very hard-working, so I'm sure she'll be _successful_ (success).

1 I don't go on social networking sites at work. I find it _____ (distraction).
2 This technology means we can _____ (production) more cars more quickly.
3 He left his last job because he found it too _____ (stress).
4 The doctor is very _____ (experience).
5 You need to be _____ (determination) to get to the top in this job.
6 In business, you have to take _____ (responsible) for your decisions.
7 How _____ (ambition) are you?
8 The book is full of _____ (imagination) pictures.
9 His business lost a lot of money – it was a complete _____ (fail).
10 My grandfather is very _____ (knowledge) about local history.

STUDY TIPS

Keep good vocabulary notes

1 What do you do when you meet a new English word or phrase that you want to remember?

1 I write it down in a special notebook that I keep just for vocabulary. ☐
2 I write it down on any piece of paper I have with me. ☐
3 I write it down with a translation. ☐
4 I write it down with a translation and an example sentence. ☐
5 I don't write it down. If it's important, I remember it. ☐
6 I mark the stressed syllable. ☐
7 I note the pronunciation in phonemic script. ☐
8 I note the 'part of speech' (noun, verb, adjective, etc.). ☐
9 I use highlighting and different colours to make the notes more attractive. ☐

2 Discuss with other students which ideas in exercise 1 work best for you. Highlight any new ideas that you would like to try.

3 Look back through Unit 5. Choose five new words and make notes about them using the ideas in exercise 1.

STUDY 1

Past perfect

had + past participle	
+	I/You/He/She/It/We/They **'d** (= **had**) **done** it.
−	I/You/He/She/It/We/They **hadn't** (= **had not**) **done** it.
?	**Had** I/you/he/she/it/we/they **done** it?

The Past perfect links one time in the past to another time further in the past.
*When we got there, everyone **had left**.*

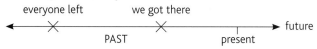

everyone left   we got there   future
PAST   present

1 Similarities with the Present perfect

• The Present perfect is 'the past of the present'.
  *It **isn't** Jane's first visit to Australia: she's **been** here twice before.*

PAST   past perfect   present   future

• The Past perfect is 'the past of the past.'
  *It **wasn't** my first visit to Australia: I'**d been** there twice before.*

past perfect   PAST   present   future

2 Time words with the Past perfect

• With the Past perfect, we use many of the same time words that we use with the Present perfect.
  *We had been in Cairo **for two months / since August**.*
  *I'd **already / just / recently** passed my driving test.*
  *It was the **first / second / third time** I'd met her.*
• The following words and phrases are also often used with the Past perfect.
  – *by / by the time*
    ***By 5:30** everyone **had left**.* (= they left before this time)
    ***By the time** we arrived, the film **had finished**.*
  – *when / after / before / as soon as*
    With these words, we use the Past perfect for the first action that happened.
    ***When** I got up, the others **had** already **left**.*
    *We **did** the washing-up **as soon as** our guests **had left**.*

3 Cases where the Past perfect is optional

• We do not usually use the Past perfect when the sequence of events in the past is clear.
  *I **had** a shower and **went** to bed.*
• If we use *when* with the Past perfect, it means that the first action was finished when the second action happened.
  *The game **had finished** when we **arrived**.*
• With two Past simple verbs, the two actions happened at more or less the same time.
  *The game **started** when we **arrived**.*

PRACTICE 1

1 Match the sentence halves using *so* or *because*. Write the sentences with the correct form of the verb in brackets.

She spoke French well because she had lived in Paris as a child.

A
1 ~~She (speak) French well~~
2 I (leave) my umbrella at home
3 My uncle (not want) to move
4 There (be) no food in the house
5 My grandparents (never / fly) before
6 When I (get) home my father was angry
7 They (already / sell) all the tickets
8 We (not have to) queue in the restaurant

B
a we (not get) into the concert.
b they (be) nervous when they got on the plane.
c I (not phone) him.
d I (forget) to go to the supermarket.
e my uncle (reserve) a table.
f ~~she (live) in Paris as a child.~~
g he (live) in the same house for 40 years.
h I (got) really wet.

2 Circle the verb that is better in the Past perfect and correct it.

1 By 7 o'clock, the place <u>was</u> completely empty – everyone <u>went</u> home.
2 It <u>was</u> the first time I ever <u>spent</u> the night away from home.
3 I <u>was</u> disappointed with my low mark in the exam because I <u>did</u> a lot of revision.
4 Before I <u>met</u> Mark at the party, I <u>saw</u> him in the street lots of times.
5 He <u>threatened</u> to leave his job many times before he actually <u>did</u> it.
6 Most of the people who <u>were</u> on the plane <u>didn't fly</u> before.
7 By the time we <u>arrived</u>, the film <u>started</u>.
8 When I <u>joined</u> the company, Jan <u>was</u> there for five years.

3 Complete the answers with the Past simple or Past perfect form of the verb in brackets. Sometimes both verbs are in the same tense.

1 **A:** Was it the first time you met him?
   B: No, I _____ (meet) him before. He _____ (be) very nice.
2 **A:** Did you enjoy the book?
   B: I loved it. Actually, I _____ (read) it before, but I _____ (forget) until the end.
3 **A:** What time did the party end?
   B: Everyone _____ (go) home by 2 o'clock. It _____ (be) quite late.
4 **A:** Did you know they are getting married?
   B: No, I _____ (not know) that, but I knew they _____ (start) going out together.
5 **A:** Are you new?
   B: Yes, I am. Yesterday _____ (be) my first day, but I _____ (not come) in because I was ill.
6 **A:** What did you do next?
   B: I _____ (walk) home in the rain. I _____ (forget) my umbrella.

Reported speech and reported questions

1 Change of tenses

When we report someone's words afterwards, the verb forms often move into the past. This is because what they said is now in the past.

Direct speech (actual words) *Years ago, John said …*	Reported (indirect speech) *A few years ago, John told me that …*
*'I **want** to get away from here.'* Present simple	*he **wanted** to get away from there.* Past simple
*'I **had** an awful time last year.'* Past simple	*he **had had** an awful time the previous year.* Past perfect
*'I**'ve found** a new job in Canada.'* Present perfect	*he **had found** a new job in Canada.* Past perfect
*'I**'m leaving** tomorrow.'* Present continuous	*he **was leaving** the next day.* Past continuous
*'I**'m going to start** a new life.'* is/are going to	*he **was going to start** a new life.* was/were going to
*'I**'ll write** to you when I get there.'* will/won't	*he **would write** to me when he got there.* would/wouldn't
*'You **can** come and see me.'* can/can't	*I **could** come and see him.* could/couldn't

REMEMBER!

- Notice the changes in place and time references in the reported statements.
  here → there
  last year → the year before
- Other modal verbs (*would, could, should, ought, might*) do not change in reported speech.
- Also notice the changes in pronouns used in reported speech.
  I → he/she

2 Verbs and conjunctions used for reporting

- In statements, *say* and *tell* are the most common reporting verbs. Look at how they are used.
  *He **said** it was true.*
  NOT *He told it was true.*
  *He **told me** it was true.*
  NOT *He said me it was true.*
  *He **said to me** it was true.*
  NOT *He told to me it was true.*
  These verbs can be followed by *that*, but it is not necessary.

- In questions, *ask* and *want to know* are common reporting verbs. In *Yes/No* questions, the verb is joined to the reported words with *if* or *whether*.

She **asked / wanted to know**	if	it was true (or not).
	whether	

- In *Wh-* questions, we do not need *if* or *whether*.
  *'**What** do you think?'*
  *He asked me **what I thought**.*

3 Word order in reported questions

The word order in reported questions is the same as in normal statements.

Direct speech	Reported speech
'Can you come early?'	She asked if *I could come* early.
'Did you see anything suspicious?'	The police officer wanted to know if *we had seen* anything suspicious.

PRACTICE 2

1 Which four sentences are incorrect?

1 He told that he was coming to the party.
2 He said he was coming to the party.
3 He told me that he was coming to the party.
4 He said me he was coming to the party.
5 He said to me that he was coming to the party.
6 He told to me he was coming to the party.
7 He told that he was coming to the party.
8 He said that he was coming to the party.

2 Put the words in the correct order to make reported questions.

1 the / was / me / teacher / why / late / asked / I

_____

2 us / home / he / were / if / we / asked / going

_____

3 her / was / asked / going / where / they / she

_____

4 brother / where / my / know / was / wanted / I / to

_____

5 him / how / didn't / was / I / he / ask

_____

REMEMBER THESE WORDS

STORIES

adventure stories	ghost stories
anecdotes	'human interest' stories
biographies	the main characters
a coincidence	mysteries
crime stories	romantic stories
fantasy	science fiction
fictional	a twist of fate

SAY AND TELL

say a prayer	tell a joke
say sorry	tell a lie
say thank you	tell someone off
say yes/no	tell someone what to do
tell the difference	tell the truth

ADVERBS FOR TELLING STORIES

eventually	suddenly
fortunately	surprisingly
gradually	thankfully
immediately	unfortunately
obviously	

OTHER

to bite	to hold on
to chase someone	to let go
a cure	to rescue
an explosion	to sink
to feel numb	to snarl
to go insane	to stare
to go shooting	to survive
(to happen without) warning	a tragedy
to have a nervous breakdown	a wave

PRACTICE

1 What kind of story do you think the extracts below come from? Choose from the types of story in the box.

a crime story   a romantic story   science fiction
a ghost story   an adventure story

1 She stopped what she was doing. There was that sound again coming from the cellar. A gentle tap, tap, tap.
2 'But where am I?' asked Leith, suddenly feeling frightened. 'You are on the planet Hex,' replied the computer.
3 Detective Jameson looked carefully at the scene. The man had clearly been dead for some time.
4 'I'll see you in Paris,' he yelled, as he grabbed the parachute and jumped from the plane.
5 Daniel looked deep into her eyes and held her hand. His heart was beating very fast.

2 Match the adverbs in A with the phrases in B. Can you remember any other adverbs used for telling stories?

A		B	
1	Fortunately,	a	something bad happened
2	Surprisingly,	b	something good happened
3	Unfortunately,	c	something happened in the end
4	Gradually,	d	something happened little by little
5	Immediately,	e	something happened straight away
6	Eventually,	f	something unexpected happened

3 Cover the word list. Which of these do you *say* and which do you *tell*? Can you remember other phrases with *say* and *tell*?

1	a lie	2	*yes*	3	the truth
4	someone off	5	a joke	6	sorry
7	thank you	8	someone what to do		

STUDY TIPS

Check your written work

1 When you hand in written work, which description best summarises your approach? (Be honest!)

1 You hand it in without looking at it again – you don't want to think about all the mistakes you've made! ☐
2 You read it through quickly, correct one or two mistakes, then hand it in. ☐
3 You check systematically for different kinds of mistakes (e.g. grammar, spelling, etc.). ☐
4 You give it to someone else to check through for you. ☐
5 You identify things you could improve then write a second draft. ☐

2 Here are some things that should be checked before you hand in written work. Which are most often a problem for you? Compare your answers in pairs.

- verb tenses
- the 's' on the third person (*he, she, it*) Present simple verbs
- using the correct preposition
- articles (*a* and *the*)
- word order
- missing out words
- putting in words you don't need
- using the wrong word (e.g. *make* instead of *do*)
- spelling
- capital letters
- full stops and commas

3 Look at the pieces of writing below and correct the mistakes. There are five mistakes in each one.

1 I'm just writing to say thank you, for the lovely pullover you send me for my birthday. It fit perfectly, and the colour great.
2 Sorry I couldn't come to the ristorant tomorrow, but I have to make my homework and study for exam. I'm very worrying!
3 I am agree – peoples should no smoking in public place.

STUDY 1

-ed/-ing adjectives

1 -ed adjectives

Adjectives ending in -ed describe our feelings about something or someone.
*I felt **bored** at the party.* (= I found the party boring)

2 -ing adjectives

Adjectives ending in -ing describe the thing or person that has an effect on us.
*Today's lesson was very **interesting**.* (= the lesson interested me)

3 Other -ed/-ing adjectives

amazed/amazing	interested/interesting
annoyed/annoying	inspired/inspiring
bored/boring	irritated/irritating
confused/confusing	moved/moving
depressed/depressing	pleased/pleasing
disappointed/disappointing	surprised/surprising
embarrassed/embarrassing	terrified/terrifying
frustrated/frustrating	worried/worrying

PRACTICE 1

1 Choose the correct adjectives.

1 That's a very *interested / interesting* suggestion.
2 The news isn't really *surprised / surprising*.
3 There's no need to feel *embarrassed / embarrassing*.
4 Why are you always late? Have you any idea how *annoyed / annoying* it is!
5 I'm afraid it was rather a *bored / boring* evening.
6 I'm really *pleased / pleasing* to see how well she's doing.
7 The news report was extremely *worrying / worried*.
8 I don't understand. I'm really *confused / confusing*.

2 Complete the sentences with an -ed/-ing adjective.

1 I was very d_____ when I failed my driving test again.
2 The instructions for this phone are really c_____ . I don't understand them at all.
3 After his divorce, Frank became more and more d_____ .
4 I was a_____ when I won the competition – I didn't expect it at all!
5 My brother taps his hands on the table all the time – it's a really a_____ habit.
6 Why doesn't this printer work? Oh, it's so f_____ !

STUDY 2

The passive

1 Simple tenses

	+	–	?
Form	subject + verb *to be* + past participle	subject + verb *to be* + not + past participle	verb *to be* + subject + past participle
Present	It's (= is) made.	It isn't (= is not) made.	Is it made?
Past	It was made.	It wasn't (= was not) made.	Was it made?
Present perfect	It's (= has) been made.	It hasn't (= has not) been made.	Has it been made?
Future	It'll (= will) be made.	It won't (= will not) be made.	Will it be made?

2 Continuous tenses

	+	–	?
Form	subject + verb *to be* + *being* + past participle	subject + verb *to be* + *not* + *being* + past participle	verb *to be* + subject + *being* + past participle
Present	It's (= is) being made.	It isn't (= is not) being made.	Is it being made?
Past	It was being made.	It wasn't (= was not) being made.	Was it being made?

3 The difference between the active and the passive

- In active sentences, the subject is the 'doer' of the verb (the person who makes the action happen).
  *The firefighter **rescued** the child.*
  (subject)   (verb)
- In passive sentences, the 'doer' of the verb is not the subject.
  *The child **was rescued** by the firefighter.*
  (subject)   (verb)

REMEMBER!

If we mention the 'doer' of the verb, we use *by* + the person.
*The building was designed **by Sir Andrew Rowley**.*

4 Reasons for using the passive

- To focus on the main topic of the sentence. The beginning of the sentence normally tells us what the sentence is mainly about. Compare the sentences below.
  Jackson won the Olympic gold medal.
  (= the sentence is mainly about Jackson)
  The Olympic gold medal was won by Jackson.
  (= the sentence is mainly about the Olympic gold medal)
- If the person who does the verb is unknown or unimportant.
  *My handbag **has been stolen**.*
  (= we don't know who did this)
  *The Petronas Towers **were built** in 1996.*
  (= we are interested in **when** they were built, not who built them)
- The doer of the action is obvious, or it is 'people in general'.
  *Dozens of people **were arrested**.*
  (= it is obvious that the police arrested them)
  *Spanish **is spoken** in more than 20 countries.*
  (= it is not necessary to say 'by people')

REMEMBER!
We often use the passive in more **formal** contexts (e.g. news reports), and less when we are speaking informally. Compare the sentences below.
*A new parking scheme **is being introduced** in the town centre.*
(= from a news report)
*I hear they**'re introducing** a new parking scheme in the town centre.*
(= from a conversation)

5 Verbs often used in the passive

- Verbs related to accidents/injuries, etc.
  was injured / was killed / was damaged / was destroyed, etc.
- Verbs related to crime
  was arrested / was sentenced / was found guilty / was sent to prison, etc.
- Verbs related to inventions, books, films, etc.
  was invented by / was discovered by / was produced by / was directed by / was written by, etc.

PRACTICE 2

1 Complete the sentences with the correct passive form of the verb in brackets.

1 Every year, 1,200 people _____ (injure) in road accidents.
2 The search for the missing man continues. Up until now, no clues _____ (find).
3 At the moment, a new shopping centre _____ (build) in the town centre.
4 Nearly $1 million _____ (steal) during the robbery.
5 The council say the work _____ (complete) next year.

2 Rewrite these active sentences using the passive form. Omit the underlined word(s).

1 The police arrested over 30 demonstrators.
_____

2 The recent storms have damaged a number of buildings.
_____

3 People destroy thousands of trees every year.
_____

4 The judge will sentence the man tomorrow.
_____

5 Someone has stolen my computer.
_____

6 Is anybody looking after you?
_____

7 They presented Sarah with a gold watch.
_____

8 Davison built the museum in 1874.
_____

3 Complete the texts with the correct active or passive form of the verb in brackets.

Famous firsts!

a On 17th July 1938, American aviator Douglas Corrigan ¹_____ (give) permission by the authorities to take off from an airfield near New York. When he ²_____ (land) several hours later in Ireland, he ³_____ (become) the first pilot to cross the Atlantic in a solo plane by accident! Corrigan ⁴_____ (give) a hero's welcome on his return to New York. Since then, he ⁵_____ (know) as 'Wrong Way' Corrigan.

b Sirimavo Bandaranaike was the first woman prime minister in the world. Her husband ¹_____ (be) the Prime Minister of Sri Lanka in the 1950s, until he ²_____ (murder) in 1959. Bandaranaike ³_____ (then decide) to enter politics herself. The following year she ⁴_____ (elect) as Prime Minister. She ⁵_____ (die) in 2000 at the age of 84.

c Almost 50 years ago, Laika ¹_____ (became) the most famous dog in the world – she was the first animal in space. *Sputnik 2* ²_____ (launch) in November 1957. Unfortunately, Laika could not ³_____ (bring) back to Earth, so she ⁴_____ (die) in space about a week after the launch. The Laika Foundation in Moscow ⁵_____ (name) after her.

REMEMBER THESE WORDS

ENTERTAINMENT AND TELEVISION

an advert	a quiz show
a chat show	a reality show
a cookery programme	a sitcom
a documentary	a soap opera
a (drama) series	a sports programme
a game show	a talent show
a murder mystery	travel news
a nature programme	the weather forecast
a phone-in	

EXTREME ADJECTIVES

astonished	freezing
boiling	furious
delighted	hilarious
excellent	ridiculous
exhausted	terrible
fantastic	terrified

OTHER

the acting	a musical
a ballet	an opera
the camera work	an orchestra
the cast	the photography
a character	to play a role
a classical/rock concert	the plot
a comedy show	a pop video
a costume	the scenery
a gig	the set
the lighting	the special effects
the lyrics	

PRACTICE

1 Underline the odd one out in each group of words. Can you explain your answers?

1 a murder mystery / a sitcom / a soap opera / travel news
2 a ballet / a character / a classical concert / a musical
3 a phone-in / a reality show / a drama series / a talent show
4 the cast / the costumes / the lighting / the special effects
5 an advert / a documentary / sports coverage / travel news
6 a musical / a comedy show / a pop video / an opera

2 Cover the word list. Write extreme adjectives which are similar in meaning to the definitions. Can you remember any others to add to the list?

1 very good _____
2 very bad _____
3 very happy _____
4 very angry _____
5 very silly _____
6 very funny _____
7 very cold _____
8 very hot _____

3 Match the sentence halves.

A

1 Jason was furious
2 It's cold out here. I'm
3 The film was superb and the acting
4 Take a coat and hat. The weather
5 We're absolutely
6 Holly used to be terrified
7 The show was hilarious
8 It's ridiculous that
9 Do you mind if I take off my jacket? It's
10 They were exhausted

B

a looks terrible.
b and he couldn't stop laughing.
c absolutely freezing!
d of spiders.
e boiling in here.
f after the long flight from Sydney.
g was fantastic!
h when someone damaged his car.
i delighted by the news.
j the bank isn't open on Saturdays.

STUDY TIPS

Using English outside the classroom

1 Here are some things you can do to improve your English outside the classroom. Tick any of these things you've done. Did you find them useful?

1 Find an English song that you like and write down phrases that you understand. Find the words online and check how well you understood it. ☐
2 Watch an English-language TV channel for a few minutes every day. ☐
3 Listen to English-language radio programmes that interest you. ☐
4 Find an article that interests you on an English newspaper website. ☐
5 Choose a graded reader (e.g. the Penguin Reader series) and start reading for pleasure in English. ☐
6 Watch a subtitled version of an English language film. Try to listen rather than read the subtitles. ☐

2 Highlight two activities you would like to try – but remember to choose things that would interest you in your own language!

STUDY 1

Polite requests

1 Asking for permission

Asking	Saying *yes*	Saying *no*
Can I ... ? Could I ... ? Could I possibly ... ? Is it all right if I ... ? Do you think I could ... ?	Yes, sure. Yes, of course. That's fine. Certainly.	Well, I'm afraid (+ reason) ... Well, the problem is that ...
Do you mind if I ... ?	No, not at all. Of course not.	Sorry, but ...

2 Asking other people to do things (making requests)

Asking	Saying *yes*	Saying *no*
Can you ... ? Could you ... ? Is it alright if you ... ? Do you think you could ... ? Will you ... ? Would you ... ?	Yes, sure. Yes, of course. That's fine. Certainly.	Well, I'm afraid (+ reason) ... Well, the problem is that ... Sorry, but ...
Do you mind + *-ing*? Would you mind + *-ing*?	No, not at all. Of course not.	

- We use *Do you mind if I ...?*, *Could I possibly ...?*, *Could you possibly ...?*, *Do you think you could ...?* when we want to sound particularly polite.
- *Could/Would you?* are a little more polite than *Can/Will you?* In all these questions, however, intonation is more important than the words you use if you want to be polite.

REMEMBER!
- After *Would you mind ...?* we use the *-ing* form of the verb.
- *Would you mind ...?* and *Do you mind ...?* mean 'Is it a problem for you?', so the polite answer is *no*!
  A: ***Do you mind getting*** some bread on your way home?
  B: *No, not at all.*

PRACTICE 1

1 Rewrite these sentences as polite requests. Use the words in brackets.

1. Pass my bag. (would / mind)
2. Take me into town. (could / possibly)
3. You cook dinner this evening. (think / could)
4. Borrow $10 until tomorrow. (think / could)
5. Use your phone. (is / alright)
6. Have a window seat. (could)
7. You turn the light off. (will)
8. I take the car tonight. (do / mind)
9. Tell Jenny about the part. (would)
10. Leave early on Friday. (could / possibly)

2 Complete the conversations. One word is missing from each line.

1. A: Would mind waiting outside?
   B: No, not all.
2. A: Do you think you give this to Maris?
   B: Yes, course.
3. A: Is alright if I sit here?
   B: Sorry, but someone is sitting.
4. A: I possibly borrow your phone for a minute?
   B: Yes, sure. Here you.

3 Read each situation. Then complete the request, making any necessary changes.

1. You want Elena to turn down her music.
   Elena, would you mind _____ , please? I'm trying to work.
2. You would like to read John's magazine.
   Is it OK _____ , John?
3. You want Ros to fetch your glasses.
   Ros, could _____ , please?
4. You want to phone Mike tomorrow because you're busy now.
   Do you mind _____ , Mike? I'm very busy right now.
5. You want to know if it's possible for Hiro to translate something for you.
   Hiro, could _____ this for me?
6. You want the shop assistant to make you ten photocopies.
   Will _____ ten copies, please?
7. You want a stranger to take a photo of you and your friend.
   Excuse me. Do you think _____ of us, please?
8. You want the bank clerk to change £50 into ten £5 notes.
   Would _____ this for ten £5 notes, please?
9. Your computer is frozen and you'd like Ann to have a look at it.
   Ann, my computer's frozen. Would you mind _____ it, please?
10. You want to go home early because you aren't feeling well.
    Do you think _____ ? I'm not feeling well.

STUDY 2

will and *shall* (for instant responses)

- If we make a decision at the moment of speaking, we use *will*.
  I suddenly feel a bit tired ... I think I'll stay in tonight.
- This use of *will* is often contrasted with *going to* (used if you've already decided). Compare the following pairs of sentences.
  A: *Do you want to play squash tomorrow some time?*
  B: *Sorry, I can't – we're going to paint the living room this weekend.*
  (= they've already decided do this)
  A: *Do you want to go and have a quick coffee?*
  B: *Good idea ... I'll finish this later.*
  (= speaker decides at that moment)

REMEMBER!

For instant decisions and responses, we always use the contracted form *'ll* and not the full form *will*.

- Very often these decisions are offers or promises.
  Don't worry – I'll give you a lift.
  If it's scary, I'll hold your hand.
- You can also use *Shall I ...?* for offers.
  Shall I help you with that?   *OK, thanks.*
  Shall I call you later?   *No, don't worry. I'll be fine.*
- *Shall we?* is used to make suggestions.
  Shall we go home now?
  Shall we have a vote?
- These are the most common uses of *shall* in modern English.

PRACTICE 2

1 Match the sentence halves.

A

1 I'll carry your books –
2 I'll try again later –
3 I'm going to get fit this summer –
4 I'll do the washing-up –
5 I'll take the red pair of shoes –
6 I'm going to cook this evening –

B

a I've signed up for a course at the gym.
b I don't like the black ones so much.
c they look very heavy.
d I bought all the ingredients this morning.
e his phone's off at the moment.
f you cooked so it's only fair.

2 Write the sentences from exercise 1 in the correct group below.

1 Decisions made at the moment of speaking
2 Decisions made before the moment of speaking

3 Read the situations below and cross out the phrase which is not correct in that situation.

1 You see an old woman carrying heavy bags.
  a Here, I'll help you with those.
  b Shall I help you with those?
  c Will I help you with those?

2 It's your dream to visit Hawaii. You've just received a letter telling you that you've won several thousand dollars.
  a I'm going to visit Hawaii.
  b Shall we visit Hawaii?
  c I think I'll visit Hawaii.

3 You are just leaving your friend's house. He's feeling ill.
  a Am I going to call you tomorrow?
  b Shall I call you tomorrow?
  c I'll call you tomorrow.

4 You are talking to your best friend on the phone. She's flying home to London tomorrow.
  a Shall I meet you at the airport?
  b I'm meeting you at the airport.
  c I'll meet you at the airport.

4 Choose the best answers.

1 **A:** It's absolutely freezing in here!
  B: *I'll close / I'm going to close* the window.

2 **A:** When is the next flight?
  B: Just a minute, *I'm going to check / I'll check* on the website.

3 **A:** Have you got any plans for tonight?
  B: Yes, *I'll have / I'm going to have* dinner with a friend.

4 **A:** I don't want to leave my laptop here.
  B: It's OK. *I'll look after / I'm going to look after* it.

5 **A:** I can't understand these instructions.
  B: *I'm going to help / I'll help* if you like

6 **A:** Are you looking forward to your holidays?
  B: I can't wait! *I'll sit / I'm going to sit* on the beach and do nothing.

7 **A:** It's raining really hard.
  B: *I'll lend you / I'm going to lend you* an umbrella.

8 **A:** What is your New Year's resolution?
  B: *I'll lose / I'm going to lose* weight.

REMEMBER THESE WORDS

SOCIAL ACTIVITIES

to go clubbing	to go to a private party
to go dancing	to grab a snack
to go driving around town	to have dinner in a restaurant
to go home early	to stay out late
to go out for a coffee	to watch live music
to go to a karaoke bar	

SOCIAL BEHAVIOUR

to go out on a date	to pick someone up (from their house)
to hug each other	to refuse an invitation
to insist on paying	to shake hands
to invite someone to your house	to share the bill
to kiss someone on both cheeks	to take someone home
to offer to pay	

TALKING ABOUT NORMS AND CUSTOMS

it's considered rude to	it's (un)acceptable to
it's good/bad manners to	it's (un)usual (for people) to
it's (perfectly) normal to	people tend / don't tend to
it's OK to	

OTHERS

to be cool/uncool	to have fun
to be offended	to head somewhere
to behave / behaviour	a host
to blow your nose	to lend
to borrow	on the whole
generally speaking	to pass someone something
to get past someone	to queue / a queue
to give someone a lift	to switch your phone to vibrate
to go round to someone's house	to take turns
a guest	to treat someone with respect
	to turn something on/off/up/down

PRACTICE

1 Match the sentences in A with the sentences in B.

A	B
1 I'm hungry.	a Let's go to a karaoke bar.
2 I've got a new car.	b Let's go home early.
3 I want to dance a lot this evening.	c Let's stay out late.
4 I don't want to go home yet.	d Let's grab a snack.
5 I'm really tired.	e Let's go clubbing.
6 I want to sing this evening.	f Let's go driving around town.

2 Complete the second sentence so that it means the same as the first.

1a Generally speaking, people shake hands when they meet.
 b It's usual ...
2a You should never blow your nose in public.
 b It's considered ...
3a People don't normally ask another person's age.
 b It's bad ...
4a Most people share the bill.
 b It's normal ...

3 Cover the word list and write the opposites of the words below.

1 to accept an invitation _____
2 to go home early _____
3 to lend _____
4 a guest _____
5 good manners _____
6 cool _____

4 Correct the mistake in each sentence.

1 On our first date, I offered paying.
2 He kissed me both cheeks.
3 On whole, children here have good manners.
4 She insisted paying for the meal.
5 Let's have a dinner in a restaurant.
6 Did you take home her?
7 I always switch my phone on vibrate in meetings.

STUDY TIPS

Record or film yourself speaking

1 Recording/Filming yourself doing speaking tasks, reading aloud or just saying new words can help your speaking. Here are some benefits. Tick the ones that you think would help you most and compare your answers in pairs.

1 When people record themselves, they often practise over and over again. This can help you to become more fluent and confident. ☐

2 Saying things over and over again can also help you to remember them. ☐

3 When you are recording yourself, you often pay more attention to being accurate. ☐

4 If you record yourself, you can listen to and assess how clear your pronunciation is. ☐

2 Here are some ways you can record/film yourself. Decide which would suit you best.

1 Film yourself on your mobile phone.
2 Download a recording app onto your phone.
3 Film or record yourself on your laptop or personal computer.
4 Other?

STUDY 1

Defining relative clauses

Defining relative clauses give us information about things, people, possessions, places and times using a **relative pronoun**.

1 Things (*that, which* or –)

*It's a machine **which** converts information.*
*A calculator is a little machine **that** does arithmetic.*

REMEMBER!

What is not possible here.
*A calculator is a machine **that/which** ~~what~~ does arithmetic.*

2 People (*who, that* or –)

*A technophobe is a person **who** doesn't use technology.*
*A newsreader is a person **that** reads the news.*
The pronoun *that* is less common than *who* here.

REMEMBER!

- We can leave out *which, who* and *that* if they are the object of the relative clause.
  *There are people (**who/that**) you can phone if you have a problem.*
  *Gloves are things (**which/that**) you wear in cold weather.*
  Notice that in sections 1 and 2 above, *which, who* and *that* are the subject of the relative clause, so they cannot be left out.
- With the passive we can sometimes miss out the relative clause.
  *A smoothie is a drink **which is made** from different types of fruit.*
  *A smoothie is a drink **made** from different types of fruit.*

3 Possessions (*whose*)

*He's a person **whose** life is dominated by computers.* (= his life)
*An orphan is a child **whose** parents have died.* (= his/her parents)

4 Places (*where, which/that* + preposition)

We can refer to places in the following ways.
*This is the house **where** I grew up.*
*This is the house (**which/that**) I grew up in.*
Notice that if we have a preposition at the end of the sentence, the relative pronoun can be omitted.

5 Times (*when*)

*The evening's a time **when** we can all relax.*
*Saturday's the day **when** I tidy the flat.*

PRACTICE 1

1 Choose the correct answers.

1 A necklace is a piece of jewellery *who / which / where* you wear around your neck.
2 A cyclist is someone *who / which / whose* rides a bicycle.
3 A helmet is a hard hat *who / whose / that* protects your head.
4 A dry cleaner's is a shop *that / where / when* you can take clothes to be dry-cleaned.
5 An air traffic controller is someone *whose / who / that* job is to control the movement of planes in and out of an airport.
6 A manager is someone *whose / which / who* is in charge of a business or part of a business.
7 A festival is a time *which / that / when* there are performances of many films, plays and pieces of music.
8 An Oscar is a prize *who / that / whose* is given each year in the USA for the best film, best actor, etc.
9 A court is a place *where / which / that* legal judgements are made.
10 A courageous person is someone *which / whose / that* is not afraid when they are in a frightening situation.
11 A nanny is a person *who / which / whose* job it is to take care of a family's children.
12 A disease is an illness *where / who / which* affects a person, animal or plant.

2 Complete the sentences with the correct relative pronoun where necessary.

1 That's the man _____ I told you about.
2 I like films _____ make me laugh.
3 Let's go to the Chinese restaurant _____ your brother arrives.
4 The woman _____ lives next door has gone into hospital.
5 That's the house _____ I was born.
6 Did you enjoy the book _____ I lent you?
7 That's the woman _____ husband had a motorcycle accident.
8 A parking meter is a machine _____ you put money into when you park your car.
9 I love buying clothes _____ are in the sale.
10 Sunday's the day _____ we usually relax.
11 The man _____ lives next door makes a lot of noise.
12 She works for the company _____ I used to work for.

3 Join the two sentences together using a relative clause. Omit any unnecessary words.

1 My brother married a woman. She's a lot older than him.
2 She showed me the ring. Her boyfriend gave her it.
3 That's the couple. I look after their children.
4 I've lost the money. You lent it to me.
5 I've got a cousin. She lives in South Africa.
6 That's the book. Everyone is talking about it.

Quantifiers

With uncountable nouns only	With countable nouns only	With both uncountable and countable nouns
(too) much a bit of a little	(too) many one or two several a couple (of) a few loads of	(not) any (not) enough a lot of / lots of no plenty of some

1 *some* and *any*

- *Some* means 'a limited quantity or number of something'. It is often used in positive sentences.
  *I like **some** pop music.* (= but not all)
- We can also use *some* in the question form when we make requests and offers.
  *Can you give **some** information about excursions?* (= request)
  *Would you like **some** more soup?* (= offer)
- *Any* is often used in negatives and questions.
  *We haven't got **any** milk in the fridge.*
  *Are there **any** questions?*

2 *a lot of* and *much/many*

- *A lot of* is usually used in positive sentences. It is common in speech or informal writing. We use *lots of* in exactly the same way.
  *We sell **a lot of / lots of** imported goods.*
- In informal speech and writing, *much* and *many* are generally used in questions and negatives.
  *We'd better hurry – we haven't got **much** time.*
  *Are there **many** clothes shops in your town?*

3 *too much/many*

We use *too much* and *too many* when there is more of something than we need.
*Let's go somewhere else. There are **too many** people in here.* (= it's too crowded)
*Do you want some of my pizza? There's **too much** for me.* (= I can't eat it all)

4 *plenty of*

We use *plenty of* to mean 'more than enough'. It has a positive meaning. It is used with countable and uncountable nouns.
*Don't worry – we've got **plenty of** time before your train leaves.*
*We've got **plenty of** sandwiches for everyone – we don't need any more.*

5 *enough*

We use *enough* to mean 'as much as we need'. It is used with countable and uncountable nouns.
*Have we got **enough** chairs for everyone?*
*We haven't got **enough** food for everyone.*

6 *several*, a *few*, a *couple*

We use these phrases with countable nouns to describe small quantities.
*We've got **several** rooms available.* (= a number of rooms)
*We've got **a few** rooms available.* (= a small number)
*We've got **a couple of** rooms available.* (= two or three)

7 *a bit*, *a little*, *a little bit*

We use these phrases with uncountable nouns to describe small quantities.
*We've got **a bit / a little / a little bit** of space.*

PRACTICE 2

1 Cross out the quantifier that can't be used in these sentences.

1 We need to buy *some / several* food for our camping trip.
2 Let's get *a few / a bit of* cakes.
3 We also need *some / a few* bread.
4 We should also take *plenty of / too much* water.
5 Have we got *too many / enough* money to buy everything?

2 Complete the text with the quantifiers in the box.

plenty	lots	much	bit	few	some	no	many
any	enough	several					

What do you need to take when you travel in the jungle?

First of all, don't carry too ¹_____ luggage. Take as little as possible so that you can carry it in a backpack. You don't need to take ²_____ sunscreen as there's ³_____ direct sunlight because of all the trees.

The most important thing is to drink ⁴_____ of water. You won't be able to carry ⁵_____ bottled water, so you'll need ⁶_____ of water purification tablets, which you can use with water from rivers.

At night you need a good fire to keep insects and animals away. Carry ⁷_____ boxes of matches (you can't have too ⁸_____ matches), but if the fire goes out, make sure you take a torch and ⁹_____ batteries.

You need to keep comfortable, so take a ¹⁰_____ changes of clothes. You will be fine if you use a ¹¹_____ of common sense.

3 Complete the sentences about your classroom or place of work with the quantifiers in the box.

1 There is/isn't _____ space for everyone to work.
2 There are/aren't _____ comfortable chairs.
3 There is/isn't _____ natural light.
4 There is/isn't _____ fresh air.
5 There are/aren't _____ notices on the wall.
6 There are/aren't _____ plants.
7 There is/isn't _____ valuable equipment.
8 There are/aren't _____ stairs.
9 There is/isn't _____ noise from outside.
10 There are/aren't _____ of people to talk to.

REMEMBER THESE WORDS

HOW GADGETS WORK

a cooker / an electric cooker	an MP3 player
a digital camera	a photocopier
a dishwasher	a tablet computer
a DVD player	a touch screen phone
a games console	a vacuum cleaner
a laptop	

VERBS FOR DESCRIBING HOW GADGETS WORK

it doesn't work	to reinstall software
to break down	to restart
to crash	to scroll down a menu
to freeze	to switch something off
to hold down a button	to switch something on
to pause	to touch an icon
to press a button	to unplug
to recharge a battery	

DESCRIBING EVERYDAY OBJECTS

a battery	plastic
fabric	rectangular
it's got	round
it's made of (metal)	rubber
it's used for + -ing	square

OTHER

a bodyguard	a GPS navigator
a boiler	a launderette
a cleaner	a personal trainer
a compass	a plumber
a decorator	a stationer's
a dry cleaner's	a torch
a freezer	wet wipes

PRACTICE

1 Match the verbs with the nouns.

A		B	
1	recharge	a	the button
2	scroll down	b	the software
3	press	c	the icon
4	reinstall	d	the menu
5	touch	e	the battery

2 Circle the odd one out in each group of words.

1	a cleaner	a launderette	a dry cleaner's
2	a bodyguard	a freezer	a personal trainer
3	a boiler	a cooker	a plumber
4	a compass	a torch	a GPS navigator
5	a photocopier	a vacuum cleaner	a decorator
6	a laptop	a dishwasher	a tablet computer
7	a battery	rubber	plastic
8	to crash	to break down	to switch on
9	round	fabric	rectangular
10	a digital camera	a freezer	a dishwasher

STUDY TIPS

Use a monolingual dictionary

1 Tick the statement(s) that describe how you use monolingual dictionaries.

1 I don't use monolingual dictionaries – I don't think I would understand them very well. ☐

2 I try to use a monolingual dictionary to find the meaning of new words, although sometimes I find it difficult to understand the explanations. ☐

3 I use a monolingual dictionary to find:
- the meaning(s) of words. ☐
- examples of how words are used. ☐
- the pronunciation of words. ☐
- the word stress. ☐
- whether a word is a noun, verb, adjective or adverb. ☐
- the opposites of words. ☐
- irregular past forms. ☐
- the prepositions that come after words. ☐
- whether new words are countable/uncountable. ☐

2 Look at the entry from a monolingual dictionary. Which information from exercise 1 part 3 can you find?

purchase[1] /ˈpɜːtʃəs $ ˈpɜːr-/ *v* [T] *formal* to buy something: *You can purchase insurance online.* | *the growing demand to purchase goods on credit* | *Where did you purchase the car?* | [+from] *Tickets may be purchased in advance from the box office.* **THESAURUS** buy.

3 The words in bold all appear in the reading text on page 87. How many questions can you answer using a monolingual dictionary?

1 Which syllable is stressed in the word *label*?
2 What is the pronunciation of the word *extreme*?
3 Is *reward* a countable noun or an uncountable noun?
4 Is the word *deserve* a verb, noun or adjective?
5 What is the opposite of the word *satisfactory*?
6 Is the verb *seek* regular or irregular?
7 Which preposition follows the verb *blame*?

10 STUDY, PRACTICE & REMEMBER

STUDY 1

Making predictions

1 Using *will* or *won't*

We often use adverbs with *will* and *won't* to show how certain we are about something.

*Our team **will probably** lose on Saturday.*
*I think he**'ll almost certainly** pass the exam.*
*We **definitely won't** be there on time.*

These adverbs (*probably, almost certainly, definitely*, etc.) come **after** *will* but **before** *won't*.

2 Using *may* (*not*) / *might* (*not*) / *could*

These modal verbs all mean that something is possible in the future. We add *well* if we are more sure it will happen.

*It **may** / **might** / **could** snow tomorrow.* (= it is possible)
*It **may** / **might** / **could well** snow tomorrow.* (= we are more sure)

We can use *may* and *might*, but not *could*, in the negative form.

He	may not	phone this weekend.
	might not	

3 (*un*)*likely to*

We use *likely to* when we think something will probably happen. We use the negative form or *unlikely to* when we think something probably won't happen.

*People **are likely to** live longer in the next century.*
*Computers **are not likely to** / **are unlikely to** replace teachers.*

PRACTICE 1

1 Put the words in the correct order to make predictions.

1 could / be / you / or / fall / careful
_____

2 university / after / will / Miran / finishes / go / she / school / probably / to
_____

3 become / Casabani / definitely / president / won't
_____

4 soon / certainly / will / get / promoted / Dominic / almost
_____

5 we / o'clock / until / probably / ten / arrive / won't / about
_____

6 likely / be / week / it / very / to / 's / next / hot
_____

7 Lorenzo / might / again / see / I / not
_____

8 at / definitely / airport / someone / the / meet / you / will
_____

9 well / evening / it / rain / later / may / this
_____

10 very / long / likely / isn't / stay / Nabil / to / for
_____

2 Complete the second sentence so it has a similar meaning to the first, using the words in brackets. Use short forms where possible.

1 It's likely that we'll go for a pizza after work.
   We _____ after work. (probably / go)
2 It's very unlikely that Maria will be on the 6 o'clock train.
   Maria _____ on the 6 o'clock train. (almost certainly / be)
3 Bill said it's possible he won't come to the barbecue.
   Bill said he _____ to the barbecue. (may / come)
4 I'm going to give you an injection. It may well hurt a bit.
   I'm going to give you an injection. It _____ a bit. (likely / hurt)
5 I'm sure your trousers will be ready by Thursday.
   Your trousers _____ by Thursday (definitely / be)
6 Be careful with that computer. It's possible that you'll drop it.
   Be careful with that computer. You _____ . (could / drop)
7 Oh, no! Another goal! It's impossible for us to win now!
   Oh, no! Another goal! We _____ now! (definitely / win)
8 It's almost certainly going to rain tomorrow.
   I think it _____ tomorrow. (may well / rain)
9 Kamari probably won't get married until he's 25.
   Kamari _____ until he's 25. (unlikely / get married)
10 Could you write down your email address? I might not remember it otherwise.
   Could you write down your email address? I _____ otherwise. (probably / remember)

3 Cross out the word or phrase which cannot complete each sentence.

1 It will **definitely** / **may** / **probably** be sunny tomorrow.
2 We **could** / **may** / **might** not be able to get tickets.
3 They **definitely won't** / **may definitely** / **will definitely** be here by 8 o'clock.
4 The road **is likely** / **may** / **won't** reopen this week.
5 There **is definitely** / **is likely to** / **will probably** be a big argument about this.
6 The President **may be** / **may not** / **may well** resign this week.

4 Add an adverb and choose the correct verb form to make the sentences true for you.

1 It ***will* / *won't*** be cold tomorrow.
   It will almost certainly be cold tomorrow.
2 It ***will* / *won't*** get dark before 7.00 p.m. today.
3 There ***will* / *won't*** be an election this year.
4 The government ***will* / *won't*** put up taxes this year.
5 Unemployment ***will* / *won't*** get worse in my country.
6 There ***will* / *won't*** be bad traffic on my way home tonight.

STUDY 2

Hypothetical possibilities with *if*

1 Hypothetical (imaginary) possibilities

- If we are talking about an imaginary/hypothetical situation, we use *would/wouldn't* + verb. Notice the contracted form *I'd*.
  I'd never lie to my friends.
  I wouldn't like to be famous.
- If we talk about a hypothetical situation or condition, we use *if* + Past simple or Past continuous. This type of sentence is often referred to as the 'second conditional'.
  If I found a wallet in the street, I'd take it to the police.
  I'd go for a walk if I wasn't feeling so tired.

REMEMBER!

- It is not correct to use *would* in the *if* clause.
  If I had enough money, I'd go abroad on holiday.
  NOT *If I would have enough money …*
- In *if* sentences, we can use *were* instead of *was*. This is especially common in the phrase *If I were you …* , used to give advice.
  If I were you, I wouldn't trust him.
- We can change the order of the sentence.
  I wouldn't trust him if I were you.
- Instead of *would*, we can also use *might* or *could*.
  If you didn't talk so much, people might listen to you more.
  I could help you if I had more time.

2 Real and hypothetical possibilities

- To talk about a real possibility in the future, we use *will*.
  I'll be worried if he doesn't phone me.
  This type of sentence is often referred to as the 'first conditional'. For more on future sentences with *if* and *when*, see Unit 5 Study 2.
- Sometimes the difference between a real and an imaginary possibility is very clear.
  I'll be very disappointed if we lose. (= a real possibility)
  I'd be absolutely terrified if I saw a ghost. (= an imaginary situation)
- Sometimes, whether we use the first or the second conditional depends on how we see the situation.
  Compare the following sentences.
  If I have enough time, I'll help you. (= it is possible I'll have time)
  If I had enough time, I'd help you. (= I don't have time)

PRACTICE 2

1 Choose the correct answers.

1 What *you would do / did you do / would you do* if a friend asked to borrow £500?
2 I *'d pretend to be / 'd pretended to be / was pretended to be* sick if I wanted to take a day off work.
3 Tom would be very disappointed if he *would lose / lost / will lose* the match.
4 I *didn't never give / wouldn't never give / 'd never give* a lift to a complete stranger.
5 If Nikol were better organised, her desk *'d be / weren't / might not be* so untidy.
6 It would be terrible if Marcos *passed / didn't pass / wouldn't pass* his exams.
7 If I *'d had / 'd have / had* more time, I'd go for long walks in the country.
8 If I asked Dennis for money, I think he *lent / will lend / would lend* it to me.
9 I'd be furious if I *think / thought / 'd think* Kim was lying to me.
10 If I *were you / 'd be you / 'm you*, I'd tell Sofia as soon as possible.

2 Complete the hypothetical sentences using the words in brackets.

1 I (avoid) paying tax if I (can)
   I would avoid paying taxes if …
2 I (never drop) litter in the street.
3 If a shop assistant (give) me too much change, I (tell) him.
4 If I (find) $100 in the street, I (not take) it to the police.
5 I (never drink) and drive.
6 If everyone (have) good manners, life (be) much easier.
7 I (not like) to be a celebrity.

3 Match the sentence halves.

A		B	
1	I'd help you	a	if I can.
2	I wouldn't help you	b	I'd tell you.
3	If I knew the answer,	c	if I could.
4	If I find out the answer,	d	if you don't want me to.
5	I'll help you	e	even if you asked me.
6	I won't do anything	f	I'll tell you.

4 Look at the sentences about real and hypothetical possibilities. Complete them with the words in the box.

···

could   had   might   were   will   would

···

1 If I _____ enough money, I'd go on holiday.
2 He _____ call you after lunch, I promise!
3 If I _____ you, I wouldn't trust him.
4 It _____ be great if I could speak Chinese fluently.
5 You _____ not enjoy that film; it's really scary in places.
6 We _____ get a takeaway pizza if you are too tired to cook.

REMEMBER THESE WORDS

SOCIETY AND CHANGE

average income	to go up
to decrease	to improve
to deteriorate	to increase
diet	life expectancy
to fall	living standards
to get better	to rise
to get worse	to stay the same
to go down	

SOCIETY AND SOCIAL ISSUES

to balance the budget	pollution
corruption	poverty
crime	a priority
defence	racism
education	to increase/reduce taxes
health care	transport
homelessness	unemployment
to increase/reduce spending (on)	to waste money on something

GROUPS IN SOCIETY

the government	the poor
the opposition (parties)	taxpayers
ordinary people	the wealthy

OTHER

to bully someone	to implant
a cure/to cure	industry
damage/to damage	to play a trick on someone
a disease	to run someone over
to flirt with someone	to scare someone
gravity	to take revenge on someone
a human cell	

PRACTICE

1 Choose the correct conclusion a–c.

1 It's official! Films this year last on average two hours 15 minutes. This is up ten percent from last year.
   a Films are getting longer.
   b Films are getting better.
   c Films are going up.
2 Twenty-two percent of rubbish comes from food packaging. It is predicted that this will be 25 percent in two years' time unless we do something about it.
   a The amount of food packaging is improving.
   b The amount of food packaging is rising.
   c The amount of food packaging is getting better.
3 Violent crimes went down last year, with only 15,000 violent crimes reported. This compares with 22,000 in 2005.
   a The number of violent crimes is falling.
   b The number of violent crimes is getting worse.
   c The number of violent crimes is becoming less dangerous.
4 US web designer Dan Koster has noticed that 15 percent of his 200 CDs can no longer be played.
   a His CDs are decreasing.
   b His CDs are falling.
   c His CDs are deteriorating.

2 Which word pairs mean the same or are very similar (S) and which are opposite or very different (D)?

to go up	to increase	S
1 to increase	to decrease	
2 to improve	to get better	
3 to cure	to damage	
4 to rise	to fall	
5 to decrease	to reduce	
6 the poor	the wealthy	

3 Match the verbs with the prepositions.

A		B	
1	to flirt	a	on someone
2	to take revenge	b	on something
3	to run someone	c	with someone
4	to play a trick	d	on someone
5	to waste money	e	over

4 Cover the word list and write the noun forms of these adjectives.

Adjective	Noun
1 unemployed	_____
2 racist	_____
3 homeless	_____
4 polluted	_____
5 poor	_____
6 industrial	_____

5 Look at the nouns in the box. Which have the same form as the corresponding verbs?

an increase   a cure   an improvement   some damage
a bully   a rise   a flirt   a reduction   a fall   a waste

STUDY TIPS

Use the internet to improve your English

1 Here are some ways you can practise your English using the internet. Tick the tips that you have already followed.

1 Read a news article in your language, then find an article on the same subject in English. ☐
2 Watch English-language videos or video clips. ☐
3 Listen to English podcasts or radio. ☐
4 Bookmark a good English-language news website and read it for a few minutes every day. ☐
5 Research a topic that you are interested in online. ☐
6 Send an email in English. ☐
7 Follow an English-speaking person who uses Twitter. ☐

2 Underline the ideas you would like to try and compare your ideas in pairs.

STUDY 1

Obligation and permission in the present

+	You	can	go.
		must	
		should	
	You	're allowed	to go.
		have	
		have got	
		ought	
–	You	can't	go.
		mustn't	
		shouldn't	
	You	're not allowed	to go.
		don't have	
		haven't got	
?		Can	I go?
		Should	
		Am I allowed	to go?
		Do I have	
		Have I got	

1 Talking about what is necessary / not necessary

- We use *must*, *have to* and *have got to* + verb to talk about something that is necessary or important.
  *We **must be** at the airport by seven.*
  *He **has to take** medicine every day for his asthma.*
  *I**'ve got to find** a telephone – it's urgent!*
- The meaning of all three is very similar, but:
  – *must* often shows that the obligation comes from the person speaking.
    *We **must be** more careful. (= I, the speaker, say it's important)*
  – *have to* and *have got to* show that the obligation comes from another person, not the speaker. It is a fact that this is necessary.
    *All young men in this country **have to do** military service.*
    (= the government says)
    *Jake**'s got to do** his exams. (= his teacher says)*
  – there are differences of formality. *Must* is often written down; for example, on public notices.
    *All visitors **must report** to reception.*
  – *have to* and *have got to* are more common in speech.
  – *must* is rarely used in question forms – *Do I have to?* is more common.
    *Must I / **Do I have to** sign here?*

- We use *don't have to* and *haven't got to* + verb to talk about something that is not necessary.
  *People **don't have to** vote if they don't want to.*
  *We **haven't got to** be there till ten.*

2 Talking about what is permitted / not permitted

- We use *can* and *be allowed to* + verb to talk about things we are permitted to do.
  *You **can park** here after 6.30 p.m.*
  *My brother's **allowed to borrow** my father's car.*
- We use *mustn't*, *not allowed to* and *can't* + verb to talk about things which we are not permitted to do (= prohibited).
  *Members of the audience **must not take** photographs during the performance. (= written notice)*
  *You**'re not allowed to** / **can't take** photos during the performance. (= spoken)*

3 Talking about what is/isn't a good idea / the correct thing

- We use *should* to say something is a good idea, or that it is correct/right.
  *You **should try** this ice cream – it's delicious.*
  *Those books are in the wrong place: they **should be** in the fiction section.*
  Should is weaker than *have to* or *must*. It is often used to give advice or make suggestions.
- *Ought to* has the same meaning as *should*. It is not usually used in the question or negative forms, where *should* is more common.
  *You **ought to be** more careful.*

PRACTICE 1

1 Match the sentence halves.

A	B
1 You can do it	a if you don't want to.
2 You've got to do it	b if you want to.
3 You don't have to do it	c because it's compulsory.
4 You're not allowed to do it	d because it's forbidden.

2 Replace the phrase in bold with an appropriate modal verb or phrase.

you should
If you go climbing in the mountains ~~it is best to~~ take a map.

1 Members of the public **are permitted to** visit the castle at weekends.
2 **It's a good idea to** check the train times before you travel.
3 **Is it necessary for me to** fill in both forms?
4 **It is forbidden to** smoke in here.
5 **Is it permitted for you to** learn to drive when you are 17?
6 At my school **it is compulsory to** wear a uniform.
7 **It is not compulsory to** wear your seat belt all the time when you are flying, but **it is the best thing**.
8 **We are permitted to** go home early on Friday afternoon.
9 **It isn't necessary for us to** buy a ticket in advance.

STUDY 2

Linking words

1 Meaning

- Words with a similar meaning to *and*:
  *My cousin's a professional footballer. He's **also** an excellent tennis player.*
  *I haven't got time to go on holiday. **Besides**, I can't afford it.*
  *Yoga is excellent exercise. **What's more**, it really helps you to relax.*
- Words with a similar meaning to *but*:
  ***Although** she's much younger than me, we get on very well.*
  *The economy seems to be improving. **Despite this**, unemployment is still high.*
  *Her father was very angry with her. **However**, he didn't say anything.*
  Other such phrases include *though*, *even though* and *in spite of* (*this*).
- Words with a similar meaning to *so*:
  *More and more people are moving to the city. **As a result**, housing is terribly expensive.*
  *At least you haven't lied to me. **For this reason**, I'm not going to punish you.*
  *He received just five percent of the votes, and **therefore** he has been eliminated.*

2 Word order

- *Although* is a conjunction – it joins two clauses (smaller sentences). There are two possible positions.
  ***Although** I don't like him, I respect his opinion.*
  *I respect his opinion, **although** I don't like him.*
  Though and *even though* can be used in the same way.
- All the other words and phrases are adverbials. There are three possible positions for them in the sentence or sentences:
  – at the beginning of the second sentence.
  *She loved him very much. **However**, he knew they could never marry.*
  All the adverbials in the box on page 109 can be used in this position.
  – in the middle of the second sentence.
  *She loved him very much. He knew, **however**, they could never marry.*
  Also, *despite this*, *what is more* and *therefore* can be used in this position.
  – at the end of the second sentence (although many people consider this rather formal/old-fashioned).
  *She loved him very much. He knew they could never marry, **however**.*
  Therefore can be used in this position.

REMEMBER!

Also comes before the main verb and after the verb *be* and auxiliary verbs.
*Adam is a very keen golfer. He **also** likes tennis.*
*Adam is a very keen golfer. He is **also** very keen on tennis.*

PRACTICE 2

1 Choose the correct answers.

1 He failed his final exam. *As a result / Although* he had to repeat the whole year.
2 *Even though / As a result* we have different opinions about everything, we never argue.
3 I'm very keen on skiing, and I *also / too* like ice hockey.
4 We don't need a swimming pool in this house. *Besides / Despite this* we can't afford it.
5 He's been refused several times already. *In spite of this / Therefore* he keeps applying.
6 Sheila is clever, ambitious and, *however / what's more*, she really wants the job.

STUDY 3

Obligation and permission in the past

Present form	Past form
I **must / have to / 've got to** go home.	I **had to** go home.
I **don't have to** go home.	I **didn't have to** go home.
They **can/can't** vote.	They **could/couldn't** vote.
We're **allowed to / 're not allowed to / mustn't** speak.	We **were allowed to / weren't allowed to** speak.

PRACTICE 3

1 Write the past forms of these sentences.

1 We mustn't take our jackets off.
2 I can't wear jeans at school.
3 We must leave early.
4 We're allowed to invite who we want.
5 I don't have to go to work.
6 We've got to write an essay for homework.
7 Do you have to work on Saturdays?
8 Are you allowed to do that?

2 Choose the correct answers.

1 My last job was really easy. I *had to / didn't have to* work very hard.
2 My school was really liberal. We *could / couldn't* do what we wanted.
3 Vera's parents were very strict. She *was / wasn't* allowed to go out in the evening.
4 Women in the 19th century didn't have many rights. They *could / couldn't* vote.
5 When I was in the army I *had to / didn't have to* wear a uniform.
6 My last boss was a complete tyrant. I *had to / didn't have to* work ridiculous hours.

REMEMBER THESE WORDS

LINKING WORDS

also	for that reason
although	however
as a result	therefore
besides	what's more
despite this	

CRIME AND PUNISHMENT

to be arrested	community service
to be/get caught	the death penalty
to be punished	a defendant
to be released	to go to prison / a prisoner
to be sent to prison	hanging
to be sentenced	a judge

CRIME AND PUNISHMENT (WORD FAMILIES)

to burgle / a burglary / a burglar
to commit a crime / a criminal
to kidnap / a kidnapping / a kidnapper
to mug / a mugging / a mugger
to murder/ a murder / a murderer
to rob / a robbery / a robber
to shoplift / shoplifting / a shoplifter

OTHER

to be banned	harsh
to be tough	to have the right to
to break the rules/law	illegal
a case	legal
to cause damage	lenient
compulsory	a life sentence
to destroy	a prison sentence
a deterrent	to solve a crime
fair	to surrender
to fight (in a battle)	unfair
to go to court	to vandalise

PRACTICE

1a Put the actions in the box into the most logical order.

to be arrested	to be released	to be sentenced
to go to prison	to commit a crime	to go to court
to get caught		

b Turn to page 129 to check your answers.

2 Is the meaning of the pairs of words similar or opposite? Write S or O.

1 harsh / lenient
2 to cause damage / to destroy
3 to get caught / to be arrested
4 to fight / to surrender
5 to be illegal / to be banned
6 to go to prison / to be released
7 to commit a crime / to solve a crime

3 Change the words below into nouns for people. Use a dictionary to help you.

a murder   *murderer*

1 a prison
2 a crime
3 a burglary
4 a robbery
5 a kidnapping
6 a mugging

STUDY TIPS

Use a dictionary to find collocations

1 You can use a dictionary to find which words go together (collocations). Which verb collocates with 'advice' in the definition below?

advice /ədˈvaɪs/ *n* [U] an opinion you give someone about what they should do: *Could you **give** me some **advice** about buying a home.*

2 Notice that you can also find this information by looking up the verb 'give'.

give /gɪv/ *v* (past tense **gave** /geɪv/, past participle **given** /ˈgɪvən/)
4 TELL SB STH [T] to tell someone information or details about something, or to tell someone what they should do: *Let me **give** you some **advice**.*

3 Look up the words in bold in your dictionary, then complete the sentences.

1 The film _____ a big **effect** on me.
2 All the noise from our neighbours _____ it **impossible** to sleep last night.
3 Did you _____ all the questions **right**?
4 When the management said no, the workers _____ on **strike**.
5 Marcel didn't _____ a **reason** for his strange behaviour.
6 I think you should _____ **advantage** of his offer.

12 STUDY, PRACTICE & REMEMBER

STUDY 1

Past modal verbs
(*could have / should have / would have*)

1 *could have* + past participle

This is used for events which were possible in the past but which didn't happen.

He could've drowned.
(= it was possible for him to drown, but he didn't)
Compare the sentences below.
Ruby could walk before she was a year old.
(= she was able to do this)
Ruby could have walked to work, but she took a taxi instead.
(= it was possible for her to walk, but she didn't)

2 *should have / shouldn't have* + past participle

This means it was a good idea to do something in the past, but you didn't do it. We often use this to **criticise** other people or to talk about **past regrets**.

You shouldn't have been so rude.
(= criticism: you were rude, and it wasn't a good idea)
I should've looked in the mirror before I went out.
(= past regret: it was a good idea to look, but I didn't)

3 *would have / wouldn't have* + past participle

We use this for imagining something in the past that didn't happen.

In his position, I would have waited for help.
(= I wasn't in his position – I am imagining the situation)

PRACTICE 1

1 Complete the conversations with the phrases in the box.

could have fallen	could have been worse
should have taken	shouldn't have opened
would have cost	wouldn't have enjoyed

1 **A:** I can't remember that lecture at all!
   B: You _____ notes.
2 **A:** He climbed up onto the roof.
   B: That was dangerous. He _____ .
3 **A:** The film was very scary.
   B: I certainly _____ it, then.
4 **A:** I clicked on the email attachment and my computer crashed.
   B: You _____ the attachment.
5 **A:** Was your car badly damaged?
   B: It _____ . I just need to replace one of the doors.
6 **A:** Why didn't you build an extra bedroom?
   B: It _____ too much.

2 Rewrite the sentences using the words in brackets.

It was a mistake to marry him. (shouldn't)
I shouldn't have married him.

1 I think it was wrong to leave her all alone. (wouldn't)
   _____
2 I was so happy, I almost kissed everyone. (could)
   _____
3 It was a mistake not to buy those shoes. (should)
   _____
4 They talked so much they almost missed the last train. (could)
   _____
5 Why didn't they buy that house? I think it was a good idea to buy it. (would)
   _____
6 It wasn't possible to help him. (couldn't)
   _____
7 It was a bad idea for them to start a business together. (shouldn't)
   _____

3 Read about the decisions some people made. What would you have done in each situation? Write responses using the prompts in brackets.

1 'I was driving alone one night and I saw two men hitchhiking. I stopped to offer them a lift.' *Kate*
   a (I / done that) *I wouldn't have done that.*
   b (they / dangerous) _____
   c (she / stopped) _____
2 'I was at the airport when a stranger asked me to carry a small package on my flight to Canada. I said *yes*'. *Joe*
   a (I / say *no*) _____
   b (it / be a bomb) _____
   c (he / say *no*) _____
3 'I was chatting to a stranger online one night. After a while the stranger asked for my address. I gave it to him.' *Paula*
   a (she / tell the stranger her address) _____
   b (the stranger / be dangerous) _____
   c (she / end) _____

STUDY 2

Hypothetical situations in the past with *if*

If you are imagining possibilities in the past, we often use *if* to describe the hypothetical situation.

If he'd stayed at home that day, he wouldn't have met his wife.
   (condition)   (result)

Notice that after *if* we use the Past perfect. This form is often called the 'third conditional'.

REMEMBER!

We can also use *might have* or *could have* if we are less sure about what would have happened.

If he'd (= he had) worked harder, he might have got into university.
We could've won the competition if our best player hadn't got injured.

Talking hypothetically about the past and present together

Notice the difference between these two forms.
- Imaginary situations generally / in the present:
  if + Past simple + *would* + verb
  If I wasn't an actor, I'd be a musician.
- Imaginary situations in the past:
  if + Past perfect + *would have* + past participle
  If I'd gone to the party, I would have seen her.

Sometimes we want to talk about the past and present together. In this case, we can 'mix' the two forms.

If she had stayed in her job, she would be richer now.
   (past)   (present)

If I didn't trust you, I wouldn't have lent you the money.
   (present)   (past)

PRACTICE 2

1 Put the words in the correct order to make sentences.

1 lost / 'd / been / careful / if / more / you / n't / have / you / it / would

    _____

2 I / passed / I / to / that / university / could / exam / have / gone / if / 'd

    _____

3 would / it / to / me / if / embarrassed / happened / I / had / have / been

    _____

4 your / now / forgotten / 'd / be / if / you / had / there / passport / n't / we

    _____

5 'd / I / started / I / known / long / it / if / would / take / how / n't / have / would

    _____

6 if / the USA, / Rick / Mia / had / stayed / would / n't / n't / in / he / have / met

    _____

2 Write sentences about the past with *if*.

I made a mistake. She shouted at me.
If I hadn't made a mistake, she wouldn't have shouted at me.

1 I felt ill. I didn't go to work.

    _____

2 My girlfriend went out without me. She met another guy.

    _____

3 He wanted to check his emails in the bath. His computer got wet and broke.

    _____

4 She didn't learn from her mistakes. She did the same thing again.

    _____

5 A storm damaged the plane. They made an emergency landing.

    _____

6 We listened to her advice. We made the right decision.

    _____

7 I answered the phone while I was driving. I crashed the car.

    _____

8 My family moved house. I had to change school.

    _____

9 It rained. We didn't have a barbecue.

    _____

10 He lost his job. He had to sell his sports car.

    _____

3 Answer the questions. Use the prompts (or your own ideas) to write complete sentences.

What would be different now if ...

you had taken acting lessons as a child? (be a Hollywood star now)
If I'd taken acting lessons as a child, I'd be a Hollywood star now.

1 you had learnt English as a child? (not be here now)

    _____

2 you had invested all your money in Google? (be rich now)

    _____

3 you hadn't learnt to read as a child? (life / be very difficult now)

    _____

4 you had felt ill this morning? (still be in bed now)

    _____

5 you hadn't stayed out so late last night? (not feel so tired now)

    _____

6 you had thought about the decision more? (not regret it now)

    _____

REMEMBER THESE WORDS

PROBLEMS AND SOLUTIONS

to be sympathetic	to make a decision
to go away	to not have a care in the world
to have a problem with	to sort a problem out
to have concerns	to talk something over
to ignore a problem	to trust your instincts/intuition
to lose sleep over something	

ROWING ACROSS THE ATLANTIC

to abandon the race	a phobia
a collision	a rescue boat
the crew (of a boat)	to row / a rower
loneliness / to be lonely	to shake with fear
a motivational speaker	to support someone
an oil tanker	a violent storm

OTHER

to accept a situation	fate
to be confused	to feel nauseous
to be fatalistic	to give/explain your point of view
to be intuitive	to give someone advice
to be logical	to make a list
to be offered a job/contract	the pros and cons
to be rational	reliable
to blame someone/yourself	to roll/throw a dice
to blow your top	to split up
a care home	to stay together
to carry on as normal	to take a chance
to criticise someone	a trick
a dilemma	to weigh something up
economical	

PRACTICE

1 Choose the correct word to complete each sentence.

1 I have a problem _____ my computer.
   a) for   b) at   c) with
2 Don't _____ the problem. Do something about it.
   a) ignore   b) go away   c) sort out
3 She's fine. She hasn't got a _____ in the world.
   a) problem   b) care   c) instinct
4 Are you _____ sleep over this problem?
   a) ignoring   b) missing   c) losing
5 If we talk it over we can sort it _____ .
   a) out   b) in   c) on
6 Have you made your _____ yet?
   a) decision   b) decide   c) solution
7 Tell me about it. What are your _____ ?
   a) cares   b) concerns   c) worry

2 Are these sentences similar in meaning (S) or different (D)?

1a He ignored the problem.
 b He sorted the problem out.
2a She decided to take a chance.
 b She weighed up the pros and cons.
3a They carried on as normal.
 b They accepted the situation.
4a I make rational decisions.
 b I make logical decisions.
5a They decided not to split up.
 b They decided to stay together.

STUDY TIPS

Revise effectively

1 Which of these statements best describes you?

1 I do well in tests because I do lots of revision.
2 I do OK in tests, but I want to revise more effectively.
3 I don't do very well in tests because I don't revise.

2 Which of these revision techniques do you use? Which have you never tried?

1 Look back through the Language focus and Vocabulary sections of the unit that you want to revise. Rub out any answers that you have written in, then see if you can still do the exercises. ☐
2 Reread the word list from the unit that you want to revise. Test yourself or a partner. ☐
3 Do the practice exercises again in Study, Practice & Remember from the unit that you want to revise. If you have problems, go back to the grammar summaries to check the rules. ☐
4 Reorganise the vocabulary that you want to learn using a diagram like this. ☐

TRAVELLING BY BOAT

verbs — problems — types of boat
to row to sink a collision a shark attack a rowing boat an oil tanker

5 Make up sentences using the vocabulary or grammar that you want to revise. ☐
6 Record sentences from the book onto your mobile phone but leave out certain words (e.g. the grammar focus or new vocabulary). Then listen and try to remember the missing words. ☐
7 Other ideas of your own? ☐

3 Underline the ideas you would like to try. Compare your answers in pairs.

Audio script

UNIT 1 RECORDING 1

1 A: What's your full name, please?
   B: It's Merhab ... M–E–R ...
2 A: Hey, great to see you! How are you doing?
   B: Yeah, I'm good, thanks. And it's really good to be here!
3 A: And ... could you tell me your full address?
   B: It's Flat 4 ...
4 A: So which part of Argentina do you come from?
   B: From near Buenos Aires. Actually, I only arrived here from São Paulo a few hours ago!
5 A: Really? How was your flight?
   B: Oh, it was fine, thanks.
6 A: So did you have a good journey?
   B: Yes, I did actually, but it was long!
7 A: What's your marital status?
   B: Single.
8 A: Have you got any family?
   B: Just my parents.
9 A: And are your parents OK?
   B: Mum is but Dad isn't very well, I'm afraid.

UNIT 1 RECORDING 2

Example
A: Is this your first visit to London?
B: Yes, actually it is.
1 What's your postcode, please?
2 Where exactly do you live?
3 How's your job going?
4 A: Do you speak any other languages apart from English?
   B: No, I don't.
5 Do all your family speak English?
6 Could you tell me your date of birth?
7 A: Did you have a nice holiday?
   B: Yes thanks, I did.
8 A: Have you got any brothers and sisters?
   B: No, I haven't.

UNIT 1 RECORDING 3

1 What's the English word for this?
2 How do you pronounce this word?
3 How do you spell your name?
4 Which page are we on?
5 Could you explain that again, please?
6 Could you say that again, please?
7 What's today's homework?
8 Could you write it on the board, please?

UNIT 1 RECORDING 5

A = Ann   J = Jess
A: Hi, Jess. So, have you got any photos of your birthday party?
J: Hi, Ann – yeah, just a second ... where are we ... oh yeah ... here's me with some friends. That's my best friend Lydia – I think you've met her, haven't you?
A: Yeah, I know Lydia, course. And who are the two guys?
J: Tom and Saliba. They're old friends of mine, too. Saliba lives in the same street as me – I've known him for years. He's going out with Lydia at the moment, actually.
A: Oh, very nice. And what's Lydia doing these days?
J: She's working in a DIY shop at the moment, which is really boring apparently, but she's decided now that she wants to be a social worker so she's applying for lots of courses and things.
A: Oh, good for her.
J: And here's another one – my little sister and my grandpa.
A: Wow – is that Isabel? She's getting so big ... I remember her when she was really small. Ha, she's pulling a face!
J: Oh, she always pulls faces in photos. I don't know why.
A: So how old's your grandfather?
J: He's 81 now, I think ... he's getting quite old.
A: He looks well for his age, doesn't he?

J: Yeah, he and my granny are still really active ... they travel all over the world and go out all the time ... they're amazing really.
A: That's brilliant.
J: And here's one of me with Luxmmi, an old school friend of mine.
A: I think you've told me about her before – she's training to be a doctor, isn't she?
J: Yeah, I think she's in her second or third year.
J: And here's some more of my family.
A: Aah, that's a nice photo ... is that your brother Joe ... the one who's wearing sunglasses?
J: Yeah, that's my big brother!
A: And what's he doing nowadays?
J: He's away at university ... well, he's home for the holidays at the moment, obviously.
A: So where's he studying?
J: Manchester – he's living in a student house with four other guys. He really likes it there.
A: Oh, that's good. And who are the others in the picture?
J: That's my dad in the middle, my cousin Harriet and Andy, my uncle.
A: Aah, it looks like a really nice party.
J: Yeah, it was great. Shame you couldn't come ...

UNIT 1 RECORDING 6

1 I spend way too much time travelling. My regular daily commute begins at about seven in the morning. Um, I leave my house, then walk to the tube station. From there I take the tube for six stops, then I hop on the train, er, for about ten minutes, then I take another tube for one stop, and then finally I take another train for about 20 minutes, and then it's a two-minute walk to work. The whole journey takes about an hour and a half, I would say, and that's on a good day; on a bad day, it could take up to three hours, and it's really, really boring.
2 I'm one of those people who just don't think there are enough hours in the day. I'm on the go the whole day long, from the moment I get up in the morning, um, to when I roll into bed at night. I have a really busy job where I'm on my feet all day. I usually end up working through my lunch break because there's so much to, to go on, um, and I would finish up work at about 5, 6 o'clock in the evening. Er, I normally would then, er, meet up with friends in the evening, um, have them over for dinner, um, and I spend a lot of time talking with my family over Skype or some friends on the phone, um, though I'd probably like to spend more of my time doing that. Um, as I said before, there just isn't enough time.
3 I spend, er, quite a lot of time looking after my daughter. Um, obviously when my wife's there we share looking after her and playing with her and things. But, um, my wife goes out to work, er, three or four nights a week, so when I get in from work, er, she goes out to work, and I finish off the dinner, look after my daughter, play with her, have dinner with her, give her a bath, brush her teeth, er, read her a couple of stories, put her to bed, sing some songs. I really enjoy it. Um, it's a great opportunity to kind of have one-to-one time with my daughter.
4 Oh, I can be so unproductive when I'm supposed to be writing an essay or, um, doing work of some kind. Um, I'll go on, on the internet to, um, to do some research for whatever topic I need to write about, um, but then I get, start looking at other things that I'm more interested in. Um, I dunno, maybe news about celebrities, or I might be downloading music. Um, and after several hours, I still haven't started researching my essay.
5 I'd like to have more time to walk my dog. Um, at the weekends I have lots of time and I take her for a lovely long walk. Um, in the week, it's always a bit of a rush and I never get a chance to really enjoy it properly, so I wish I had more time for that.

UNIT 2 RECORDING 1

1 Last English lesson I was wearing jeans and a white shirt … I think.
2 I can clearly remember walking on my own for the first time. I was about 13 months old and I was walking with my parents – they were holding my hands. Suddenly, my favourite aunt appeared at the door and I walked towards her … on my own.
3 At that time I was watching football on TV, probably.
4 Her name was Miss Spivey and she was quite young – about 25, I think – and she had very dark hair and dark eyes, and she always wore a lot of make-up on her eyes, I remember.
5 While I was shopping in town, I saw the news on the TVs in a shop window. I went into the shop and asked the assistant what was happening. Everyone in the shop was talking about it. They were really shocked.

UNIT 2 RECORDING 2

The most romantic story I know is the way my grandparents met. They were travelling from London to Newcastle by train, and in those days it was a long journey, so after a while they started talking. They soon discovered that they had a lot in common. Both of them were from Newcastle, but both of them were training to be journalists in London, and both of them were going home to see their families for Christmas.

The weather was terrible; apparently it was snowing really badly all the way to Newcastle. At one point, the train stopped for quite a long time, but it obviously wasn't a problem, because somehow during the journey, they fell in love and decided to get married. By the time they reached Newcastle, they were engaged! The wedding took place a few weeks later, and amazingly they are still happily married 50 years later!

UNIT 2 RECORDING 6

1 I remember when I was about eight or nine, I had a pet; it was my first pet actually, and it was a little budgie called Ollie. I named her Ollie because it was, er, the year of the Olympics … um, I can't remember which year it was. But this bird was really unusual because, um, quite quickly she became very tame. And I used to come home from school and I'd pick her up, er, off wherever she was perching and I'd take her upstairs and she'd sit on the side of the bed while I did my homework, and then she'd jump onto my pen while I was writing, or she'd jump onto my hair and chew it. Er, sometimes during dinnertime she'd actually jump onto the plate and skid around in the sauce, which wasn't very hygienic, but … um, I don't actually know what happened to her because one day, we all got so used to just her being round the house, that one day my mother came in with some washing, the back door was open, and she just flew off and, er, we never found her again. It's a bit sad really.
2 Right, er, this is a story of something that happened to me when I was, I think, about 11 or 12, so I was actually quite old, which makes it more embarrassing. Um, I was in the garden at my parents' house, and I think they were having a party because there were lots of people there – family members and their friends – and I had this swing on, um, a cherry tree in the garden that my dad had made me when I was quite little, and on this day I jumped onto the swing, um, as I would do any other day, and the branch that the swing was attached to fell clean off the tree, and the swing hit me in the head and I blacked out, um, very briefly. I was fine, but it was so, so embarrassing in front of lots of people that I know and who still remember it today.
3 Right. So, it was a time when I was really frightened, and, er, it was about two years ago, when I was on holiday in Sicily. And one afternoon we decided to hire a boat to go and sail round the coast. Um, it started off quite nicely – it was, the sun was shining and, er, you know we were sunbathing. But then we, er, we decided to drop the anchor and, er, stay still for a little while, but I didn't know that you shouldn't use the, er, engine when the anchor is dropped. So somehow the rope got tangled up in the engine, and the, um, engine stopped working.

So, um, we were stuck. The boat started floating out towards the sea, um, and also at the same time the, er, the weather changed; it became very windy and the sea got choppy, um, and we were quite scared. So when we looked in the boat, the radio didn't work, so we couldn't ask for any help.

We thought we were gonna be stuck there all night, um, because we had no way of contacting anybody. Um, there was water coming in the boat, we were cold, it was windy, and we didn't know what to do; it was desperation really.

But, in the end it was OK because my girlfriend managed to find the telephone number of the people who gave us the boat, so after about half an hour maybe, they came and rescued us, but at the time it was, er, we were very worried and very scared.

UNIT 3 RECORDING 6

1 Times Square in the 1950s looks **very similar to** Times Square now.
2 The adverts then were **exactly the same as** modern ones.
3 The buildings then were **completely different from** buildings now.
4 In the 1950s, all the cars were **very similar to** each other.
5 The taxis then were **a bit different from** the taxis now.
6 The traffic then was **a lot worse than** the traffic now.
7 The pollution then **wasn't as bad as** the pollution now.
8 In the 1950s, there were **a lot fewer** adverts than now.

UNIT 3 RECORDING 11

T = Tom   C = Carla
Part two
T: It's hard to know where to start. London's great for parks … museums … markets and just … street life, really. There are lots of great places to just walk about and have a coffee and, you know, just enjoy the atmosphere. I guess Covent Garden's the most famous place for that sort of thing, but personally I much prefer the South Bank … you know, the area next to the River Thames on the south side. There are lots of theatres and concert halls on the South Bank, but there are also cafés and shops, and you can walk up and down the river and look for books at the bookstalls and just hang out. It's a great place to watch people. I'd definitely recommend going there.
C: Cool, it sounds great. What about markets? I love markets!
T: There are loads of great markets in London, but personally I'd recommend Brick Lane. That was my favourite.
C: Oh, I haven't heard of that. What's it like?
T: Brick Lane's the traditional Bangladeshi area of East London, so it's famous for its curries and ethnic food. London's a great place to eat food from all over the world, and it's not too expensive in Brick Lane.
C: Good.
T: But there's a lot more there, too. It's a really arty area … there are a lot of art students and fashion students living and studying there. You can buy cool vintage stuff and individually designed clothes – you know, things you won't find anywhere else – and it's good for clubs and nightlife, too. You'll love it.
C: Sounds great. And what about parks? London's famous for its parks, right?
T: Yeah, there are loads. Hyde Park's the biggest park in central London and it's the most famous. But if you want to have a relaxing day away from the city centre, you should go to Richmond Park. That was my favourite park when I lived there.
C: Yeah?
T: Yeah. It's the biggest park in London and you can almost forget you're in a big city. I mean, at the weekend there are lots of people jogging and cycling and walking with their families and having picnics and stuff, but you can get away from everyone if you want to … and there are deer – lots of deer. You should definitely go.
C: Ooooh, I love deer – I have to go there! … What about museums? I'm not really a museum person, but I'd like to go to one or two while I'm there. Which ones do you recommend?
T: Do you read detective stories? Sherlock Holmes? There's a Sherlock Holmes museum.
C: Really? I love Sherlock Holmes stories. Where's the museum?
T: It's on Baker Street in central London. In the books, Sherlock Holmes lived on Baker Street and the museum tries to show what a London house was like in the 19th century. It's small but really fascinating.
C: OK, I am definitely going there! Well, thanks a lot – that's been great …

Audio script

UNIT 4 RECORDING 1

Some people are so famous that it's hard to believe they have other skills, but this week in our 'Fabulous facts' slot, we're focusing on famous people and their hidden talents!

Barack Obama, for example, is not only one of the most famous politicians in the world, he has also published several books, including a book for children called *Of Thee I Sing: A Letter to My Daughters*. He wrote the book in 2008 for his two daughters – as you might guess from the title!

Obama isn't the only politician to appear in bookshops. Winston Churchill, the famous British prime minister, was also an author and an artist. Over the course of his life, he wrote over 70 books and painted more than 500 pictures. In 1953, he won the Nobel Prize for Literature – the only world leader who has ever done this!

And what about modern celebrities? Do they have the same hidden talents? Well, some of them do. Pop singer Shakira, for example, doesn't just produce international hit records – she has learnt to speak six languages! Wow! And since she became successful in 1995, she has also founded schools for poor children all over Columbia, her native country, and has raised tens of millions of pounds for charity. What a woman!

And Brad Pitt is not just Hollywood's leading actor, he's also an architect! He has apparently been interested in architecture since he was young and has studied the subject for many years. He has even designed a restaurant and an apartment building!

Even royals these days have surprising talents. Kate Middleton, the Duchess of Cambridge, is a keen sportswoman, and before she was engaged to Prince William, she trained to row across the English Channel to France – a total of 34 kilometres – as part of an all-woman team. Unfortunately, she couldn't take part in the end. It was too dangerous because so many photographers were planning to follow her boat … what a shame!

UNIT 4 RECORDING 2

1 A: What's the matter?
 B: I've lost my mobile. Have you seen it anywhere?
 A: I can't believe you've lost it again! Why don't you keep it in your pocket?
 B: OK, so I've lost it again. Have you seen it?
 A: Have you looked on the coffee table? It's usually there.
 B: Yes, I have. It's not there, I've looked. Hang on. Oh! It was in my pocket all the time!
2 A: … I didn't recognise you for a minute. You look so different. You've changed your hair – it's really nice. I like it!
 B: Oh, thanks, and you look really well, too. You've lost weight, haven't you?
 A: Well, yes, a bit. I've joined a gym.
3 A: Tony, is Jiang still here?
 B: She was here a minute ago. Perhaps she's just gone out for a minute.
 C: If you're looking for Jiang, she's gone home – she left about ten minutes ago.
 A: Oh, no. I've missed her. Has she locked her office?
 C: I think she has.
4 A: Miss?
 B: Yes.
 A: We've finished the test. Can we go now?
 B: Not before the others have finished. Adam, how are you getting on? Have you finished?
 C: Sorry, I haven't finished yet. Can I have another five minutes?
 B: Yes, OK.
5 A: Let me see … er … Pierre, have you met Karimah, Karimah Safar?
 B: Yes, I think we have. We met at the conference last year, didn't we?
 C: That's right. I remember. Nice to see you again.
 B: You too.
 A: Karimah has joined our London office so you'll see a lot of each other.

UNIT 4 RECORDING 3

1 A: What's the matter?
 B: I've lost my mobile. Have you seen it anywhere?
 A: I can't believe you've lost it again! Why don't you keep it in your pocket?
 B: OK, so I've lost it again. Have you seen it?
 A: Have you looked on the coffee table? It's usually there.
 B: Yes, I have. It's not there, I've looked. Hang on. Oh! It was in my pocket all the time!

UNIT 4 RECORDING 4

Meltem

OK, so I was born in Ankara in 1990 and I spent my childhood there. Er, I started school, um, primary school, in 1996. And it was at primary school, when I was … eight, that I started learning English. I remember my teacher was really strict in class, but we all loved her. I've been learning English ever since, because, well, because my primary school teacher taught me to love the language, I guess!

And then, when I was 12, we moved – my family and I – to Istanbul … so that was in … 2002. I really didn't want to move, I remember, so my dad had to buy me a guitar when we moved, you know, as a present, and I started having guitar lessons.

So, what's next? Um, I left high school and started university in 2008 … studying business … er, I was there for four years. And … in 2011, I met Selim and, um, we've been going out together since then. And, do you want to know if I'm in love? Ha! I'm not telling anyone; it's a secret! And after I left university, in 2012, I started working for my uncle's import–export business. It's a really nice job and I get to use my business skills, so that's great.

What else can I tell you about my life? Well, all those guitar lessons weren't a waste of time because now I'm in a band … it's called Yedi Kizler. It means 'seven girls' in Turkish. And we're called that because … it's obvious really … there are seven of us in the band and we're all girls! Um … actually, I've been in three different bands, but this one is definitely the best. Anyway, Yedi Kizler started in 2010 and we've played about 20 gigs and we've got a few fans – I think we've got about 500 followers on Facebook.

And what else? Well, I'd really like to get a flat of my own – it's really crowded in my parents' flat. I've been looking for ages, um, for something I like and that I can afford, just to rent … and today I think maybe I've found the right one! Finally! I'm so excited!

UNIT 4 RECORDING 8

1 I'd like to nominate the English actress Emma Watson. Emma became famous playing the role of Hermione in the Harry Potter films. She started acting in those films when, when she was just 11 years old and continued for the next ten years. She's won many awards for her acting skills and she's appeared on the cover of magazines all over the world. She's exceptionally talented and clever.

But the reason I really admire her is because she hasn't let fame and money change her. While she was playing Hermione, she continued to work hard at her studies and she refused to leave school and become a full-time actress. When she finished the Harry Potter films, in 2009, she decided to go to university. She went to the famous Brown University in the US. It's inspiring to find a celebrity who still believes in the value of education.

UNIT 4 RECORDING 9

2 My nomination for the Inspiration Award is the Argentine footballer Lionel Messi. He's the most talented footballer of his generation, but he's still charming and dedicated. When Messi was 11, he was diagnosed with an illness. The treatment cost $900 a month. Messi's family weren't rich, so Messi left home to join FC Barcelona and the club paid for his treatment. This was a good deal for Barcelona, because Messi went on to score hundreds of goals for the club.

Messi has done a lot for children in his home country. He founded a charity which helps children get the education and health care that they need. I think he's an excellent role model for boys and young men everywhere, because he shows that you don't have to be selfish and egotistical to be successful.

UNIT 4 RECORDING 10

3   I'd like to nominate American Mark Zuckerberg for the Inspiration Award. He's the founder and president of Facebook. I want to nominate him because he's changed the way we live and how we communicate. And he's done all this while he's still a young adult.

Zuckerberg's also done a lot for education. In 2010, he gave $100 million to schools in Newark in the USA. He's very rich, so it's probably not a lot of money for him, but it still shows that he cares about other people. He's an excellent role model for young people everywhere, because he wanted to change the world – and he succeeded.

UNIT 4 RECORDING 11

4   My nomination for the Inspiration Award is Aung San Suu Kyi. She's a politician and leader in Burma. She won the Nobel Peace Prize in 1991, but she's spent most of her life since then under house arrest.

What's amazing about Aung San Suu Kyi is her courage and her strength. She's got strong principles and she inspires respect. Um, I think she deserves to win because she has led and inspired people for more than 20 years, even when she has been unable to walk outside of her front door.

UNIT 4 RECORDING 12

5   My choice for the Inspiration Award is Jamie Foxx. Jamie is an American actor, singer-songwriter, comedian and radio show presenter. He's won many awards for his acting, including an Oscar for the film Ray, and his music has gone to the top of the charts in lots of different countries. He's one of only four artists to have won an Oscar and had a number one album in the USA.

What's amazing about Jamie Foxx is the number of things that he is good at. Apart from all his performing skills, he's also a talented sportsman. I think he deserves to win because he is simply incredibly talented.

UNIT 6 RECORDING 1

When Tamara Rabi met Adriana Scott at a local McDonald's ® restaurant, their lives changed forever. 'I didn't know what to say except "hi". I was just so shocked – it was like seeing myself,' says Adriana. They were both students at neighbouring universities in Long Island, New York, and they had grown up only 30 kilometres apart. They shared a birthday, they were exactly the same height and both loved hip hop. But the most important thing they shared was the same Mexican mother. Both girls grew up knowing that their mother had given them up for adoption when they were born, but they had no idea that they had an identical twin. Then, Justin Lattore, a friend of Adriana's, went to Tamara's 20th birthday party. When he walked in and saw Tamara, he couldn't believe his eyes. 'I was just shocked – she looked so much like Adriana,' says Justin. Then it got clearer – they had to be sisters. In fact, Tamara had already noticed that strangers on her university campus often smiled and said hello, clearly mistaking her for someone else.

Following the birthday, Justin put the two girls in touch and they arranged the McDonald's meeting by email. 'As she came towards me, she was walking like me, talking like me,' says Tamara. 'We have the same mannerisms, the same interests and got the same grades at school,' adds Adriana. The girls even discovered that as children they had often had the same nightmare: of a really loud noise followed by a very quiet one. They had another sad factor in common. Both of their adoptive fathers had died a few years before they met.

Now the twins are finishing their studies, and they meet often. 'I feel she's my sister, but our relationship right now is more like friends,' says Tamara. She's optimistic and excited that their futures will be together: 'We will always have each other. We don't have any other brothers and sisters – we'll grow old together!'

UNIT 6 RECORDING 2

1   She lived in Paris.
2   I'd left my umbrella at home.
3   I left my umbrella at home.
4   They sold all the tickets.
5   My uncle had reserved a table.
6   She'd lived in Paris.
7   They'd sold all the tickets.
8   My uncle reserved a table.

UNIT 6 RECORDING 3

J = Josh   M = Maria   HZ = Hui Zhong   L = Liam

J: A few years ago I had an argument with my girlfriend. She said that I was obsessed by work. As I was driving home, I turned on the radio and the first thing I heard were the lyrics 'She said it wasn't working, she told me she was leaving'. When I got home there was a voicemail from my girlfriend. She said that she didn't want to see me anymore. And that was the last I heard from her.

M: My favourite coincidence story is about Mark Twain, the American author. He was born in 1835, two weeks after Halley's Comet appeared. In his autobiography, Twain said that he had come in with the comet and he expected to go out with it (Halley's Comet comes back every 76 years). Sure enough, Twain died in 1910, the day after the comet reappeared.

HZ: A few months ago, I was thinking about an old friend from university. His name was Jung Xiu. He always said that we would get married one day. The next day I checked my email as usual. To my amazement, there was an email from Jung Xiu. He asked me if I was still living in Bejing and he told me what he was doing. He said he'd just had a dream about me and had found my email address online. We've met up a couple of times since then. Who knows, perhaps he was right after all!

L: My friend and I from Thomas Abney Secondary School in South London did a gap year together when we were 18. We went to Australia and found a job in a small insurance office in Melbourne. It was really boring work but quite well paid. One day the manager said he was hiring another worker to help us. The next day a guy of about 20 walked into the office. He looked familiar. We asked him where he was from and he told us he was from South London. Then we asked him which school he'd gone to and he said Thomas Abney. We were so surprised. He'd been in the class two years above us.

UNIT 6 RECORDING 4

1   Do you often tell jokes? Can you tell any jokes in English?
2   Do you have an elder brother or sister? Did he or she tell you what to do as a child?
3   Can you say hello, goodbye and thank you in four different languages?
4   If you hated your friend's hairstyle and she asked your opinion, would you tell the truth?
5   Can you tell me something about your last holiday?
6   In your family, do you usually say a prayer before meals?
7   Did your teachers in primary school tell you off a lot?
8   If you had a minor car accident and it was your fault, would you say sorry to the other driver?
9   Can you tell the difference between British and American English?
10   If one of your classmates was cheating in a test, would you say something to the teacher?
11   Do you think it's always wrong to tell lies? When is it acceptable?
12   If a homeless person asks you for money, do you usually say yes or no?

Audio script

UNIT 6 RECORDING 5

Part one

'My aunt will be here soon, Mr Nuttel,' said a self-confident young lady of 15. 'Until then, I'm afraid, you have me.'

Frampton Nuttel tried to say something polite. Privately, he was wondering whether this visit to total strangers would really help to cure his bad nerves, as his sister had hoped.

'I know what will happen,' his sister had said, as he was leaving for his rest cure in the country, 'you will never meet or speak to anyone, and your nerves will be worse than ever. So, I'm going to give you letters of introduction to all the people I know there.'

'Do you know many people round here?' asked the niece after a silence.

'Hardly anyone,' said Frampton.

'Then you know nothing about my aunt and her great tragedy ...' continued the self-confident young lady.

'Her tragedy?' asked Frampton.

'Yes, you may wonder why we keep the windows open in October,' she said, pointing towards the large French windows that opened onto the garden.

'It's quite warm for the time of year, but has the window got anything to do with the tragedy?' asked Frampton.

'Out through that window, exactly three years ago today, my aunt's husband and her two younger brothers went off for a day's shooting. They never came back. All three sank in a terrible bog. We never found their bodies – that was the worst thing.' Here the girl's voice lost its confidence. 'Poor aunt thinks that they will come back someday. She believes they will walk in through that door with their little brown dog, just as they used to. That's why we have the door open every evening. Poor dear aunt, she has often told me how they went out: her husband was carrying his white coat over his arm, and her brother Ronnie was singing. Do you know sometimes on a quiet evening like this, I have the strangest feeling that they will walk in through that window ...'

Frampton felt relieved when at last her aunt came into the room. 'I hope Vera has been amusing you?' she said.

'She's been very interesting,' said Frampton.

'I hope you don't mind the open window,' said Mrs Sappleton. 'My husband and brothers will be home soon from shooting, and they always come in this way.'

UNIT 6 RECORDING 6

Part two

She continued to chat happily about shooting. To Frampton it was all absolutely horrible.

Attempting to change the subject, he told them about his illness. 'The doctors have told me to have complete rest, with no excitement at all,' explained Frampton.

'Really?' said Mrs Sappleton, but she was not paying attention. Her eyes were staring past him to the open window and garden beyond.

Suddenly, she jumped up. 'Here they are at last,' she said. 'Just in time for tea!'

Frampton shivered, and looked at the niece with sympathy. The young girl was staring out through the window with a look of pure horror in her eyes. In a cold shock of fear, Frampton turned round, and looked in the same direction.

In the twilight, three figures were walking across the garden towards the window. They were all carrying guns under their arms, and one of them also had a white coat over his shoulders. A tired brown dog was walking close to them. As the figures came nearer to the house, a young voice began to sing.

Frampton grabbed his hat wildly and ran out through the hall door, across the front garden and through the front gate. Outside in the road, he almost knocked a man off his bicycle in his terrible panic.

'Here we are, my dear,' said the man carrying the white coat, as he came in through the window. 'Who was that who ran out as we came in?'

'A very strange man – a Mr Nuttel,' said Mrs Sappleton. 'He could only talk about his illnesses, and then he ran off without saying goodbye when you arrived. It was as if he had seen a ghost!'

'I expect it was the dog,' said the niece calmly. 'He told me he had a terrible fear of dogs. A pack of wild dogs once chased him on the banks of the River Ganges in India, and he hid all night with the dogs snarling just above him. It's enough to make anyone suffer with their nerves.'

Telling stories at short notice was her speciality.

UNIT 7 RECORDING 3

1 One of my favourite movies is, er, *Lord of the Rings*, er, which is based on the book written by Tolkien. Classic, um, trilogy and fantastic read. I read the book, um, and, well, it was recommended, um, by a friend and I absolutely loved the book – it was absolutely amazing.

   Um, and then when the films came out, um, I thought that they would probably be a little bit disappointing because the book was just so good – I mean, there's no way you can put that, um, you know, into a film – but the films were actually, you know, they did the book justice, um, and the cinematography was amazing. The performances were great – I mean, the casting was great because the characters really did justice to the characters in the book. Um, and I loved the fact that it was all filmed in New Zealand. I've never seen a better movie, I don't think.

2 A TV show that I really like at the moment is *Modern Family*. It's about four different families, um, that are quite modern. Whereas in the past people used to think that you'd have a mum, a dad and two children, um, in *Modern Family* you've got one family, for instance, where the dad is about 50 or 60 maybe, and his wife is in her early 30s, and she's got a son as well from a previous marriage. Um, so that's quite modern.

   Um, the other family is a typical family, but they're all a bit crazy. You've got mum, dad, two girls and a boy, and obviously the siblings, er, go mad all the time.

   The series is really funny because they say and do things that you normally think about doing or saying but in real life obviously you can't do it. I, I remember one episode, for instance, where the dad cancelled Christmas because one of his children lied, and I've always wanted to do that. I would recommend everyone to watch it, cos it's a really good show.

3 Oh, I saw a television programme last week, um, Saturday night, really main peak-time television programme, and, er, it was called *The X Factor* and I just hated it – I really don't like singing competitions on television. Um, the people on the programme were just not very good singers. The judges weren't judging them for singing: they were judging the way they looked and they were judging their image. Um, I think really the judges were thinking about who would sell the most records. So it was very much about image and not about singing. I think if we're going to have a singing competition, then the contestants should just be judged on singing and not the way they look or how their image will sell lots of records.

4 I want to tell you about, er, the first time I went to a ballet. Um, it was called *Alice in Wonderland*, and it's based on the book by Lewis Carroll. Um, I went with my friend who, er, it was her birthday, er, so we went to see it in the, the, um, in Covent Garden in the Royal Opera House in London. Um, absolutely adored it. It was, er, I thought it was just really, really amazing. The, the set and the, er, the design of the stage were just terrific. Um, particularly liked, er, the, the Queen of Hearts – she was, um, an absolutely brilliant character, er, really, really funny, um, which I, I thought, I think maybe that was the best part about it, was that, er, I was at a ballet, which was all about the dance, but the whole audience was, um, was laughing – it was a real comedy show as well. Er, I'd recommend it to anybody.

UNIT 8 RECORDING 4

A **A:** Come on. Shall we go on the roller coaster?
   B: Are you joking? I'm not going to risk my life on that.
   A: Don't worry. I'll look after you. Nothing can go wrong.
   B: Everything can go wrong! Look, I'll go on the big wheel with you but not the roller coaster.
   A: But this is the best one! You'll love it. Come on. Shall I help you?
   B: Oh, alright. I'll give it a go. But I can't believe I'm doing this.
   A: There. We're in. Don't worry! I'll hold your hand.
   B: Oh yeah. That's really going to help.

B **A:** ... so I said, 'No, you can't', and I walked out.

B: No! Really? ... Oh no. Is that the time? I really need to go.

A: Shall we have a quick coffee?

B: I'd love to, but I really should go. I'm going to try and go to the gym tomorrow morning ... my New Year's resolution!

A: Oh yeah? Well, I'll give you a lift if you like. I'm parked just over there.

B: I think I'll get the bus. I'm going to do some shopping on the way home.

A: Shall I take you to the supermarket?

B: That's really kind, but there's no need. The bus is fine.

A: OK. I'll give you a call next week.

B: OK. Speak to you then. Bye!

UNIT 8 RECORDING 6

A = Aleksander   M = Mei   LK = Lee Kuan   S = Simone
R = Rosa   RN = Ramon   K = Khalid

1 A: In my country, people usually shake hands when they greet each other – not only the first time they meet, or if they haven't seen each other for a long time, but every day. When you enter a room, it's normal to shake hands with everyone in the room.

2 M: When you first start going out with someone, I think you should always act fairly cool. I mean, you shouldn't answer their texts immediately and things like that; it's uncool. On the other hand, if people wait too long, that's a sign they're not interested. I mean, if a guy doesn't answer your texts after two days, then you should forget about him and move on.

3 LK: When you go out here, people expect you to dress smartly. The way you dress is important. Your clothes can't be dirty or crumpled or old. And it's important to be fashionable, especially for women, with nice make-up and jewellery. It's what people expect.

4 S: If you've only just started seeing someone, don't request to be their friend on Facebook! I mean, if you've only been on a few dates, you don't necessarily want to get involved with all their friends, do you? You should definitely wait and decide if you want to be in a relationship with each other before you accept each other as friends.

5 R: In Peru, if you go visit your friends you should never arrive on time. No one arrives on time. It's perfectly OK to arrive an hour late, nobody cares – it's expected! If you really want people to be punctual, you have to say *hora inglesa*, which means 'English time'!

6 RN: People tend to go out late in Spain, really late – not just young people but everyone. I mean, I often don't meet my friends until 11 o'clock. If you want to eat in a restaurant, it's perfectly normal to eat at that time, and if you want to go dancing or go to bars, in Madrid, you can stay up until five, six, seven in the morning. There are still lots of people out at that time.

7 K: Generally speaking, people my age eat with their family in the evening. My mother and my sisters cook it and we all eat together. It's not acceptable to go on dates in the evening with a girlfriend, unless you're engaged first. After dinner, I normally go for a drive with my friends. Or we go to the shopping mall and hang out with our friends.

UNIT 9 RECORDING 1

1 A: They told me it was the very latest model, but I've had nothing but trouble with it over the last week. It's driving me mad, to be honest, cos I need to use it, y'know, every day.

B: So what's the problem exactly?

A: Well, it just crashes all the time without warning. The screen just freezes – I've no idea why. And I have to restart it and I keep losing my work – losing things I've done. It's so frustrating.

B: Um. That's not good, is it? I suppose you've tried reinstalling the software?

A: Yeah, but it didn't make any difference.

B: You should take it back to the shop then, definitely.

2 ... and you should all be aware of a few basic safety measures. Firstly, if some paper gets stuck or the machine breaks down at any time, don't just leave it and hope someone else'll fix it. Switch the machine off here at the wall. There's no need to unplug it. Just switch it off here, and you open it here, by holding down this button here. Now, it can get extremely hot inside, especially if you're making a large number of copies, so do take care you don't touch anything. Oh, and by the way, if you ever see smoke coming out of it ...

3 A: Is that new?

B: Yeah, I just got it the other day. Nice, isn't it? I'm just choosing a ringtone.

A: Mmm, can I have a look?

B: Yeah, it's so easy to use. You just touch the icons with your finger.

A: Cool.

B: Then you just scroll down the menu with your finger like this.

A: And so does that icon mean that you need to recharge the battery?

B: Yeah, that's right. The battery is a bit low at the moment.

4 A: Oh dear, is this new? I've never seen one like this before.

B: Don't worry, Gran. It's switched on and the film's in. When you're ready to watch it, you just press the OK button here.

A: Yes, I see. Oh, that's easy, isn't it?

B: Yeah, it's really easy. And if you want to pause it for any reason, then just press this button here.

A: Mmm, I'll do my best, but if it doesn't work for me, you'll be in the other room, won't you?

B: Yes, Gran, I'll be in the other room.

UNIT 9 RECORDING 3

F = Fadil   A = Abigail   J = Joel

F: There are a few things that we always tell our customers to bring with them. For example, we tell people to bring a couple of packs of wet wipes. We travel in four-by-fours so we bring plenty of water with us, but that's for drinking, not for washing. Wet wipes are really useful for staying clean. Another thing we recommend that you bring is your swimming gear. Obviously, a lot of people wonder why you need your swimming gear in the desert. The reason is that we always try to stop at an oasis when we're on a trip. That's really an unforgettable experience. People who don't bring their swimming gear always regret it. What else ... ? It's good to bring several plastic bags. They're useful for organising things and they stop sand getting everywhere. And you need to bring a hat and plenty of sunscreen, of course – at least factor 15. And of course a lot of people forget that the desert is freezing cold at night, so you need to bring some warm clothes.

A: I've been going climbing in the Rockies since I was a child, so I'm really aware of the dangers – particularly the way the weather can change really quickly. I see far too many people out climbing in just a pair of shorts and a T-shirt. They haven't packed enough warm clothes to deal with a change in the weather.

And I always advise people to take some insect repellent and a bit of food, even if they're only going for a few hours. If the weather changes and they get stuck, they might really need both of them. High-energy food is best – things like raisins and peanuts. You can add a little bit of your favourite chocolate, too.

Too many people these days rely on a handheld GPS navigator. Now most GPS navigators are great; it's definitely a good idea to take one – they tell you exactly where you are – but they can also break or run out of battery, so you need a back-up – a map and a compass. And don't forget a plastic bag. You don't want your map to get wet.

J: I'm a real festival-lover, you know. I just love the atmosphere and the music and the social scene. And I've learnt, over the past couple of years, what I need to bring. Number one on my list is a tent and a sleeping bag. They're your home, so it's worth spending a bit of money on a good tent and a warm sleeping bag. Then you need a torch with a few spare batteries. When you're trying to find your tent in the dark, it's really essential. What else ... well, with the British weather, you really need a pair of wellies.

Often people bring too much food with them and they always regret it, because they spend a lot of time carrying it around and, actually, there are plenty of places to buy food. To be honest, these days you can buy most of the stuff you need at the festival. So really, when you think about it, all you need is enough money!

Audio script

UNIT 10 RECORDING 2

1 Seventy-one percent of the Earth's surface is covered in water.
2 The lowest temperature ever recorded was -89°C.
3 In 2030, the football World Cup will be a hundred years old.
4 The closest distance between Earth and Mars is 55,680,000 km.
5 It is estimated that the world population in 2029 will be 8.2 billion.
6 The speed of light is 300,000 km/sec.
7 The population of Japan is 127,000,000.
8 The world's largest shopping mall is 892,000 m².
9 Seventeen percent of British people are over 65.
10 The largest crowd ever for a sporting event was 199,859.

UNIT 10 RECORDING 8

1 I'll probably travel a lot.
2 I think I'd probably have several different careers.
3 I'd invent one that could tidy my flat.
4 I think I'll probably go camping.
5 I'll probably move out of the city centre.
6 I'd live somewhere hot and beautiful.
7 I'd definitely give up work.
8 I'll buy a new car probably.

UNIT 10 RECORDING 9

1 I am a hotel owner from the north of Peakoilia, and I am really worried about the economy of our island. Businesses just aren't making enough money and the government is not doing enough to help us. They haven't put enough money into promoting tourism in particular, in my opinion. If we have more tourists, then we'll have more businesses, and if there are more businesses, there will be more jobs and everyone will be able to pay more taxes. Then we'll be able to improve schools and hospitals, but first we have to develop business. I'd suggest that we spend more on promoting tourism, and we really must have the new airport that they are talking about in the north of the country. This is really important for local businesses.
2 I'm a teacher, and to me the biggest problem is the state of our schools. Classrooms are getting really old, we don't have enough books and we need computers if we want to train young people for the modern world. It's really important, in my opinion. Young people are the future of our country after all. But at the same time, we cannot reduce spending on hospitals or the army, because these things are very important, too. I think the government should increase taxes on wealthy people to pay for improvements to our schools. There are plenty of rich people in Peakoilia – and they don't pay very high taxes, so they can afford it.
3 For me there are two big problems: unemployment and defence. I feel really worried for our young people. It's getting more and more difficult to find a job and I just don't know what they can do. I feel really sorry for them. At the same time, I think we have a big problem with our neighbour, Expandia. I really believe that they want to attack us and they're just waiting for an opportunity. So I think the government should increase spending on defence and increase the army to, say, 5,000 soldiers. This would help to solve two problems. It would make the country more secure against our neighbours and it would give young people jobs, and useful training. It would give them something to do and a focus for their lives. Of course, the problem is: where does the money come from? Hm, I don't have an answer to that ...
4 The best option is to reduce taxes on ordinary people. I'm a mother of a young family. My husband and I both work, but we just don't have enough money to live. Everything is so expensive these days. We want to be able to buy clothes for our children and ... have a better standard of living generally. But it's just not possible. And I don't think the government needs to spend all this money on hotels and golf courses and things. That's all for rich tourists. The government should help ordinary people like me ... now that would be popular!

UNIT 11 RECORDING 3

1 I think, um, it should be compulsory to have a trial licence, the ones you get for motorcycles. Normally when you have a motorcycle licence, you get a trial licence, and after about two years, um, you can convert it to a real licence. I think that should be, um, implemented for cars as well. Cars are more dangerous than motorcycles, I think.

  And a lot of people don't really know how to drive properly, especially when they've just gotten their licence. Before you get your full licence, you have to do an extra test. Um, I think the driving test is thorough enough, but people need a lot more practice before they're actually ready to go out on the roads. And that second test should be able to prove that a person is a competent driver. And I think that should be a law.
2 Er, I'm going to talk about, um, hunting and hunting laws, um, and my opinion about hunting, basically. You know, I'm not against hunting, um, I am against hunting for sport, though – I think there's a big, big difference. Um, you know, people traditionally have needed to hunt to eat and to live, and to me, um, that's fine. Um, what I don't agree with is hunting for sport, um, because I don't see the pleasure in going and, um, killing an innocent, beautiful creature just for the sake of killing it. Um, to me that doesn't make sense. I mean, you would hope that, that people would use the meat and, um, you know, they would do something with the animal, but unfortunately a lot of the time people don't; they just kill the animal and that's it. Um, so I don't think it should be banned, but it needs to be controlled. Um, and I also think that it would be better if people didn't hunt for sport, and they just hunted to sustain themselves and to use the food.
3 I'd make it a law that if you go and live in a foreign country, it should be compulsory to learn the language of that country. Um, I think that otherwise if you don't speak the same language as the people around you, you're never going to be able to integrate into society.

  Um, I lived in Brussels before, um, where the language is either French or Dutch, and, er, I, I had a good bit of French, which I found really helpful – people always found it, um, much nicer when you went into a shop or, er, into a restaurant and you were able to make an effort to speak in their language.

  Er, it was also, um, a m-, a much better way to get to know the country that you're, you're, you're living in. Er, it helps you be a bit, a big part of it more if you can actually communicate with the people and make friends with those people. Um, I think that's probably the most important part about it.
4 I think there should be a law that, um, if you're fit and able and you've been unemployed for say six months or more, and you're receiving money from the government to help you, you should have to do some kind of voluntary work. Er, there are lots of projects that I'm sure aren't being done because there isn't the money or there aren't the people to do the jobs. So if you're out of work, then why not do something constructive to help society and, and, er, your local community?

  The sort of things that could be done are, for example, er, fixing up local community centres or painting churches, er, doing work on local schools to make them better places for learning. I think if people did that, um, did some kind of, er, work or helping the community, it would, it would get them used to the routine of working; it would make it easier for them to get back into work when they eventually find a job.

UNIT 12 RECORDING 5

1 If Andrew had known about his phobia, he wouldn't have entered the race.
2 If Andrew had stayed on the boat, his phobia would have got worse.
3 If Debra's boat had hit an oil tanker, it would have sunk.
4 If they had continued the race together, the couple might still be married now.
5 If Debra hadn't had this experience, she wouldn't be a successful motivational speaker now.

Verb list

VERB	PAST SIMPLE	PAST PARTICIPLE
be	was / were	been
beat	beat	beaten
become	became	become
begin	began	begun
bend	bent	bent
bite	bit	bitten
blow	blew	blown
break	broke	broken
bring	brought	brought
build	built	built
burn	burned / burnt	burned / burnt
burst	burst	burst
buy	bought	bought
can	could	been able
catch	caught	caught
choose	chose	chosen
come	came	come
cost	cost	cost
cut	cut	cut
dig	dug	dug
do	did	done
draw	drew	drawn
dream	dreamed / dreamt	dreamed / dreamt
drink	drank	drunk
drive	drove	driven
eat	ate	eaten
fall	fell	fallen
feed	fed	fed
feel	felt	felt
fight	fought	fought
find	found	found
fly	flew	flown
forget	forgot	forgotten
forgive	forgave	forgiven
freeze	froze	frozen
get	got	got
give	gave	given
go	went	gone / been
grow	grew	grown
hang	hung	hanged / hung
have	had	had
hear	heard	heard
hide	hid	hidden
hit	hit	hit
hold	held	held
hurt	hurt	hurt
keep	kept	kept
kneel	knelt	knelt
know	knew	known
lay	laid	laid
lead	led	led
learn	learned / learnt	learned / learnt

VERB	PAST SIMPLE	PAST PARTICIPLE
leave	left	left
lend	lent	lent
let	let	let
lie	lay	lain
light	lit	lit
lose	lost	lost
make	made	made
mean	meant	meant
meet	met	met
must	had to	had to
pay	paid	paid
put	put	put
read	read	read
ride	rode	ridden
ring	rang	rung
rise	rose	risen
run	ran	run
say	said	said
see	saw	seen
sell	sold	sold
send	sent	sent
set	set	set
shake	shook	shaken
shine	shone	shone
shoot	shot	shot
show	showed	shown
shut	shut	shut
sing	sang	sung
sink	sank	sunk
sit	sat	sat
sleep	slept	slept
slide	slid	slid
smell	smelled / smelt	smelled / smelt
speak	spoke	spoken
spend	spent	spent
spill	spilled / spilt	spilled / spilt
spoil	spoiled / spoilt	spoiled / spoilt
stand	stood	stood
steal	stole	stolen
stick	stuck	stuck
swim	swam	swum
take	took	taken
teach	taught	taught
tear	tore	torn
tell	told	told
think	thought	thought
throw	threw	thrown
understand	understood	understood
wake	woke	woken
wear	wore	worn
win	won	won
write	wrote	written

Pearson Education Limited
Edinburgh Gate
Harlow
Essex CM20 2JE
England
and Associated Companies throughout the world.

www.pearsonelt.com

© Pearson Education Limited 2013

The right of Sarah Cunningham and Peter Moor to be identified as authors of this Work has been asserted by them in accordance with the Copyright, Designs and Patents Act 1988.

First published 2013

ISBN: 978-1-4479-3687-9

Set in Bliss Light 10.5pt/12pt
Printed in Slovakia by Neografia

Acknowledgements
The publishers and authors would like to thank the following people and institutions for their feedback and comments during the development of the material:
Emily Bell, International House, Santander, Spain; Stephanie Dimond-Bayir, Bell Educational Trust, Cambridge, UK; Timothy Foster, Madrid, Spain; Elizabeth Gregson, Università degli Studi di Trento, Trento, Italy; Denise Metzger, Navitas English Services, Sydney, Australia; Marie O'Connor, Auckland, New Zealand; Michael Parrish, Kwansei Gakuin University, Nishinomiya City, Japan; Zane Ritchie, Kwansei Gakuin University, Nishinomiya City, Japan; Andrew Sowter, Kwansei Gakuin University, Nishinomiya City, Japan; Kylie Tyler, Navitas English Services, Sydney, Australia; Will Varney, Cambridge English Studies, La Coruña, Spain; Damian Williams, Rio de Janeiro, Brazil; Lech Wojciech Krzeminski, Maria Curie-Sklodowska University, Lublin, Poland

Text acknowledgements
We are grateful to the following for permission to reproduce copyright material: Extract 4. from *Open*, HarperCollins (Andre Agassi 2010) pp.28-29, reprinted by permission of HarperCollins Publishers Ltd © 2010 Andre Agassi; Extract 6. from *Pearson Longman Dictionary of Contemporary English*, Pearson Education (2009) © Pearson Education Ltd; Extract 6. adapted from 'The people who fell to earth', *The Guardian*, 21/02/2009 (Interview with Josh Peltz by Charlotte Northedge and Ros Anderson) © Guardian News & Media Ltd 2009; Extract 6. adapted from 'What it feels like to ... get shipwrecked' and 'Get attacked by a shark', *The Independent on Sunday*, 22/08/2004 (Jacques, A.) © *The Independent*, www.independent.co.uk; Extract 8. adapted from 'I love to exchange phone numbers with strangers', *Colors Magazine*, Autumn 2009, Issue 76 (Pani Akhavan), Reproduced with permission; Extract 9. from 'I couldn't live without ...', *The Independent*, 27/02/2005, pp.14-16 (Peyton, O., Moore, P., Billington, R., Pereira, S., and Cartwright, J.) © *The Independent*, www.independent.co.uk; Quote 10. from Dr Aubrey de Grey, Chief Science Officer at SENS Foundation, www.sens.org, reproduced with kind permission; Quote 10. from Ray Kurzweil from 'The future will surprise us; our brains will merge with machines' in 'Reinventing Humanity: The Future of Machine-Human Intelligence' by Ray Kurzweil for *The Futurist Magazine* (www.wfs.org) March–April 2006, Reproduced with permission

Photo acknowledgements
The Publisher would like to thank the following for their kind permission to reproduce their photographs:

(Key: b-bottom; c-centre; l-left; r-right; t-top)

4Corners Images: Roberto Rinaldi / SIME 64–65t; **Alamy Images:** 84, 89bl, 104–105, Paul Abbitt rf 11tl, AF Archive 68br, 92b, Yuri Arcurs 83b, Adie Bush / Cultura RM 38br, David Crausby 106 (under 21), Curtseyes 42t, GL Archive 45tl, Juice Images245 / Juice Images 96b, 99, David Kilpatrick 107b, Russell Kord 31b (New York now), Alistair Laming 74, Mary Evans Picture Library 110r, Moodboard 7r, Gianni Muratore 32 (juggler), Oberhaeuser / Caro 106 (texting), Oramstock 106 (staff only), PhotoEdit 107tl, Photosindia Batch7 / PhotosIndia.com 38bc, Radius Images 76b, 82c, Pat Shearman 107tr, Lynne Sutherland 92 (cb), Washington Imaging 113tr, Chris Wayatt 106bl, 113tl, Finnbarr Webster 89br, Chris Willson 32 (street art), Lisa F. Young 113cr; **Bridgeman Art Library Ltd:** Convicts on Their Way to Botany Bay (Litho), by Richard Caton Woodville, (1825–56) / Private Collection 111tl, Jonathan Wild Pelted by the Mob on His Way to the Place of Execution, From the 'Tyburn Chronicle', English School, C18th / Private Collection 111tc; **Caters News Agency Ltd:** 87r; **Corbis:** Bettmann 24tr, Imaginechina / Corbis Wire 30tl, 30tr, Julie Lemberger / Terra 73t (ballet), Tim Pannell / Ivy 21, Seppo Sirkka / epa / Corbis Wire 73b (Turandot), Richard Franck Smith / Sygma 24b, Ken Welsh / Design Pics 106 (speed limit); **DK Images:** Dave King 90 (torch); **Fotolia.com:** 84–85 (background), alanmc67 106 (no ball games), Yuri Arcurs 67c, Atelier W. 50 (rings), BeautyofLife 90 (hooded top), Beboy 102, beleberda 26–27 (buildings), Eky Chan 44–45 (background), 60–61 (green background), cucumber images 93t, Cult12 41, Danussa 50 (postmark), E.baille 32 (background), Gaman Mihai-Radu 111b, hugolacasse 50 (Paris, Rome), Kamaga 26–27 (silhouettes), Mee Ting 86, karam miri 32 (plate), Natis 50 (mortar board), petrafler 72l (The Crying), PictureArt 90–91 (Colorado background), Patrick Poendl 90 (Sahara background), Eduardo Rivero 66b, Sashkin 110, Scanrail 46bl, 50 (legal scales), 90 (batteries), sel 40 (guitar), Kate Shephard 26b, 29bl, Tsian 67t, Valua Vitaly 55, Valerii Zan 44b; **Getty Images:** 77l, 85tl, 97b, AFP 125, Tony Anderson / Taxi 34, Antoine Antoniol / Bloomberg via Getty Images 42b, Nicolas Asfouri / AFP 66tl, Eileen Bach / Lifesize 94, Paul Bradbury / OJO Images 15, James Braund / Digital Vision 51tl, Paula Bronstein 43r, Buyenlarge / Moviepix 109l, Fabrice Coffrini / AFP 42cl, Comstock Images 52cl, Nick Daly / Workbook Stock 51b, Digital Vision 52cr, Shannon Fagan / Taxi 101cr, Jon Feingersh Photography Inc / Blend Images 30b, Priscilla Gragg / Blend Images 29 (right inset), Digital Vision 52cr, JGI / Jamie Grill 38bl, Taylor Hill / FilmMagic 36l, Steven Hunt / Photographer's Choice 98l, Jasper Juinen 42cr, Jupiterimages / Comstock Images 17bl, Jupiterimages / Workbook Stock 51tr, Keystone-France / Gamma-Keystone via Getty Images 31t (New York 1950s), Jonathan Kirn / Stone 40 (Meltem), David Levenson 93 (cbl), Cynthia Lum / WireImage 38c, Dan MacMedan / WireImage 56b, 68t, Mike Marsland / WireImage 43l, David McGlynn / Taxi 121t, Antonio Mo / Iconica 82tr, Stuart Mostyn / Redferns 91 (festival background), PhotoAlto / Laurence Mouton 6t, 7l, PhotoAlto / Laurence Mouton 6t, 7l, Thomas Northcut / Lifesize 123b, Sarma Ozols / The Image Bank 11b, Push / Digital Vision 82b, Will Ragozzino 97t, Gabe Rogel / Aurora 91 (Abigail), Shelby Ross / The Image Bank 82tl, John Russell 36bl, 38t, Philip and Karen Smith 124–125, UIG via Getty Images 25l; **Eyevine LTD:** © Phil Mcauliffe / Polaris 108; **Harriet M Connor:** 8tl, 8bl, 9tr, 9br; **Pearson Education Ltd:** BananaStock 52bl, Jon Barlow / Pearson Education Ltd 91 (Joel), Hola / photolibrary.com 83t, Mitch Hrdlicka / Photodisc 40 (mortarboard), The Illustrated London News. Ingram Publishing 44tr, Image Source 101r, MindStudio / Pearson Education Ltd 100r, MindStudio. Pearson Education Ltd 100l, Photodisc 95, Phovoir / Imagestate 29 (left inset), Nigel Riches / Image Source 76t; **Press Association Images:** Steven Day / AP 60–61b, Xu Jiajun / Landov 24tl; **Reuters:** David Mercado 65; **Rex Features:** 37r, 72r (The House of Eliott), Matt Baron / BEI 37l, Kristin Callahan 36r, John Chapple 57, David Crichlow 118cl, 118bl, 118br, c.20thC. Fox / Everett 68bl, Paul Grover 93b, Andy Hooper / Daily Mail 93 (ct), ITV 92 (ct), Alex Lentati / Evening Standard 93 (cbr), Geoff Moore 33 (Sherlock Holmes Museum), Newspix 113b, Picture Perfect 43c, Clive Postlethwaite 109r, Tim Rooke 36c, Sipa Press 25, 66cr, Times Newspapers Ltd 92tr; **Science Photo Library Ltd:** Roger Harris 98r; **Shutterstock.com:** 113cl, Yuri Arcurs 116t, 122, ARENA Creative 77r, bioraven 40 (key), Danicek 90 (sleeping bag), Tereshchenko Dmitry 87l, doglikehorse 50 (Sofia), Fenia 20r, Iakov Filimonov 92tl, Fotoline 116b, 121b, Sergey Furtaev 52t, hartphotography 11c, Jostein Hauge 6b, 11tr, jocic 89cr, Robert Kneschke 114, kropic1 35, Chaiwat Kwannoi 33 (chair), Lerche&Johnson 90 (boots), Losevsky Photo and Video 29tr, mangostock 101cl, nilovsergey 50 (rose), nrt 40 (briefcase), Vakhrushev Pavel 40, 50 (rose), Edyta Pawlowska 123t, Nicholas Piccillo 90 (Fadil), Podfoto 40 (backpack), ra2 studio 18, karen roach 40 (booties), Rodho 13 (leaves) and 23, 33, 43, 53, 63, 73, 83, 93, 103, 113, 123, Dasha Rosato 119, R. Gino Santa Maria 52br, sianc 101l, SVLuma 50 (crossroads sign), takayuki 20l, tele52 89tc, Yakobchuk Vasyl 16t, Richard Waters 33 (stag); **Thor Swift Photography:** 96; **The Art Archive:** Thomas Rowlandson (1757–1827)Judges / Birmingham City Art Gallery 111tr; **The Kobal Collection:** Titanic (1997) / 20TH Century Fox / Paramount 60tl

All other images © Pearson Education

Cover photo © *Front:* **Shutterstock.com:** Rodho tr

Illustrated by: Clementine Hope (NB Illustration) p.79; In-house p.15, p.17, p.28, p.34, p.46, p.55, pp.74–5, p.94, p.114; Fabio Leone (Bright Agency) p.62; Andrew Lyons (Handsome Frank) pp.22–3; Julian Mosedale p.12, p.26, p.48, p.49, p.67, pp.80–1; Michael Ogden (The Inkshed) p.120; Jamie Sneddon p.78